CUNNING

CUNNING

Don Herzog

Princeton University Press ❀ *Princeton & Oxford*

Copyright © 2006 by Princeton University Press

Published by Princeton University Press, 41 William Street, Princeton,
New Jersey 08540

In the United Kingdom: Princeton University Press, 3 Market Place,
Woodstock, Oxfordshire OX20 1SY

Library of Congress Cataloging-in-Publication Data
Herzog, Don, 1956–
Cunning / Don Herzog.
p. cm.
Includes bibliographical references and index.
ISBN-13: 978-0-691-12415-5 (hardcover : alk. paper)
ISBN-10: 0-691-12415-9 (hardcover : alk. paper)
1. Deception.   I. Title.
BJ1421.H47 2006
179'.8—dc22   2005015343

British Library Cataloging-in-Publication Data is available

This book has been composed in Adobe Caslon

Printed on acid-free paper.∞

pup.princeton.edu

Printed in the United States of America

1 3 5 7 9 10 8 6 4 2

FOR LINDA

" 'Skin me, Brer Fox,' sez Brer Rabbit, sezee, 'snatch out my eyeballs, t'ar out my years by de roots, en cut off my legs,' sezee, 'but do please, Brer Fox, don't fling me in dat brier-patch,' sezee."

—JOEL CHANDLER HARRIS
Uncle Remus: His Songs and His Sayings

CONTENTS

INTRODUCTION

🎚 "I do not marvel in any ways to see such a multitude of people assembled . . . to behold the unfortunate tragedy of this my wretched life. For the case is rare. . . ."[1] He loved his wife, insisted John Kello at the scaffold. He denied that he'd dabbled in magic. But "the wicked spirit" had urged him to kill his wife to advance his career. (He never explains how she was an obstacle. Was she just set against his promotion? or having to move to some wretched small town? Then, you'd think, they'd talk about it or endure some marital spats. But murder? It sounds like a parody of men devoted more to their jobs than to their families.) He tried poisoning her, but she vomited. So he strangled her instead, leaving himself with the usual dilemma, how to dispose of the corpse. Picture him, please, the jittery husband, gingerly embracing his wife as if trying to patch things up after a fight and awkwardly presenting a valedictory gift, a necklace too cumbersome to please, still, his wife complaisant, sweetly uncomplaining: he circled a noose around the corpse's neck and left the body hanging as if she'd committed suicide.

Kello already had drawn up his will, leaving all his property and the children's care to her. A loving husband could do no more. And he already had spread rumors that she was "tempted terribly in the night." Leaving his house keys inside, he slipped out the seldom-used back door of his study. A later tradition of uncertain provenance has it that after killing her, he sailed off to preach—Kello was a minister—and then invited some of the congregation back to his home, where he was shocked, shocked, to discover the dangling body.[2] Then he anguished over whether those commit-

[1] *The Confession of Maister Iohn Kello Minister of Spot, togidder with His Ernist Repentance Maid vpon the Scaffald befoir His Sufferring, the Fourt Day of October. 1570* (Edinburgh, 1570). The pamphlet is reproduced with extensive variations in spelling and punctuation in Richard Bannatyne, *Journal of the Transactions in Scotland, during the Contest between the Adherents of Queen Mary, and Those of Her Son* (Edinburgh, 1806), pp. 39–51. I've modernized spelling in the text throughout, but only capitalization in footnoted titles, to assist those wishing to track down the sources. Yes, Kello was a real historical figure: see Hew Scott, *Fasti Ecclesiae Scoticanæ: The Succession of Ministers in the Church of Scotland from the Reformation*, new ed., 9 vols. (Edinburgh: Oliver and Boyd, 1915–61), 1:417; *The Diary of Mr John Lamont of Newton: 1649–1671* (Edinburgh, 1830), p. 227.

[2] William Roughead, *Twelve Scots Trials* (Edinburgh: William Green and Sons, 1913), pp. 1–15.

ting suicide could be saved. "And that my affection towards her might appear the greater," he denied that God would suffer so innocent a creature to succumb "to the temptation and rage of Satan."

Kello was hanged in Edinburgh in 1570. The historical context makes the episode a bit less murky. After the Reformation hit Scotland, just ten or twelve years before Kello's turn at the scaffold, the kirk or church was severely understaffed,[3] so he could well have glimpsed attractive job openings. By 1574, Scottish ministers were prosperous enough to provoke sumptuary legislation prohibiting them and their wives from wearing fine clothes, jewelry, and silk hats.[4] The locals were used to duels and assassinations, also to "seizers," zealous officers who the year of Kello's death had two men burned alive for sodomy—and who kept up their savage enforcement of religious commandments into the 1700s.[5] (Remember them the next time someone assures you that Islam just needs its own Reformation.) As far as I know, though, the execution of a minister was no everyday yawner. None of this tells us what Kello had in mind for his career or what his wife objected to. Here, too, the historical record is frustratingly opaque.

Kello might have gotten away with it, but the grumbling and gossiping of some of the faithful were getting under his skin. And "above all," another minister penetrated "the inward cogitations of my heart" and interpreted a troubled dream he'd had. Staggered by the interpretation, Kello "persuaded myself God spoke in him." *I persuaded myself* will easily bear the sense of *I came to believe*. But it's tempting to construe it as admitting that he talked himself into it. Now why would he? And why would he report the dream in the first place? Was he afflicted by the fabled guilty conscience, plaguing the perpetrator, confronting him with knowing accusers at every turn, transmuting others' casual glances into caustic glares? Maybe, but

---

[3] Rosalind Mitchison, *The Old Poor Law in Scotland: The Experience of Poverty, 1574–1845* (Edinburgh: Edinburgh University Press, 2000), p. 11. For an incisive overview of kirk history, see Jenny Wormald, *Court, Kirk, and Community: Scotland 1470–1625* (London: Edward Arnold, 1981), chaps. 5–8.

[4] David M. Walker, *A Legal History of Scotland*, 6 vols. to date (Edinburgh: T. & T. Clark Ltd., 1988–), 3:279.

[5] Allan Massie, *Edinburgh* (London: Sinclair-Stevenson, 1994), pp. 37–38; Ebenezer Henderson, R. L. Wright, and William Haldane, *The Annals of Kinross-Shire*, ed. Hon Rhoderick and Alison Moncreiff (n.p.: Fossoway & District Community Council, 1990), p. 30; Ebenezer Henderson, *The Annals of Dunfermline* (Glasgow, 1879), p. 377.

many guilty people don't seem to suffer from such inexorable consciences. Some innocent people do.

What is a guilty conscience, anyway? Just the detritus of years of conditioning, some irrational quirk that happens to be shared by others and vigorously promoted by pompous authorities? If so, can the agile murderer wriggle away from morality? Imagine the psychotherapist's ad: "Counsel for those in the clutches of the indefensible superstitions of morality. Triumphant testimonials on offer from prior clients now viewed by the base cowards around us as psychopaths." No, she's not offering merely to help out those in sweaty paroxysms of guilt over trivial faults. She's offering her patients the chance to burst the confines of morality into lives where they never hesitate over what's right or wrong, good or bad. Would you enter such therapy? Should you? Do you flinch at the prospect?

Or is a guilty conscience the still, small voice of God within?[6] Recall how it feels when you want to do something questionable, when you've persuaded yourself that it is the right thing to do, and then you suddenly know that it's wrong. Even then, is conscience inescapable? or are some tone-deaf to its stern song? Are they culpable? negligent? or, not to put too fine a point on it, damned? Maybe Kello succumbed to visions of hellfire and the desperate seductions of being a deathbed convert. But how religiously orthodox could he have been? Yes, there's a distinguished tradition of people killing for God, even when they embrace Him as the Prince of Peace. But not killing their wives to advance their careers.

What kind of minister does such a thing? Linger over Kello's activities during the weeks he's planning the murder. Sometimes he's writing his will, figuring out how to get poison without leaving an incriminating trail, and sadly confiding in his parishioners about his wife's alleged nocturnal temptations. Sometimes he's officiating at marriages, baptizing infants, and solemnly urging the faithful to repent for their sins. You'd think he has to be play-acting in those latter activities, right? After all, he's dead serious

---

[6] See 1 Kings 19:12. The crucial text in the reception and transformation of this notion in ethics is Bishop Butler's *Sermons* of 1726, an argument for the authority of conscience. (In his sixth Sermon, Butler flirts with blasphemy by casting "our nature" as "the voice of God within us.") For intellectual context and commentary, see J. L. Mackie, *Hume's Moral Theory* (London: Routledge & Kegan Paul, 1980), esp. pp. 35–43; and Stephen Darwall, *The British Moralists and the Internal "Ought": 1640–1740* (Cambridge: Cambridge University Press, 1995), esp. chap. 7.

about disposing of his wife and you'd think he'd have to be shuddering inside—or at least be ironic?—when he issues his menacing or beseeching warnings of damnation. But maybe not. Maybe he's entirely serious in both sets of activities. Maybe there's a sort of firewall in his mind separating the lethal plotting from the earnest praying, so that when doing one he never thinks of the other. Then again, maybe both sets of activities run seamlessly, promiscuously, together. As he launches into his homily, he says to himself, "No, damn it! can't use a knife, I'd never be able to hide it"— and maybe he says it without even breaking stride, his earnest cadences washing over the assembled faithful. Maybe when he paints his lurid portraits of hell, he grimly concedes to himself that he'll roast there, too. Maybe; maybe not. It's hard to imagine what's buzzing around in his head. Then again, it's often hard to imagine how we handle the conflicting demands of our own lives. Does the predatory real estate broker flinch when she leans over to embrace her granddaughter? Does the unctuous used car salesman, whose sales commissions depend on his glib dishonesties, flinch when he assures his suspicious wife that she can trust him? Does she smirk?

But the question is not just, what kind of minister does such a thing? It's also, what kind of person does such a thing? True, there's an especially pointed conflict between his role and his action. But it's not as though an insurance broker or a potter may murder people without a second thought. Even a butcher, who can slash other animals without a second thought, knows not to deploy his professional expertise or cutlery on human beings. The problem with Kello isn't or isn't only that he departed from the demands of being a minister. Then too, some roles seem to permit or even demand unscrupulous actions. If Kello seems remote, consider instead the dirty little not-so-secrets of our own world, close at hand. Should a prison guard beat a prisoner now and then, just to remind everyone who's boss? Should a criminal defense lawyer suborn perjury—or let slide testimony she knows to be false? Sure, the rules prohibit such things. But maybe she should break the rules sometimes. Should a department store clerk shoplift choice merchandise to help a needy friend?

Each could plead that the actions in question would make good sense or that they'd be rational. "You want me to keep order in this prison, right?" our guard might demand. "I know that cruelty is bad and I'm no sadist. But I don't propose any gratuitous cruelties. If I don't keep the inmates in line, we'll need to use far worse violence on them." The defense lawyer might acidly note that the local DA is not above his own cheating—everyone knows that cops on the witness stand lie all the time—and so insist that it isn't only unfair to make her play by Queensberry rules, it's also perverse: it keeps her from offering her client the vigorous advocacy to which he's entitled. The clerk might sigh, "I suppose it's wrong to steal others' property. But I'm not doing it for myself. My friend needs it much more than the corporation does. Besides, they already figure shrinkage into these prices. Why do you think this stuff costs so much?"

Here's an enticing labyrinth full of problems, with the paths of morality, roles, and rationality crossed, confused, confusing. Tradition bequeaths us stirring rhetoric on these matters: "do the right thing"; "go about your allotted business in good cheer"; "choose means calculated to efficiently advance your ends." I want to seduce you—or corrupt you; you can decide later—into seeing these time-honored slogans not as shining nuggets of wisdom but as laughable bromides. And I want to proceed not with stirring visions of what's good, but by pursuing the twists and turns of cunning, my thread through the labyrinth. So we'll meet rogues as fiendish as Kello, even worse, but also more quirky and amiable types: a political astrologer, a car salesman, an outfit offering online exorcisms, and more, some of them from history and literature, some from our own world. Some really are rogues—I don't propose to defend wife-murdering as a tactic for advancing your career. But some of them can rightly plead powerful excuses to mitigate their faults, and others, however we may initially cringe, are probably doing the right thing. Just don't think you already know who falls into each category and why.

But why cunning? Was Kello cunning? I grant that he wasn't the most cunning guy around. Had he been, we'd have no gallows confession to savor. Maybe the really cunning leave no traces, unless indeed they choose to gloat in posthumous autobiographies. But in his faltering way, was Kello cunning? To be coy, that depends partly on what you mean. Kello was self-consciously scheming, deceptive, selfish—or so he must have thought, but he could have been mistaken—and amoral. So is that what *cunning* means? There's no point in trying to stipulate a definition of cunning. Definitions come at the end of the day, if at all. Anyway, dictionaries are often unhelpful. (Try looking up *love* or *justice*.) Notice, though, that *cunning* brings to mind *crooked*, *shifty*, *slippery*, *elusive*, *evasive*. The cunning actor bobs and weaves past obstacles to prevail. As Dewey noticed, that's just to say he's intelligent.[7] But it's also to raise the worry that some obstacles should be respected, not dodged, that some kinds of intelligence are sleazy or worse. *Cunning* suggests *clever*, not *wise*, and promptly forces us to wonder about being too clever by half. So the familiar contrast between "low cunning" and genuine wisdom. We might well applaud Houdini's daredevil stunts, his wiggling his way out of ropes, chains, and locked trunks. But when the obstacles are the dictates of morality or our social obligations, should we applaud those who evade them? Ambrose Bierce's *Devil's Dictionary*, delightfully exempt from my complaints about dictionaries, nails some problems:

> *Cunning, n.* The faculty that distinguishes a weak animal or person from a strong one. It brings its possessor much mental satisfaction and great material adversity. An Italian proverb says: "The furrier gets the skins of more foxes than asses."

Can you be cunning in pursuit of an unambiguously good end? Try this: "Mother Teresa cunningly extracted a pledge of support for the Home for the Dying Destitute." Do you balk? Because you can't imagine such a saintly figure stooping to cunning tactics? Or because nothing done for such a lofty reason could properly be described as cunning? Or again, can't you be cunning and selfless? What about the dad who secretly works for gangsters in order to keep bread on the table for his beloved children? Or the politician who wallows in sleaze not to secure his reelection but to cut a better deal for the workers or the environment? Yet again, can you be cunning without noticing it? Wouldn't it be cunning to deceive not just those around you, but yourself? A wary onlooker challenges you: it's got to be easier to insist vehemently on the utmost integrity of your actions when you believe in it yourself. Can you cunningly tell the truth? What if you're talking to someone who distrusts you and you want deliberately to muddy the waters? "You bet," you chuckle, "I'm the kind of person who would seduce your partner." Then you go ahead and do just that. As you imagine these scenarios, do you cast them with men or women? Why? And how does the style of the performance depend on that choice?

---

[7] John Dewey, *How We Think: A Restatement of the Relation of Reflective Thinking to the Educative Process*, new ed. [1933], in Dewey, *The Later Works, 1925–1953*, ed. Jo Ann Boydston et al., 17 vols. (Carbondale and Edwardsville, IL: Southern Illinois University Press, 1981–90), 8:223.

I want to sharpen our grasp of cunning, to reckon with its twists and turns, allures and horrors, insights and blindnesses. But I also want to use it for my own purposes and blithely shove it aside when I've exhausted its usefulness. So cunning will be front and center much of the time, but it will also be my stalking horse for sidling up to some vexing puzzles about rationality, roles, and morality. I tend to worry about focusing on what's good. It makes it too easy to sound syrupy, high-minded, like a bad Sunday school sermon or an inspirational greeting card. The sheer nasty cleverness of the cunning will keep me honest. It will force me to give the devil his due, every step of the way.

The book falls into three parts. First, I explore some canonical moments of cunning: stories about Odysseus and texts by Machiavelli. I introduce a time-honored but radically deficient scheme, the thought that the world is divided into knaves and fools. (Perhaps we should add honest people, who need only to unmask the knaves to protect themselves.) Second, I explore a host of ways in which the familiar distinction between appearance and reality is an inadequate guide to social life, ways then in which unmasking can't be a matter of stripping away pretext and revealing underlying reality. I also chart what qualifies as another sort of problem with appearances: for our knowledge of the world, we're inescapably dependent on what others tell us. But the way it seems to them may not be the way it really is, and anyway they might want to paint a misleading picture. Such complications make the problems of cunning look bleaker, more intractable, than the scheme of knaves and fools suggests. Third, then, I amplify our grounds for despair. The villain conscious of his knavish intentions is another stylized and deceptive figure. Cunning is compatible with self-deception, with simple ignorance too. No consolation is to be found in the prospect of doing one's duty or adhering to the obligations of one's roles, nor in turning to the resources of religion or a familiar strategy of justification from moral philosophy. I close by telling a tale not wholly unlike Kello's, this one from early seventeenth-century England.

My goal throughout is to deepen and refine our sense of what's troubling in this terrain, not to reassure. I go narcoleptic when theory starts feeling like the view of the social landscape from three miles up in a hot-air balloon—and I'm cranky enough to suspect it starts feeling that way too often. Is the right prior to the good? Do expressive considerations muck up the appeal of efficiently marshalling one's means in the pursuit of one's ends? Does reason itself dictate the pursuit of some ends or the respect of moral side constraints? Does nature? Or are we left only with passion? Plenty of people write about these abstract issues head-on, with the occasional Tinkertoy example introduced to illustrate a broad theoretical point. I know how to talk and write in this mode, but I don't trust it. To be blunt, even peremptory, about it, I think that such work reveals far more about the intelligence and sensibility of the author than it does about the predicaments of social life.

Every day, we wrestle our way through a tangle of competing commitments that show up in extravagantly stylized and artificially coherent ways in theories of instrumental rationality, deontology, consequentialism, and so on. That we should adopt one such theory and live by its dictates seems to me intellectual madness worthy of the projectors Gulliver marvels at in Lagado, indeed worthy of the more malodorous experiments of that distinguished academy. Here I stage a mock tragedy in which familiar overbearing creatures descend from the airy heights of Theory's Cloudcuckooland and do each other in, leaving the stage full of bloody bodies. But I allow them to dispatch each other—actually I urge them on with some sadistic glee; an astute critic might insist it's a comedy—not to defend skepticism, nor to remind us of what we knew all along, despite theory's false consolations, namely that the world is weird and complicated and that theories tend to be oversimplified. I am not a Kantian, I am not a utilitarian, and I am not going to offer any intriguing conceptual structure to explain how to merge the best of each tradition. But mine finally is no counsel of despair: going local is a strategy for gaining knowledge, not a surrender to some exotic skepticism. So I return to the nitty-gritty grounds of practice and puzzle afresh over tantalizing dilemmas. I think the examples are richer, more provocative, than the off-the-shelf abstractions that have dazed our senses and dulled our imaginations.

As a reader, I have my wits about me and I instantly try to position myself as a mischievous equal of the author, not a slack-jawed receptacle of whatever she has to say. I'm glum when I feel like the author is condescending, catechizing, deigning to spoon-feed me answers. I'm happy when the author furnishes illuminating devices to help me find my way through dark and uncertain terrain. As a writer, I assume my readers are the same, that they can take—and will welcome—teasing and insinuation right alongside ordinary declarative sentences and logical arguments. Put differently, I've nothing against a rhetoric that goads and provokes objections. Nor do I have anything against laying out a dispassionate account of the way things seem to me. Just don't expect me to tell you which I'm doing at any moment. And don't trust me if I do.

That stormlet of brash pique subsiding abruptly, I lapse back to my usual serene melancholy about the state of theory. Let me amplify some earlier comments and offer an only slightly disingenuous sketch of how cunning gives us a tractable handle on three annoyingly puffy theory dilemmas. One: what is captivating, what disgusting, about what economists have enshrined as hardboiled instrumental rationality, efficiently using one's means to realize one's ends? Sometimes we admire the rational actor for his discipline; sometimes we revile him for his ruthlessness. Two: think of a social role as a bundle of rights and obligations and distinguish two ways you can occupy the role. You can distance yourself from the role and demand some further account of why you should adhere to its rights and obligations. ("I know I'm supposed to hold office hours, but why should I?") Or you can identify with the role and more or less automatically follow its dictates, at least if no pressing worries come up. Sometimes we embrace role distance as autonomy; sometimes we denounce it as alienation. Sometimes we embrace role identification as happy or secure; sometimes we denounce it as bovine or robotic. Three: what is the justification of morality? Why be a slave of duty? Wouldn't a little furtive cheating be sensible? Then why not more than a little? Why not as much cheating as you can prudently hope to get away with? I suspect that these three dilemmas are closely connected, that they may even be at bottom the same dilemma. And I suggest that cunning lets us see how. The cunning agent is unflaggingly methodical in the pursuit of his ends, insistently distant in his roles, lethally ready to be immoral at the drop of a hat. Or anyway he seems to be, or we fear that he is, or he flirts with that stance, or he taunts us for not daring to adopt it as our own.

"*Cunning*," warned a 1770 advice manual, "wears the face of a *virtue*, but is the base representative of it, and no more like it, than an *ape* is like a *man*. It is the art of dissimulation and deceit, which foolish people practice, because they know no better; or being wickedly inclined, act against their better judgment." Raising the stakes, the manual continued, "It deforms the beauty of truth, and renders the charms of simplicity and sincerity, as haggard, as one of those poor old women, who in days of ignorance, were called *witches*."[8] As we'll see, there's a lot packed in here. But can the manual's ready moral condemnation be vindicated?

Perhaps in style, surely in strategy of attack, this essay is different from much of my previous work. I take it no one has any burning interest in my intellectual biography, so suffice it to say that I continue exploring what an unvarnished pragmatist sensibility might mean for doing theory. I remain resolutely antifoundationalist about justification, fascinated by contingencies, bored and stolidly unmoved by the fact/value gap, and temperamentally more inclined to pick apart flabby categories than to try to find sweeping generalizations. But you needn't sympathize with any of that, you needn't even have a view about it, to enjoy reading this essay, or to find it disturbing. Or so I hope.

I presented previous work on these materials at Harvard University, Indiana University, Ohio State University, Stanford University, Swarthmore College, the University of California at Berkeley, the University of Chicago, the University of Virginia, the University of Wisconsin at Madison, and Vanderbilt University. Thanks to patient audiences there for helping me to see what I'm up to. Thanks to the usual suspects, and some new ones, for comments on drafts: Liz Anderson, Jill Horwitz, Sue Juster, Jennet Kirkpatrick, Larry Kramer, Danielle LaVaque-Manty, Mika LaVaque-Manty, Daryl Levinson, Katie Lorenz, Kirstie McClure, Bill Miller, Deborah Moores, Adela Pinch, Jim Reische, Lynn Sanders, Andy Stark, J. David Velleman, Adrian Vermeule, Mark West, and Liz Wingrove. And thanks to the University of Michigan Law School, a fabulous place to work.

[8] Jonas Hanway, *Advice from a Farmer, to His Daughter, in a Series of Discourses*, 3 vols. (London, 1770), 3:253.

DILEMMAS

�֍ Odysseus has a problem. Actually, Odysseus has many problems. The Trojan War is over—he and his fellow Achaians are splendidly victorious—but he is facing an arduous trip home: ten years of sailing from one dangerous adventure to another, with not just his biceps but his considerable wits to guide him. Odysseus is almost the incarnation of *mêtis*, the ancient Greek word we translate as *cunning*.[1] He is, Homer tells us, *polutropos*, many-sided.[2] Rehearsing the history of the Trojan War for Odysseus's son Telemachus, wise old Nestor underlines the point: "no one there could hope to rival Odysseus, / not for sheer cunning— / at every twist of strategy he excelled us all."[3] Endlessly resourceful, quick on the rebound, he successfully navigates perils that would doom more unimaginative, plodding types. The *Odyssey* is in part a celebration of the cunning of Odysseus, a cunning put, we're often told, to exemplary use: Odysseus longs for Ithaca, for his home, his son, and especially his long-suffering wife, Penelope. The brilliant schemes that finally get him back are replayed endlessly in folklore and literature, not to mention comic books and television shows. Odysseus has himself lashed to the mast so he can hear the haunting songs of the Sirens without jumping ship. He ruthlessly steers his boat through the impossibly narrow channel between Scylla, a six-headed monster, and Charybdis, a voracious whirlpool, even though he knows Scylla will snatch and devour six of his sailors, knowledge he doesn't bother sharing with them. Finally back in Ithaca, he enters his own home posing as a beggar. The disguise lets him survey what is now enemy territory and figure out

---

[1] See generally Marcel Detienne and Jean-Pierre Vernant, *Cunning Intelligence in Greek Culture and Society*, trans. Janet Lloyd (Sussex: Harvester Press, 1978); for a comparative extension, see Lisa Raphals, *Knowing Words: Wisdom and Cunning in the Classical Traditions of China and Greece* (Ithaca, NY: Cornell University Press, 1992). The range of the Greek word is wider: *A Greek-English Lexicon*, comp. Henry George Liddell and Robert Scott, rev. and aug. Sir Henry Stuart Jones, 9th ed. (Oxford: Clarendon Press, 1996), p. 1130, offers "wisdom, skill, craft; . . . counsel, plan, understanding."

[2] On this theme, see the suggestive if overly exuberant Pietro Pucci, *Odysseus Polutropos: Intertextual Readings in the Odyssey and the Iliad* (Ithaca, NY: Cornell University Press, 1987).

[3] Throughout, I've quoted from Homer, *The Odyssey*, trans. Robert Fagles (New York: Viking, 1996), and removed occasional italics.

how to kill the suitors besieging Penelope. He'll have help only from Telemachus and two loyal servants. (Well, and a hand from Athena, the goddess of wisdom who dotes on Odysseus and ensures that the suitors' lances never find their mark.)

There is no doubt great cunning in all this. But there may well be more. Consider the savage punishments Odysseus metes out to the disloyal servants. A dozen servant girls have made themselves sexually available to the suitors. After the domestic battle, they get to clean up the gore and for their reward are hanged out in the yard. Melanthius has his ears, nose, hands, and feet severed, his genitals hacked off to feed the dogs, too, all for daring to taunt and kick the still-disguised Odysseus. Why proceed this way? It looks like rage, revenge, punishment for their past misdeeds: a kind of justice, understandable even if overheated and so finally indefensible. This answer looks backward in time for its justification. And there's nothing particularly cunning about it. It's not calculating or devious or self-interested. But now consider a second answer, relentlessly forward-looking, with cunning written all over it. Odysseus, in this view, kills these servants—or should kill them—wholly with an eye to the future behavior of his other servants or maybe more generally his reputation as someone you don't want to cross. (Modern economists insist that rationality is wholly about calculating future consequences. Pay no attention to sunk costs, they insist. Folk wisdom sometimes chimes in. Don't cry over spilt milk; it's water under the bridge; let bygones be bygones.) Of course, he can't *say* that that's why he's doing it. He has to look as vengeful, as obsessed with the past, as he can or else the surviving servants won't be as horrified. They'll take refuge in the thought that if they misbehave, Odysseus will punish them if and only if he thinks that will redound to his future advantage. But savvy observers should see through his apparent vengefulness as just a pose. Now which answer seems to capture Odysseus in the closing books of the poem? Which exhibits him as rational? or as admirable?

It's possible that even as blood and guts are spewing around his living room, Odysseus is contemplating the future. Or that before whipping himself into his not particularly deliberative frenzy, Odysseus steels himself by thinking, "Killing these guys in cold blood opens the best future available to me, so it's time to go berserk." But another of Odysseus's adventures reveals that he can't be the allegorical figure of unadulterated cunning. He and his men are trapped in the loathsome cave of one of the Cyclopes, a brutish giant named Polyphemus who apparently intends to eat them all, two at a time. Odysseus gores Polyphemus in his single eye with a burning log. Better yet, when Polyphemus turns to his fellow Cyclopes for help, his request goes nowhere because Odysseus has dubbed himself Nobody: the other giants can't fathom what's bothering Polyphemus when he wails that Nobody has hurt him. (The Greek has a nice pun. When they respond, "if Nobody has hurt you," *Nobody* is *mê tis*.[4] So it's, "if cunning has hurt you." As it has.) With the blind giant desperately groping around for them, Odysseus and his men steal out of the cave by hanging from the undersides of Polyphemus's sheep. Then a momentary loss of self-control costs Odysseus dearly. Succumbing to the usual desire of heroes smitten with honor and glory, he gloats and tells Polyphemus who he really is. Even a grown giant knows how to run whimpering to daddy—or how to launch a majestic curse. Polyphemus does just that, and his father happens to be Poseidon, god of the seas. When you have to sail home over (and sometimes under) dangerous un-charted waters, you probably don't want Poseidon steaming mad at you. But Odysseus's costly lapse looks like a further advertisement for the conspicuous merits of cunning. Even this notoriously cunning hero, it seems, wasn't cunning enough to keep his mouth shut. Look what hap-pened.

Indeed, it's tempting to read the *Odyssey* as a celebration of cunning more generally. Penelope, for instance, has her own problem. Loutish suit-ors are consuming her estate, abusing her coerced hospitality, while wait-ing for her to choose a new husband to replace the presumably dead Odysseus. So she says that she will choose once she finishes weaving a shroud for Odysseus's father. Every day she weaves, every night she unrav-els: she purchases several years' delay with this stunt. We're often in-structed to applaud this famous sample of feminine wiles, but I'm decid-edly unimpressed. What passes for Penelope's cunning seems more like the gross stupidity of the suitors. ("Gosh, fellas, she works day after day and the thing never gets done. What's going on?" "Beats me.") Or better, like the cunning opportunism of the suitors, if they're playing dumb. Look at the problem from the point of view of any individual suitor. Force the

---

[4] *Odyssey*, trans. Fagles, pp. 509–10.

issue, call Penelope on her ludicrous pretense, and she's all too likely to choose someone else. Even if she's not antagonized by the effrontery, there are plenty of other suitors mobbing the premises, so the odds of being chosen are low in the first place. Meanwhile, the servant girls are offering free food and drink and their lascivious selves to boot. Not a bad deal. Let the lady ravel and unravel. So we should pause when Antinous indignantly repels Telemachus's tearful accusation that he and his fellow suitors are cads sponging off the estate by shifting the blame to Penelope, whom he brands "the matchless queen of cunning." There's a scam here, but who's running it? Maybe Penelope is after all—if she grasps the strategic dilemma her threadbare pose leaves the suitors in.[5]

Or take Athena. When she wants to goad Telemachus into setting off to find his father, she tells him that he has inherited Odysseus's cunning. Now Telemachus does manage to develop a slender backbone and to acquit himself decently, but he is innocent in the arts of cunning. Athena is lying. It's a useful lie, but it's still a lie. She plays more tricks when Odysseus finally returns to Ithaca alone, every one of his men having died along the way. She covers the land with mist to give her time to disguise Odysseus. Here, too, he can use being a nobody as he figures out how to reclaim his home. The mist distresses Odysseus: he doesn't recognize Ithaca. Athena then disguises herself as an elegant young man to reveal to Odysseus that he is back home. She asks who he is. He responds as he so often does when asked about his identity, by rattling off a glib pack of outrageous lies. She laughs—ah, she says, we're both so cunning—and then assures him that she's unflinchingly loyal to him and that she'll help him reclaim his home. Some of this deceitfulness, too, sensibly advances her ends. If she wants Odysseus to prevail, as she does, she needs to disguise him. But some of it isn't necessary. She could just greet Odysseus on the beach and put her cards on the table. Odysseus doesn't need to be tricked or manipulated, because she and he want the same things. The extra cunning on offer here—the shapeshifter adopting the guise of the young man, for instance—is pure playfulness. It allows her to revel in their shared skills—"We're both old hands / at the arts of intrigue"—but it advances no project, skirts around no obstacle. This is cunning for its own sake, for the exhilaration of performance.

[5] I owe this last thought to Katie Lorenz.

Odysseus's routine lying is strategic through and through. He does it to help himself, not for the fun of it. If you can't get away with being nobody but you want to maintain some wiggle room, you might as well be someone else. When you hide behind a mask, an assumed identity, others can't get a fix on you. You'll need some of Odysseus's fluency in the arts of deception—it isn't easy to keep your stories straight when you're inventing them on the fly—and you'll have to hope that those you're trying to fool can't check up on you or just won't bother. Homer reminds us that Odysseus is no slavish lover of the truth, that we needn't believe what he says. Disguised by Athena, ready to deal with the people of Ithaca again, Odysseus encounters his old devoted swineherd, Eumaeus, who lavishes this apparent stranger with hospitality and only then asks for his history and identity. "The great teller of tales[6] returned at length, / 'My story—the whole truth—I'm glad to tell it all.'" Here the narrator emphatically warns the audience: remember, the guy is a liar. So we chuckle at the hilariously detailed picture Odysseus paints of himself as a rich Cretan who fought at Troy and then spent seven years getting fabulously wealthy in Egypt. But we pause when Odysseus introduces none other than Odysseus into his picture. Eumaeus pauses, too. Mystified by the stranger's repeated insistence that Odysseus will return, he wonders aloud, "who are you, I ask you, to lie for no good reason?"

ODYSSEAN PREDICAMENTS

I'm tempted by an eccentric reading. Odysseus, I suspect, is telling lies even when we imagine he's telling the truth. A formal feature of the text is suggestive: we owe Odysseus's most eye-popping tales to Odysseus himself, not the narrator. Asked by gracious King Alcinous to explain why he's moaning at a musical recital of the Trojan War, Odysseus promptly produces the Cyclops, Aeolus's sack of winds that will help him sail home, Circe turning his men into swine, even his trip to the underworld and interviews with famous dead people. No wonder Homer introduces this fan-

---

[6] Milman Parry famously argued that Homer's choice of descriptive epithets is driven by the demands of meter: see *The Making of Homeric Verse: The Collected Papers of Milman Parry*, ed. Adam Parry (Oxford: Clarendon Press, 1971), esp. chaps. 1–2. I don't need to deny the point to say that this epithet is deliciously pointed.

tastic eruption by again branding Odysseus "the great teller of tales." No wonder an enraptured Alcinous declares that he could listen to such wonderful stories all night long. (Odysseus will solemnly reward him with another eruption, this time belching remarkable accounts of skirting Scylla and Charybdis and slaughtering the cattle of sun god Helios.) "One look at you," the king assures Odysseus, "and we know that you are no one who would cheat us—no fraud, such as the dark soil breeds and spreads / across the face of the earth these days." One look? Is Odysseus's credibility written so unmistakably on his face? Could it be? The guileless eyes and their candid unflinching gaze: isn't that exactly the look that the expert con man displays? The king doesn't know how his language—"you are no one"— echoes through the rest of the poem, but we do.[7] We know that Odysseus is no one, a nobody, from his exchange with Polyphemus and we know that when he's a nobody, the instantiation of cunning, he is indeed a cheater. Maybe Alcinous doesn't believe a word of Odysseus's tale, pleasurable as it is to listen to. Maybe he winks when he announces that Odysseus's sincerity is written on his face. True, he showers Odysseus with gifts and sends him on his way. But that customary regal hospitality doesn't mean he's been taken in.

So we know that Odysseus is lying when he treats Athena and Eumaeus to stories about himself. Why not think he's lying when he recounts the amazing tales we usually accept as real? Groaning at the *Odyssey*'s excesses, ancient literary critic Longinus complains that Homer's incredible tales lapse into nonsense.[8] Even Aristotle concedes that only Homer's poetic ability masks the sheer absurdity of some episodes in the *Odyssey*.[9] Homer isn't only feeding Odysseus his lines. He might be adding some of his own. Opening the poem, Homer (or anyway his narrative voice) endorses some of Odysseus's tales, but that can't settle what we should believe. There's no reason to think that Homer's own words are guaranteed to be true. Maybe Homer is in cahoots with Odysseus; maybe Homer is an unreliable narrator, right at the start of the Western literary tradition.[10]

---

[7] Thanks to Arlene Saxonhouse for confirming that Homer's Doric Greek here again deploys the word for "nobody" Odysseus uses with the Cyclopes.

[8] *On the Sublime*, 9.

[9] *Poetics*, 24.

[10] On how slippery Homer and Penelope can be, see John J. Winkler, *The Constraints of Desire: The Anthropology of Sex and Gender in Ancient Greece* (New York: Routledge, 1990), chap. 5.

Indeed, maybe he's only sometimes in cahoots with his literary creation. Maybe the two are uneasy allies, working sometimes at cross-purposes, wary of one another. So too Zeus himself mentions Odysseus's blinding the Cyclops. But we know that that god isn't above lying—or being deceived.

Pause at the timing: it takes Odysseus ten years to get home. That's a dilatory or downright lazy trip, even by ancient standards. (As the crow flies—not, I grant, an available travel option—it's well shy of four hundred miles from Troy to Ithaca.) The war itself took another ten years. So he's been away twenty years. It could be that Penelope isn't the sweet soul of constant devotion. I don't mean to cast any aspersions. On the contrary! I have my doubts about how flattering it is to make Penelope so vacuous, my doubts too about whether we can find that sort of romantic love in this far-off cultural setting. Maybe she harbors doubts, suspicions, okay, out with it, vivid hostile fantasies. Maybe she imagines herself greeting her errant husband with an imperious demand, something along the lines of, "Where in the world have you been?" Or, to sharpen the point, "What the hell have you been doing?"[11]

So what has Odysseus been doing? The *Odyssey* doesn't unfold its ten years with the monotonous regularity of the calendar. It skips huge chunks, puts others under a microscope, jumps back and forth, and so on. But we learn that Odysseus spends seven years sleeping with gorgeous Calypso. Yes, during the day he thinks of Penelope and cries. He loves her or misses her or feels guilty or ambivalent—sentiments not unusual in the litanies of unfaithful husbands—but he doesn't return to his journey until Calypso sends him packing. Now this, some will respond indignantly, is patently unfair. Odysseus is stranded without a ship until Calypso offers him one, and even this mortal would be hard-pressed to outwit a nymph. So what about the further year he spends sleeping with Circe? This time he leaves only when his men scold him. Homer fails to mention any tears. So it's ten years' wandering, eight of them spent sleeping around. He'll need an awfully good story when he finally gets home. It's helpful of Homer to distract his audience's attention from this elapsed time. Imagine 80 percent of the poem dwelling on Odysseus's extramarital sexual performances.

---

[11] Helene P. Foley, "'Reverse Similes' and Sex Roles in the Odyssey," *Arethusa* 11:1 (Spring 1978):7–26 is shrewd on gender and deception in thinking about Penelope and Odysseus.

I don't expect to persuade many of the merits of this vantage point on the *Odyssey*. After all, we like our literary texts, especially the ancient ones, high-minded, and a heroic Odysseus is more seductive than a stray husband with sorry excuses. Regardless, the *Odyssey* offers tales within tales, and our first impressions about which to believe may be sorely mistaken. We have not just the cunning of Odysseus, the swashbuckling man of action, to reckon with, but also that of Homer, the poet using dazzling words to teach and delight and confuse us. Our knowledge of Greek mythology is complicated further: their poets and playwrights retailed different versions of these stories. (I still remember how baffled I was on my first reading of the *Iliad* to find the Achaians prevailing at Troy without spiriting themselves into the city walls inside a giant wooden horse, then how much more baffled to find a passing reference to the Trojan horse in the *Odyssey*.) What we make of Odysseus will depend too on which stories we turn to. Those inclined to think well of him because of the *Odyssey*'s deft escape routines might want to think again.

So consider Sophocles's *Philoctetes*.[12] Before the play opens, Philoctetes, proud possessor of Heracles's bow, has trespassed unwittingly on sacred terrain. Rewarding his blunder, a divinely mandated snake bite leaves him with a suppurating, stinking wound that never heals. He's disgusting, prone to crippling fits too, and his agonized cries disturb his fellow Achaians' religious observances. So they've ditched him on an uninhabited island where he's eked out a living death. Now, though, an oracle instructs them that they need his bow to conquer Troy. Odysseus returns to the island with Neoptolemus, noble son of his noble father, Achilles. Odysseus patiently explains to a wide-eyed Neoptolemus that the only way to lure Philoctetes back to Troy is to trick him. Philoctetes hates Odysseus, who was instrumental in the decision to ditch him. So there's no chance of persuading the wounded man to rejoin the fray. (Talk of his future advantage will go nowhere when he's fixed on the past, nursing a grudge. Does that make Philoctetes irrational?) Given his prowess as an archer, they can't try to take him by force, either. Odysseus pulls no punches. "You must

---

[12] I quote from David Grene's translation in *The Complete Greek Tragedies*, Centennial Edition, ed. David Grene and Richmond Lattimore, 4 vols. (Chicago: University of Chicago Press, 1992), 2:401–66. Aeschylus and Euripides wrote plays on the same episode which alas don't survive. For discussion, see Dio Chrysostom, *Discourse* no. 52; and see too Dio's *Discourse* no. 59 for some dialogue apparently based on Euripides's play.

sharpen your wits," he advises Neoptolemus, "to become a thief / of the arms no man has conquered."

Neoptolemus balks: "I have a natural antipathy / to get my ends by tricks and stratagems." He's willing to fight Philoctetes, he says, and we shouldn't harbor any sentimental illusions about his conception of a fair fight. "Surely a one-legged man / cannot prevail against so many of us!" He acknowledges that Odysseus is his military superior, that he's reluctant to be called traitor. "Still, my lord, / I would prefer even to fail with honor / than win by cheating." He doesn't doubt the value of prevailing at Troy. But he's not willing to adopt just any means promising to realize that end. An honorable man will not stoop so low.

Odysseus responds in the patronizing tones of a cynical—or is it wise? or shall we split the difference and label it worldly?—parent addressing an idealistic teenager. "I was young, too, once, and then I had a tongue / very inactive and a doing hand." Since then he's learned that "it is the tongue that wins and not the deed." Yet Odysseus's advice appalls Neoptolemus. "Do you not find it vile yourself, this lying?" Odysseus's response must sound calm, even relentless: "Not if the lying brings our rescue with it." One might think his position is modest. In an emergency or when the stakes are astronomically high, you have to be willing to stoop, to do things that ordinarily would be disqualified as dishonorable or immoral. If you want to sack Troy, you can't afford scruples. Or perhaps Odysseus is leaning on his position as emissary of the army. It's not up to me, he might be thinking, to decide what's right or wrong. I'm on a mission, entrusted by my peers—he can't honestly call them superiors—with a task; it would be wrong to disappoint them, and they're responsible for whatever choice they've made. But the continuing exchange reveals that Odysseus's position is radical, not modest. "How can a man not blush to say such things?" demands Neoptolemus. Odysseus shoots back, "When one does something for gain, one need not blush." Not just something splendid or crucial, like taking Troy. Not just something dutiful or loyal, like serving one's friends or army. Just something: any old thing. This nobody will stop at nothing. The modest position implicitly concedes that it's sleazy to deceive Philoctetes, but adds that that can be outweighed by a more compelling reason. The radical position denies that there's anything objectionable to be outweighed. That's what makes Odysseus's response breathtaking. After all, earnest young Neoptolemus understands that lying to Philoctetes might work. He thinks it unacceptable anyway. That further thought, that some successful tactics ought to be rejected, indeed ought not be considered in the first place, is precisely what Odysseus resolutely denies. Why care about dishonor when gain beckons?

The play is not alone in casting Odysseus as blithely unmoved by dishonor when gain beckons. In the *Iliad*, he and Diomedes slaughter sleeping Trojan soldiers. It's a tactical winner, thinning the enemy ranks at little risk and, as it turns out, no cost. But there is no honor in such butchery. Consider too another moment of lopsided combat. Expert with his own bow and arrow, Paris, the Trojan who grabbed Helen and so provoked the war, hangs back from hand-to-hand combat and picks off enemy soldiers. But when he wounds Diomedes in the heel, Diomedes sneers at him as a dirty fighter and an effeminate wretch to boot. Should Paris respond that he can kill with his bow and arrow, so he needn't blush or worry about fairness or his masculinity? Should Diomedes be joining Odysseus for his nocturnal carnage and then mocking Paris?

Odysseus's unswerving pursuit of results has its appeal, but it isn't anachronistic or mawkish to hesitate over it. The ancient Greek sources themselves register or invite hesitation. Fidelity to the historical sources aside, let's distinguish Odysseus's resourcefulness from his willingness to adopt any means that works. On offer in the careening adventures of the *Odyssey*, whether we are to believe in them or not, is ingenious creativity, the ability to come up with clever schemes to get out of one scrape after another, also to improvise on the fly, react quickly to new challenges, not get stuck in bureaucratic ruts. Not everyone is so resourceful, and I've no hesitation in admiring this facet of Odysseus. Are you confident you could figure out how to escape from Polyphemus's cave? or the traps of our more manicured world? But that resourcefulness isn't the same as Odysseus's disregard for what might be objectionable in adopting some means. Still, there's room to be resourceful without dipping into a bag of immoral or otherwise dubious tricks. We tangle both notions (and others) together in our concept of cunning. That helps explain why we're of (at least) two minds about whether or in what sense it's a vice or a virtue. Blind Polyphemus when he's threatening to kill you? Sure, unless you're a pacifist. Abandon six of your sailors to Scylla to navigate a channel that could kill you and all your sailors? Maybe. Trick Philoctetes so shamelessly? Maybe not.

Let's dwell on our hesitation—I conscript you in sharing it—about Odysseus's stance in *Philoctetes*. Suppose we accept the play's premise that the only way to get Philoctetes and his bow back to Troy is to trick him. (One incredulous writer of antiquity complains that obviously they can overpower him: his bow and arrow will be useless once they're close by.)[13] Should they do it? Neoptolemus overcomes his instinctive revulsion and spins his own lies, casting himself as a bitter foe of Odysseus who's leaving Troy and would be happy to bring Philoctetes home. Those lies work: Philoctetes hands over the bow as he succumbs to another debilitating fit. Yet when Philoctetes recovers, he finds Neoptolemus oddly hesitant. "Is it disgust at my sickness?" asks the archer. "All is disgust when one leaves his own nature / and does things that misfit it," responds Neoptolemus. Torn between the "terrible compassion" he feels for Philoctetes, the ties of justice and interest that he says militate in favor of following his orders, and the nausea cascading over him at his own deceptive performance, Neoptolemus has to witness a bullying tirade from a newly returned Odysseus, who insists that Philoctetes must indeed sail for Troy. Odysseus and Neoptolemus, still clutching the bow, relinquish the stage for a miserable colloquy between Philoctetes and Neoptolemus's sailors. Then Neoptolemus strides back onstage, intent on undoing what he now sees as his wrong by returning Philoctetes's bow. Odysseus threatens him with the army's reprisal, but now the younger man won't be bullied. Philoctetes thinks somehow there is another trick. Even his pious invocation of Zeus doesn't assuage his doubts. Still, he gets back his bow.

So should they trick him out of the bow or not? Is Neoptolemus redeeming himself, making amends or offering restitution, at the end? Or is he revealing that he's a spineless wonder, sabotaging the expedition against Troy and grievously disappointing—and injuring—his fellow soldiers? It's easy to denounce Odysseus.[14] There's something cold, even fiendish, in his ruthless campaign to get the desired result, his utter lack of interest in what is vexing in using or abusing poor Philoctetes. And his language is harsh, even brutal.[15] Manipulating Philoctetes is treating him as if he were not a person but a stubborn obstacle, a stone that needs to be kicked aside.

---

[13] Dio Chrysostom, *Discourse* no. 52.

[14] See for instance Martha Nussbaum, "Consequences and Character in Sophocles' *Philoctetes*," *Philosophy and Literature*: (Fall 1976):25–53; and James Boyd White, *Heracles' Bow: Essays on the Rhetoric and Poetics of the Law* (Madison: University of Wisconsin Press, 1985), chap. 1.

[15] For another rendition of how we might idiomatically construe the Greek, see Anne Carson, "'Echo with No Door on Her Mouth': A Notional Refraction through Sophokles, Plato, and Defoe," *Stanford Literature Review* 3:2 (Fall 1986):255–56. Thanks to Yopie Prins for the reference.

We shrink from such callous contempt, and Sophocles isn't trying to make it look pretty.

Then again, maybe it's too easy to denounce Odysseus. When he threatens Neoptolemus at the end, he's just blustering. We could supply him more persuasive lines. "What?" he could jeer, "you care so much for your precious clean hands that you dare not sully yourself with a bad deed? You flatter yourself that it's integrity; you want to respect your nature. You vain idiot! I think it's self-indulgence or, worse yet, outrageous selfishness. The Achaians are depending on you. Your moral regard richly benefits our Trojan enemies. Funny, isn't it, that such a scrupulous fellow is doing just what a traitor would! I wouldn't call your moral sensibilities exquisite. I'd call them perverse." Deceiving Philoctetes may be cunning, even dastardly. It may also be the right thing to do. If you are sure it's wrong, say because it treats Philoctetes only as a means, would you stick to that view no matter how great we make the reward? What if they have to trick Philoctetes not in order to take Troy, but to save dozens, hundreds, thousands of lives?

I see no obvious way to decide what ought to be done here. Neither, I conjecture, did Sophocles. The play ends with that infamous contrivance of ancient Greek drama, the *deus ex machina* or god from the machine: Heracles himself descends to instruct Philoctetes to make his peace with the world and help take Troy. The contrivance is usually deemed a sign of dramatic weakness or failure. Here, though, it has to be a merit of the play. It's as if Sophocles wants to say that there is no way of adjudicating the competing claims of Neoptolemus and Odysseus, no way of persuading wounded Philoctetes to abandon his island even if he'd be better off doing so. Only divine intervention could pretend to resolve anything. Those of us not lucky enough to rely on it will have to flounder through. Before leaving the play, though, I want to suggest that at stake is not just the famous question of practical judgment, "What ought to be done?" At stake too is the question of what sort of person to be. Not a wholly independent question, either. Deeds require doers, and the play also brings into arrestingly sharp focus the differences between Neoptolemus and Odysseus.

We've already seen one. Neoptolemus, remember, thinks a man should blush to utter aloud the thoughts that Odysseus unblushingly defends. We know that Neoptolemus cares about his honor. That means that if his peers would disapprove hearing such talk, he should keep his lips zipped.

But we know too that Neoptolemus cares about justice. When he's bent on returning Philoctetes's bow, Odysseus scolds him: "In your own case / neither the words nor the acts are clever." "Still," Neoptolemus snaps back, "if they are just, they are better than clever." Justice, unlike honor, doesn't depend in any straightforward way on what others think. So Neoptolemus's real position is even stronger than the one he articulates. A man should blush not only to speak as Odysseus does, but even to have Odysseus's thoughts occur to him in the first place. If he is a just man, he will have settled dispositions, ways of doing things and not doing them, ways of seeing and not seeing. When he's disgusted with himself, it's because he has flouted those dispositions—or because he's learned that they weren't as deep as he'd thought. At the play's opening, realizing that Neoptolemus will shrink from his advice, Odysseus tries this gambit: "For one brief shameless portion of a day / give me yourself, and then for all the rest / you may be called most scrupulous of men." (Imagine Satan asking you not to sell him your soul, but to rent it overnight.) But is scrupulousness something you can effortlessly turn on and off? Is a self something you want to entrust to another? If that other is as emphatically unscrupulous as Odysseus? The language of giving yourself away is obscure. However we construe it, though, it's ominous in this context.

So what kind of person is Odysseus? What does it mean to be unscrupulous, literally to have no scruples, no doubts or hesitations over right and wrong? Sympathizing with Neoptolemus, Philoctetes hurls a stinging accusation at Odysseus: "Your shabby, slit-eyed soul taught him step by step / to be clever in mischief against his nature and will." Exploiting his age and status, Odysseus has corrupted the younger man. Odysseus's retort is eye-opening: "As the occasion / demands, such a one am I." He is a shapeshifter able to don any disguise, any mask, and instantly deliver a compelling performance in role. It's not that he has a bad or shabby character. He has no character, no settled dispositions, at all. So is he immoral? He adds that "When there is a competition of men just and good, / you will find none more scrupulous than myself." As the occasion demands, if gain is to be had, morality is fine, too. "What I seek in everything is to win," so he can't afford to swear off justice or goodness, either—they might always come in handy. The villain devoted to deception and evil isn't nearly cunning enough.

Is it possible to be so accomplished and flexible? There are actual cases of versatile shapeshifters.[16] Eric Dolphy excelled on flute, alto sax, and bass clarinet, all before dying at thirty-six. Could he have mastered half a dozen more instruments? And then become, oh, an oil painter, a neurosurgeon, a composer of poignant sonnets, an astrophysicist, an innovative sculptor, a loving husband, a financial analyst, an ethnographer of the Siberian steppes, a charitable pastor, a bare-knuckled ward politician, and a French chef? Karl Marx indicted the division of labor for consigning a man to be a hunter, a fisherman, a shepherd, or a critical critic, and to stay in one role on pain of losing his income. Under communism, he promised, that man would hunt in the morning, fish in the afternoon, and so on, just as he pleased, without ever being imprisoned in a given job. The indictment's terms are tongue in cheek—Marx was no fan of the critical critics—but not, I think, Marx's underlying worries about role differentiation.[17] Regardless, time is scarce. Worse, the more intriguing options you have, the scarcer time gets. So choice always entails renunciation. Whatever evils you're prepared to lay at capitalism's feet, this can't be one of them. If you crave grim melodrama, think of all those selves you could have been but chose to murder by becoming who you are now instead. Even those betting on great longevity will have to face the unpleasant fact that some skills are contradictory. If you enlarge and harden your hands as a bricklayer or a boxer, you're going to have a hard time with laser surgery or miniature needlepoint.

Worse, a reputation for flexibility itself prevents some possibilities. In the *Iliad*, Odysseus leads a delegation imploring Achilles, sulking majestically in his ship, to rejoin the fray. Achilles announces that he will answer bluntly, so he doesn't have to listen to one speaker after another. "I hate that man like the very Gates of Death / who says one thing but hides another in his heart."[18] It's a polite apology for his own bluntness: he doesn't

---

[16] See for instance *The Unparallel'd Impostor: Or, The Whole Life, Artifices and Forgeries of Japhet Crook, Alias Sir Peter Stranger, Bart.* (London, 1731); Steven C. Bullock, "A Mumper among the Gentle: Tom Bell, Colonial Confidence Man," *William and Mary Quarterly*, 3rd ser., 55:2 (April 1998):231–58; Frank W. Abagnale with Stan Redding, *Catch Me if You Can: The Amazing True Story of the Most Extraordinary Liar in the History of Fun and Profit* (New York: Broadway Books, 2000).

[17] *The German Ideology*, pt. 1; see Terrell Carver, "Communism for Critical Critics? *The German Ideology* and the Problem of Technology," *History of Political Thought* 9:1 (Spring 1988):129–36.

[18] *Iliad*, bk. 9; the translation is from Homer, *The Iliad*, trans. Robert Fagles (New York: Viking, 1990), p. 262.

want to be despicable. Or is it? The comment doubles as a brazen assault on Odysseus. He, not Achilles, is that man who hides one thing and speaks another. That means his plea to Achilles is doomed. Achilles knows Odysseus more than well enough to know what a shapeshifter he is. That makes his deeds remarkable, but his words untrustworthy. "As the occasion demands, such a one am I": yet he can't meet the occasion demanding a speaker of known integrity.

So Odysseus's retort names an impossible aspiration. But plenty of aspirations are out of reach but still valuable. Engineers can't give us frictionless surfaces and, face it, Windows 2020, with all its bells and whistles, will still crash. Suppose Odysseus growls, "Of *course* you can't be infinitely flexible and infinitely skilled, but the more the better." Really? Is constancy always to be derided as a rut, never to be embraced as character or integrity? It's hard to imagine what it would be like to be whatever the occasion demands, what kind of person you'd be, whether you'd be a person at all. Whom is Penelope in love with, anyway? Try this: as the occasion demands, he is sexual athlete with Calypso and Circe, devoted husband with Penelope. But he can't be both. To be a devoted husband is in part not to play sexual athlete with other women. It makes no difference that he's far from home, no difference whether Penelope eventually finds out. So there's something suspect or incoherent in being whatever the occasion demands. Meeting the demands of some occasions will preclude meeting those of others.

Can't Odysseus still give Penelope the impression that he's a devoted husband? He'll keep some facts dark. She'll learn that inquiries into his ten years' voyage distress him, so she'll discreetly avoid the topic. He may not be a devoted husband, but he'll expertly act the part. She'll never know the difference. Is there anything worrisome about her blissful ignorance? It might come crashing down. Maybe a bitter sailor who survived will roll his eyes at tales of domesticated Odysseus cuddling Penelope by the fireside. Maybe he'll land in Ithaca with a blackmail threat—or a wagging tongue. Suppose Odysseus casually dismisses such prospects as exceedingly unlikely. Suppose he's right to do so. Or suppose he's willing to take his chances—the risk of exposure adds a spicy thrill to his newly cozy life— and suppose she never finds out. Now their marriage is built on a lie or anyway a significant omission. But what precisely is wrong with that? Suppose you knew the sordid truth and you were magically there. Would you make her better off if you told her? ("I don't want to meddle, dear, but [pause, sigh, doleful gaze, impulsively clasped hands] there's something you simply must know about Odysseus.") Or might she rightly complain that you'd wrecked her life?

It seems plausible that Penelope is worse off married to an Odysseus pretending to be faithful than a genuinely faithful Odysseus, even if she can't tell the difference. If that sounds paradoxical, try it in two steps. Suppose she does see through pretend-Odysseus. He brandishes a magic spell and she instantly subsides into taking appearances at face value. Has the spell made her better off or, as I'm inclined to think, further injured her? Or imagine that your own partner is a robot, an alien, a dream, a super-duper hologram with all the other sensory dimensions provided by miracles of engineering. Can you honestly shrug and say, well, makes no difference to me, after all I can't tell the difference between that and a real human being? Then too it seems plausible that Odysseus himself is worse off being a successfully deceptive husband than a faithful one. The easy point is that he has to scour the horizon for arrivals and news requiring special explanations. But let's shelve that easy point and imagine that he finds the deceptive performances simple, pleasurable, choiceworthy. He silently rejoices at how clever he is. Still it seems plausible to say that he is missing out on the good of a relatively honest relationship. He can't be wholly intimate, open, vulnerable; he can't unburden himself of whatever's on his mind. Those possibilities are good whether he happens to prefer them or not.

Let's take stock of some of these Odyssean predicaments. Front and center are some worries about how to connect morality and rationality. Next—and connected—are a couple of puzzles about time. Finally there's a quandary about the rightful domain of cunning tactics.

A tantalizing picture, now canonized as instrumental or means/end rationality, shapes up this way. Your ends are given. Reason figures out how to realize them. A trivial case: you're thirsty and reason has you stroll over to the fountain for some cold water. More complex cases have the same structure. You want to be a doctor and reason discovers that you have to go to medical school, that you'll need to do well as an undergraduate, and so on. But reason has nothing to say about the validity of the ends, unless we can take an apparent end and cast it as a means to an even higher end. Maybe you want to be a doctor solely to make lots of money. Then reason might apprise you of the salary implications of managed health care and advise you to consider investment banking or corporate law.

Now let's distinguish two accounts of just how your ends are given. One: your ends are what you want, the verb trading on *lack* and *desire*. In the seventeenth century, we find Hobbes urging that "the Thoughts, are to the Desires, as Scouts, and Spies, to range abroad, and find the way to the things Desired."[19] In the eighteenth, we find Hume insisting that "Reason is, and ought only to be the slave of the passions, and can never pretend to any other office than to serve and obey them." He conceded that "this opinion may appear somewhat extraordinary,"[20] but today it counts in many circles as screamingly obvious. So suppose you want to see how many stale donuts you can eat on Tuesday mornings in airport terminals during the next year. Maybe you have a reason—say you've bet a friend that you can generate a new entry in the *Guinness Book of World Records*— or maybe you have no reason at all, just whimsy. Then reason diligently investigates the schedule of local donut production and distribution, travel connections to nearby airports, how to keep your Tuesday mornings open, and so on.

Two: your ends are set by what's good for you—what's in your interests or advances your welfare—whether or not that engages your desires. It's good for you to eat a balanced diet and get regular exercise, but you want to snarf down lots of saturated fats and love being a couch potato. Then rationality counsels that you eat more leafy green vegetables and that you actually use that exercise bike you've been hanging damp laundry on. Indeed rationality may counsel that you work on changing your desires, that you learn to savor pungent rapini and sweaty exhaustion alike. Some strenuously resist the thought that your interests or welfare could be anything besides what you want. But the example of health should make clear that the two notions are independent.[21] They may overlap. You may happen to like regular exercise. They may have a tighter internal link. Sometimes it's good for you to do something—relax with a novel, say—simply because

---

[19] Thomas Hobbes, *Leviathan*, chap. 8.

[20] David Hume, *A Treatise of Human Nature*, bk. 2, pt. 3, sec. 3.

[21] See Thomas Scanlon, "Preference and Urgency," *Journal of Philosophy* 72:19 (November 1975):655–69; Stephen Darwall, *Welfare and Rational Care* (Princeton, NJ: Princeton University Press, 2002). I'm not persuaded, though, by Philippa Foot, *Natural Goodness* (Oxford: Clarendon Press, 2001).

you want to. And once you want something, you may gain interests you wouldn't otherwise have. If you want to be a doctor, you gain an interest in excelling in undergraduate chemistry and biology courses. (Which doesn't mean you'll find them interesting, a similar locution with a sharply different meaning. Even if they're deadly dull, you'll have an interest in mastering them. Though you might want to reconsider your desire to be a doctor if the nuts and bolts of the trade are anathema.) I grant such connections, but we can't stipulate that your interests or welfare are always and necessarily what you want, no more and no less.

The first view of ends leaves open how selfish you are. Maybe you're a wretch who wouldn't go two steps out of your way to save a life or would do so if and only if you thought you might win a reward. Maybe you're a saint who takes in crack babies for foster care and then fights to adopt them. Maybe you're partly selfish, partly altruistic, and have many other motivations, too. Maybe, for instance, you're disinterestedly obsequious and play lickspittle toady even when others can't help you and even when they're dismayed by your groveling.[22] The second way of thinking about ends seems to link rationality to selfishness, but that depends on how we construe "good for you." There's surely room to say that it's good for you to be considerate of others absent the further thought that they will duly reward you.

But I acknowledge the temptation to link rationality and self-interest. In some moods, we think that selfish action raises no puzzles about explanation or justification, but that self-sacrifice demands a further story. In a raging storm, the boat capsizes, people scream, and two people dive in. One snatches a life preserver and heads for shore. The other keeps looking for flailing survivors, not loved ones he can't imagine abandoning, but strangers. He's shivering, exhausted, no longer able to make it to shore. Luckily a rescue boat picks him up, but he couldn't have known that would happen. The first, you might think, is merely prudent: and indeed this kind of instrumental rationality gets dubbed prudential rationality. So his action is unremarkable. But why does the second risk his life? It's tempting to look for some hidden or indirect bit of self-interest. Maybe he was hoping for fame or the hand in marriage of the woman who had brutally rejected

[22] See Stephen Holmes, "The Secret History of Self-Interest," in Jenny Mansbridge, ed., *Beyond Self-Interest* (Chicago: University of Chicago Press, 1990).

him as a coward. I don't doubt that sometimes such hidden or indirect bits of self-interest motor action. Amiably misanthropic writers—la Rochefoucauld and Mandeville are my favorites—delight in detecting them, in trying to puncture what they see as our fatuous complacency in believing we have loftier motivations. But it's absurd to think that self-interest motors everything we do. News flash: Mother Teresa was not secretly gunning for the Nobel Prize.

The terrain here is littered with familiar equivocations. Here are three. One: some collapse the category self-interest into voluntary action. "You chose to do it, didn't you? So it must have been good for you." That rescues the claim that all human action is self-interested by making it trivial. If Mother Teresa voluntarily washes lepers' feet to serve the needy or mortify her flesh or try to sanctify a dismal corner of our profane world, it's pointless to insist her action was selfish.

Two: it makes no difference whether the formal scheme of instrumental rationality is pliable enough to accommodate anything and everything. Some will assert that Odysseus and Neoptolemus are both instrumentally rational, that they just assign different costs and benefits to various actions and outcomes. I don't believe that we can always tinker with our descriptions of means and ends, costs and benefits, to accommodate anything and everything. But even if we can, that shows only that we can stretch the model to Silly Putty lengths. After we're done, we still have to confront the conflict between Neoptolemus and Odysseus. Fans of self-interest or utility maximization may think that they've uncovered some deep unity in the world. So does the caricatured Eastern mystic who intones that all is one. But maybe they just need a more discriminating vocabulary. Put differently, instrumental rationality looks empty only on paper and blackboards. In the world, it has a recognizable social personality or a series of them. One is Odyssean scorn for worries about honor and justice, a relentless focus on securing desired outcomes. Another is Puritan discipline, the fussy, even neurotic, gathering and allocation of resources. Rather than think of instrumental rationality as empty, it would be better to unmask it as a shapeshifter.

Three: sometimes our apparent departures from instrumental rationality turn out to serve the demands of the theory. It's often efficient, for instance, to rely on habits and rules of thumb because it's costly to spend lots of time calculating. Some are willing to swallow hard and say that the rationality of an action has nothing to do with the self-understandings or motivations of those performing it—indeed, that it might be rational not to be motivated by the grounds that actually justify your action.[23] But the conjecture that our apparent departures invariably realize our ends efficiently is a scrap of magical thinking or secular theodicy masquerading as hardheaded realism. Even if it's true, it's irrelevant in guiding deliberation. If it's bad to calculate, it's bad to calculate. So if we're looking for an account of what considerations properly guide you when you're acting, we needn't worry about whether an external observer could successfully describe it as instrumentally rational for you not to attempt to be rational, or even to attempt not to be rational.

I don't expect these hasty remarks to persuade the enthusiastic fans of self-interest. I don't imagine anyway that they are persuadable. The fans have been championing their pet view for centuries, and others have patiently refuted it again and again. So I will assume without further discussion that not all human action is self-interested. Yet that doesn't dissolve the puzzle about how to connect rationality and morality. You have an end, selfish or not. You seize on a means to your end. Then morality, like some thuggish traffic cop banishing you to an annoying detour, forbids the means. (You want to close that contract, but no, you may not bribe the clerk.) Worse, maybe morality forbids the end. (No, you may not murder your enemy.) Now it looks like you're stuck, paralyzed, between the counsels of rationality and morality, like one of those stricken cartoon characters with a leering devil perched on one shoulder, a beseeching angel on the other. Morality looks mysterious, unmotivated, indefensible. It gets in the way of doing what's rational. No wonder Odysseus declares, "When one does something for gain, one need not blush." Maybe Neoptolemus, with his curious attachments to honor and morality, should be blushing at his sheer stupidity in balking at achieving his ends. The end is given, whether by desire or by the agent's welfare or interests. The means are available. What more need be said?

On either account of ends, rationality is all about means. As Hume emphasizes, it can't pretend to judge ends: "'Tis not contrary to reason to prefer the destruction of the whole world to the scratching of my finger." To

---

[23] See Derek Parfit, *Reasons and Persons* (Oxford: Clarendon Press, 1984), chap. 1, especially pp. 23–24 on self-effacing theories.

dispel the illusion that reason has anything to do with egoism, he adds, "'Tis not contrary to reason for me to choose my total ruin, to prevent the least uneasiness of an *Indian* or person wholly unknown to me."[24] Much more can be said to refine the picture. Economists have worked wonders (no, I'm not being ironic)[25] in formalizing a mathematically tractable account of utility maximization. Yet already we can sense that this picture of rationality, however successful in illuminating market domains, is wrongheaded for several reasons. For now I want only to emphasize its unflinching focus on the future. I cheerfully concede that sometimes that's what rationality is concerned with. But not always. Many of our practices are profoundly backward-looking. We punish criminals; we grieve at funerals, even when we've had plenty of time to anticipate the deaths of our loved ones, even when we're relieved by their deaths and think they and we are now better off; we ritualistically, even lovingly, retell the stories of our traditions. More ambitious economists will pounce. Don't we punish criminals not because they deserve it, but to deter future crime? Maybe. But couldn't it be both? Does the hostility to retributive theories of punishment arise because desert is allegedly mysterious or because they direct our attention to the past and we're in the clutches of a picture of rationality that forbids that? Or again, do we grieve at funerals to show other mourners that we're caring friends? Should we? Lizzie is stony, frigid, becalmed in an ocean of enigmatic memories at her sister's funeral. Her mother beckons. Does she hug Lizzie and whisper that it's fine to bawl? No, she has an economics Ph.D. and she murmurs, "Dear, you're missing a prize opportunity to send a lucrative signal." What is wrong with this picture?

So instrumental rationality directs our attention exclusively to the future. But in plenty of settings we're riveted on the past. Some of that is doubtless neurotic: there must be some kernel of sense in all the psychological blather about letting go of childhood. And some of it is politically lethal: the year 1389 still drenches the Balkans in blood. But sometimes we properly care for the past. Your best friend from high school shows up on your doorstep. Then she was popular, fun-loving, and she generously saw you through some rough stuff. Now she's unkempt, distraught, scattered.

---

[24] *Treatise*, bk. 2, pt. 3, sec. 3.

[25] But yes, the apparently rigorous categories of economics can mask a lot of confusion. See my "Externalities and Other Parasites," 67 *University of Chicago Law Review* 3 (Summer 2000): 895–923.

Her life has gone badly, yours well. She could use some money. Quite a bit, as she blurts out. On this scanty description, you're not obliged to help her out. But doing so could be perfectly sensible. Not because you were hoping to rekindle your friendship. Indeed you might hope that she would disappear and put herself back together far away. You might be confident she'll disappear whether you lighten your wallet or not. Still, if giving her money is rational, it needn't be because you were hoping to bask in others' admiration of your charitable works: remember the traditions that enjoin you to keep your good works secret. Nor is it helpful to insist on the future impact on your own mental states. Yes, maybe you'll preen yourself in front of the mirror—"What a loyal friend and charitable soul am I!"—and maybe you'd suffer gnawing remorse if you spurned her. But there's something contrived about thinking that you act to control your own later emotions. Those emotions are parasitic on appraisals of what you've done, whether you've acted well or badly. So yes, the remorse is in the future. But it hangs on the judgment that you should have helped her out. That judgment responds to your past. It doesn't promise to realize any future goal. But it seems rational for all that. However pliable it's supposed to be, instrumental rationality does assume action wholly devoted to future consequences. But we have histories as well as futures. There's something worrisome in the image of being relentlessly uninterested in our pasts.[26]

Let me distinguish the point from two uncontroversial ones. Everyone agrees that the past helps shape who we are. The causal story about our current desires and interests has to pull extensively on our histories. And everyone—let's abandon skeptical fretting about induction—agrees that the past is the storehouse of experience we can draw on in predicting the shape of the future. We know that water will relieve your thirst because it always has. The further point I want to press is that the past can provide good reasons or justifications for action. Try this problem: your partner is diagnosed, at a tragically young age, with Alzheimer's disease. The disease has a predictable downward curve. Should you bow out the moment future costs outweigh future benefits? Or might you properly think yourself

---

[26] For connected worries, see, in different idioms, "Rational Conduct," in Michael Oakeshott, *Rationalism in Politics and Other Essays*, new and expanded ed. (Indianapolis, IN: LibertyPress, 1991), pp. 99–131; Amartya Sen, "Rational Fools: A Critique of the Behavioral Foundations of Economic Theory," *Philosophy & Public Affairs* 6:4 (Summer 1977):317–44.

bound to care for the loved one to the bitter end? Yes, you prefer the future in which your old best friend has funds to that in which you turn her away destitute; you prefer the future in which you care for your partner to that in which you pack your bags and sneak away. Again it's tempting to stretch the formal structure of instrumental rationality and again I think that shows its Silly Putty pliability. It is the comic gargoyle of the social sciences masquerading as a hardheaded realist. And again notice that we care not just about outcomes, but about how they arise. It's one thing for your old friend to be destitute, another for her to be destitute because you spurned her plea. An account of rationality should illuminate these matters, not hide them.

So too—here's my second point about time and rationality—the contrast between Odysseus's flexibility and Neoptolemus's integrity has a chronological dimension. "As the occasion demands, such a one am I": not only, I'll be whatever it takes to solve the problem at hand; but also, I'll be whatever fits the moment. Not that Odysseus refuses to adopt any end that can't be realized quickly. Nor that he's unwilling to take detours. No one hoping to conquer the pinnacle can be sure that every step will be uphill. Rather that he disavows any interest in character, integrity, settled dispositions, which he sees as straitjackets denying him the flexibility he needs to realize his ends. Modern philosophers have fretted that personal identity is elusive, even fictive. They've nominated different kinds of continuity over time as serviceable candidates answering to our intuitions about identity. Is Odysseus intent on not having any identity? He's still disguised when he first returns home. But Euryclea, who nursed him when he was an infant, recognizes a scar on his thigh. So there are physical limits to his shapeshifting. Would Odysseus be better off as Proteus, the sea god he wrestles into submission, who actually can change his shape at will? Is the scar an emblem of failure, a contemptible limit? Criminals splash acid to try to eradicate their fingerprints, and plastic surgeons obligingly try to supply us with others' bodies. What about Neoptolemus's disgust at departing from his nature? Is his integrity a psychic scar?

One last quandary. Where—in what social settings—does Odysseus belong? Where is cunning alluring, even choiceworthy? Where should it be resisted? For that quandary, I want to turn to that infamous genius of modern politics.

CUNNING: ALWAYS AND EVERYWHERE?

Poor Niccolò Machiavelli. A forgettable Florentine functionary, he fell from favor in 1512—a conspiracy knocked his faction out of power—and soon after landed in jail. There he was tortured with the strappado: his wrists were tied behind him; then he was dropped from a height and left suddenly hanging in midair. The jerk was often enough to dislocate the victim's shoulders and always enough to ignite blazing pain. Four times was customary, usually plenty to elicit whatever confessions the authorities sought, but Machiavelli endured the ordeal six times. A few weeks later, he was released. He hoped briefly to regain employment; that hope disappointed, he took refuge in a nondescript village outside Florence and consoled himself with his writing. He didn't live to see the publication of *The Prince*, though he did witness a butchered plagiarism of it. His book was published several years after his death with the approval of one pope, but less than thirty years later another pope slapped all his work onto the Church's first Index of Prohibited Books.[27]

He rapidly gained a European reputation as evil, even satanic. Wasn't the devil named Old Nick? No wonder *Machiavellian* became an English epithet for the cunning or duplicitous, Machiavelli himself—or his legendary reputation—a major tributary feeding an English river churning with baleful fear of Italy as popish, politically corrupt, sexually irregular, morally depraved, dissolute, dissipated.[28] As the first to publish an English translation put it, "Mine Author was a Florentine, whose national attribute among the Italians is subtlety, and whose particular eminence in cunning hath styled the most cunning, as his Sectaries, *Machiavellians*."[29] We've lost an English play of 1613 called *Machiavel and the Devil*.[30] But we do have Marlowe's *Jew of Malta*, first published in 1633 but probably written around 1591, where Machiavelli himself appears onstage and delivers a

[27] The standard biography remains Roberto Ridolfi, *The Life of Niccolò Machiavelli*, trans. Cecil Grayson (Chicago: University of Chicago Press, 1963).

[28] A splendid study of these matters is Victoria Kahn, *Machiavellian Rhetoric: From the Counter-Reformation to Milton* (Princeton, NJ: Princeton University Press, 1994).

[29] E[dward] D[acres], *Machiavels Discovrses upon the First Decade of T. Livius Translated out of the Italian; With Some Marginall Animadversions Noting and Taxing His Errours* (London, 1636), Epistle Dedicatory, sig. A4 recto.

[30] John D. Cox, *The Devil and the Sacred in English Drama, 1350–1642* (Cambridge: Cambridge University Press, 2000), p. 211.

prologue designed to make the audience shudder, I suppose with the usual mix of abject horror and guilty pleasure:

> Admired I am of those that hate me most.
> Though some speak openly against my books,
> Yet will they read me, and thereby attain
> To Peter's chair: and when they cast me off,
> Are poisoned by my climbing followers.
> I count religion but a childish toy,
> And hold there is no sin but ignorance.

Some four centuries ago, the nefarious image is in place. Yes, declares Machiavelli, I wrote the politicians' guidebook. They pretend to hate me, they even condemn me, but my advice wins them the papacy and remains crucial if they wish to hold onto it. We might look askance at the thought that clambering onto Peter's chair is a vicious political struggle, but the history of the papacy isn't pretty. Marlowe's immediate audience, Protestants steeped in propaganda branding the Church of Rome the Whore of Babylon and the Pope the Antichrist, wouldn't have blinked. *Plus que ça change*: some three decades ago, Henry Kissinger, who wrote an admiring study of Metternich, another wily diplomat, and whose semisecret bombing campaign in Cambodia has something to do with the millions killed by Pol Pot, stressed that he owed nothing to Machiavelli.[31]

Some bathos in these matters seems inevitable. Never shy about quantification, experimental psychologists have devised a Mach scale to measure how prone people are to manipulate others. Subjects record how strongly they agree or disagree with such claims as "It is wise to flatter important people" and "Anyone who completely trusts anyone else is asking for trouble." The companion Kiddie-Mach scale dumbs down the language but supposes the same sensibilities available to the young.[32] More recently yet, Machiavelli has been expropriated to explain how to navigate the shoals of big business. In *What Would Machiavelli Do? The Ends Justify*

---

[31] Henry Kissinger, *A World Restored: Metternich, Castlereagh and the Problems of Peace, 1812–22* (Boston: Houghton Mifflin, 1957); William Shawcross, *Sideshow: Kissinger, Nixon and the Destruction of Cambodia* (New York: Simon and Schuster, 1979); "Kissinger: An Interview with Oriana Fallaci," *New Republic* (16 December 1972), p. 21.

[32] *Measures of Personality and Social Psychological Attitudes*, ed. John P. Robinson, Phillip R. Shaver, and Lawrence S. Wrightsman (San Diego, CA: Academic Press, 1991), pp. 376–85.

the Meanness, we learn that "not giving a shit is big mojo."[33] Disavowing any interest in exposed cleavage, the author of *The Princessa: Machiavelli for Women* urges her gentle reader, "Turn your chest toward a problem. Stand straight. Your breasts send powerful messages of femininity into the fray, and you stand a good chance of prevailing."[34]

I'll turn soon to the gender dynamics in play here, but first I want briefly to rehearse some of the decidedly less amusing advice Machiavelli dispenses in *The Prince*. There he insists—or seems to insist—that a leader consolidating control of a newly conquered territory adopt evil tactics. Take the infamous Cesare Borgia, dubbed duke of Valentino. He needed to pacify Romagna, "full of robberies, quarrels, and every other kind of insolence"[35] after being governed by weak and corrupt leaders. So the duke installed Remirro de Orco and authorized him to use "the fullest power" to subjugate the people. De Orco did such a brutally good job that he won himself "the very greatest reputation," but also hatred. Quick to seize a promising opportunity, Borgia had de Orco murdered and his body, cut in two, displayed in the piazza. "The ferocity of this spectacle," Machiavelli drily reports, "left the people at once satisfied and stupefied." A faithful henchman, de Orco had done Borgia's dirty work, but he also had emerged as a potential rival. Borgia's tool having outlived his usefulness, Borgia disposed of him and so earned the locals' grateful affection. (We have to assume the locals didn't understand principal/agent relations.) The tactic wouldn't occur to everyone. Maybe it never occurred to de Orco. (Or maybe he didn't watch his back carefully enough.) But it did occur to Borgia, so we must count him clever, imaginative, resourceful. Decisive, too. Nothing in Machiavelli's account suggests that Borgia vacillated or fretted about morality or honor. Nor does Machiavelli fret. He introduces Borgia by writing, "I do not know what better teaching I could give to a new prince than the example of his actions," and introduces the story I've just told by writing, "because this point is deserving of notice and of being imitated by others, I do not want to leave it out." In case the reader dozes through the lesson, Machiavelli returns to it after reviewing the duke's further career (more murders, more conquest, and his best efforts to infiltrate

---

[33] Stanley Bing, *What Would Machiavelli Do? The Ends Justify the Meanness* (New York: HarperBusiness, 2000), p. 65.

[34] Harriet Rubin, *The Princessa: Machiavelli for Women* (New York: Doubleday, 1997), p. 139.

[35] I quote throughout from Niccolò Machiavelli, *The Prince*, trans. Harvey C. Mansfield, 2nd ed. (Chicago: University of Chicago Press, 1998).

the College of Cardinals to control the choice of the next pope): "If I summed up all the actions of the duke, I would not know how to reproach him; on the contrary, it seems to me he should be put forward, as I have done, to be imitated by all those who have risen to empire through fortune and by the arms of others."[36]

Many contemporary readers would have known how to reproach the ruthless duke. Some would have declared that he was destined for hell. Others would have insisted that his actions were vicious. Doubtless anticipating such stock responses, Machiavelli has understated but unmistakable rejoinders. He praises religious principalities only to shunt them aside; he can't resist toying with his reader's pious preconceptions. Yes, Moses was an excellent prince, but the actions of Cyrus and others "appear no different from those of Moses, who had so great a teacher." God is politically irrelevant. Not that belief in Him is. Machiavelli's prince must traffic boldly in appearances, must "be a great pretender and dissembler," and above all must "appear to have" religion. But he won't waste his time on any genuine Christian piety. Nor will Machiavelli. Consider his account of fortune. He begins, "It is not unknown to me that many have held and hold the opinion that worldly things are so governed by fortune and by God, that men cannot correct them with their prudence." Then God vanishes again. Actually, Machiavelli sunnily continues, fortune controls only about half our actions. The young prince has a chance even with that half if he won't shrink from rape or something perilously close to it: "It is better to be impetuous than cautious, because fortune is a woman; and it is necessary, if one wants to hold her down, to beat her and strike her down."

It's not just that God has vanished. It's that a pagan goddess abruptly has reappeared. Fortuna, fickle ancient goddess of fortune, was armed with a wheel to steer men's lives or to show how cyclical their fortunes were. She had a cornucopia to shower down good or bad fortune on them. Leading Christian writers had maintained some of the imagery, but had been pushing fortune toward brute contingency, casting her as a remote handmaiden of God impassively dispensing the inexorable dictates of providence to which men must passively submit.[37] (Monotheism has never come easily.) Ever fond of the ancients—if we can take his correspondence

---

[36] For similar language, see Machiavelli to Francesco Vettori, 31 January 1514.

[37] For a summary of the preceding tradition and a study of what Machiavelli does to it, see Hanna Fenichel Pitkin, *Fortune Is a Woman: Gender and Politics in the Thought of Niccolò Machiavelli* (Berkeley: University of California Press, 1984), chap. 6.

seriously, he donned court garb to speak with them every evening and, you bet, they answered;[38] so was our staunch realist nutty as a fruitcake?— Machiavelli makes fortune vividly female again. Not any old female, either, but a particular, peculiar, one, an obnoxious dominatrix to wrestle with. In a poem, he expanded on the compressed references of *The Prince* with some acidulous harridan imagery. On high, rewarding the unjust, punishing the just, ever capricious, leaving no one at the top or bottom of her wheel (even wheels) for long, well pleased by those who shove her around: this capricious, even bitchy, Fortune, an "aged witch," rewards men only to prepare their punishments. Machiavelli permits himself a caustic conclusion: "In days gone by few have been successful, and they have died before their wheel reversed itself or in turning carried them down to the bottom."[39] The sentiment is not that of the Christian who bewails our pilgrimage through this vale of tears. The blasphemy is transparent, as it is when he boasts, "I love my native city more than my soul."[40] On his deathbed, Machiavelli reported dreaming of wretches in heaven and ancient philosophers in hell and quipped he'd rather join the latter to talk politics.[41] Sounds like Machiavelli was willing to take his chances on hell.[42]

Let's put hell on hold. Isn't the duke vicious? Isn't it then vicious of Machiavelli to recommend emulating him? Well, what are virtue and vice, anyway? Machiavelli inherits a concept of *virtù* stamped by the classical tradition with three notable features.[43] First, a virtue is a quality of a *vir* or

---

[38] Machiavelli to Francesco Vettori, 10 December 1513.

[39] "Tercets on Fortune," in *Machiavelli: The Chief Works and Others*, trans. Allan Gilbert, 3 vols. (Durham, NC: Duke University Press, 1965), 2:745–49.

[40] Machiavelli to Francesco Vettori, 16 April 1527, in *Machiavelli*, trans. Gilbert, 2:1010.

[41] Ridolfi, *Life*, pp. 249–50, reports the episode as fact; Maurizio Viroli, *Niccolò's Smile: A Biography of Machiavelli*, trans. Antony Shugaar (New York: Farrar, Straus and Giroux, 2000), p. 3, says it's apocryphal.

[42] Contrast the approach in a recent extravaganza: Sebastian de Grazia, *Machiavelli in Hell* (Princeton, NJ: Princeton University Press, 1989), esp. chaps. 2–4. Granted, elsewhere Machiavelli writes with more apparent conviction about religion: see for instance the "Exhortation to Penitence." But *Discourses on the First Ten Books of Titus Livy*, bk. 1, chaps. 11–15, and bk. 2, chap. 2 clinch the case that Machiavelli's pressing interest in religion is whether it is politically useful or harmful. Gramsci found in Machiavelli "the basis for a modern laicism and for a complete laicization of all aspects of life and of all customary relationships": *Selections from the Prison Notebooks of Antonio Gramsci*, ed. and trans. Quintin Hoare and Geoffrey Nowell Smith (New York: International Publishers, 1971), p. 133.

[43] Quentin Skinner, *Machiavelli: A Very Short Introduction* (Oxford: Oxford University Press, 2000), pp. 38–46, is helpful on some of these connections.

true man. So it slips freely between moral virtue and manliness. Even modern English betrays this etymological link in the word *virility*.[44] Or, if you like, Machiavelli's virtue is at home in a world comfortable thinking that virtue is gendered, for instance that men should be courageous and that cowards are at once unmanly and vicious. (Feminine virtue, in this way oxymoronic, comes to consist in fidelity, chastity, silence, and the like.) Second, a virtue is a means leading to a prized end, a trait enabling excellent performance. Again modern English retains the connection: it is the virtue of a knife to hold a sharp edge and cut cleanly. Third, as a matter of strict denotation we can identify the virtues. Cicero lists the four cardinal virtues—wisdom, justice, courage, and temperance—and he adds others, not least willingness to deal with others in good faith.[45] By Machiavelli's day, the mirror-of-princes literature had piled on with a goopy cloying vengeance. Dozens of books sedulously recommended dozens of conventional virtues to princes who seemed, shall we say, not entirely receptive to the lesson, however incessantly repeated.

The Prince dutifully mimics the formal conventions of the mirror-of-princes literature. So Machiavelli anticipates the sneer that he is too lowly to advise princes by likening himself to one on the plains who can better see the mountains. Yet Machiavelli means to subvert the easy moralisms of his predecessors,[46] just as he means to mock and demolish Cicero and other classical sources. For he has seen that the three features of virtue don't cohere. Borgia's murder of de Orco was ungrateful and unjust, but splendidly successful in helping him consolidate power. The example is anything but unique. Sometimes—often? especially in politics?—the conventional virtues will not pay off in prized ends. Then what's a would-be *vir* to do?

Machiavelli puts increasing pressure on the concept of *virtù*. Take cruelty. Early on, Machiavelli surveys those who become princes by committing crimes. Agathocles, he reports, had "such virtue of spirit and body" that he rose from his humble beginnings to rule Sicily and Syracuse. Indeed, "whoever might consider the actions and virtue of this man will see

---

[44] Throughout I've relied on the second edition of the *OED* for etymology.

[45] *De officiis*, bk. I, v; bk. III, xiii.

[46] Felix Gilbert, "The Humanist Concept of the Prince and *The Prince* of Machiavelli," *Journal of Modern History* 11:4 (December 1939):449–83, reprinted in Gilbert, *History: Choice and Commitment* (Cambridge, MA: Belknap Press, Harvard University Press, 1977), chap. 4.

nothing or little that can attributed to fortune." He did it himself. The next passage is crucial:

> Yet one cannot call it virtue to kill one's citizens, betray one's friends, to be without faith, without mercy, without religion; these modes can enable one to acquire empire, but not glory. For, if one considers the virtue of Agathocles in entering into and escaping from dangers, and the greatness of his spirit in enduring and overcoming adversities, one does not see why he has to be judged inferior to any most excellent captain. Nonetheless, his savage cruelty and inhumanity, together with his infinite crimes, do not permit him to be celebrated among the most excellent men. Thus, one cannot attribute to fortune or to virtue what he achieved without either.

Logically, the passage is reeling, staggering, dead drunk. It lurches among patent contradictions: it is virtue, it can't be virtue, his virtue makes him the equal of the most excellent, and we may not celebrate him as excellent. His virtue won him a princely rule that he cannot owe to virtue. Literarily, the passage is teasing, feinting, wonderfully mischievous. It jabs at the reader, even slaps him around, insinuating that his prior beliefs about virtue are incoherent. Agathocles's cruelty leads to success, so it must be a virtue; but cruelty can't be a virtue because it doesn't appear on the laundry list stipulating the virtues. That "one cannot call it virtue" means that saying so does violence to the concept. It sounds confused, not something a fluent speaker would say. But we may have to learn how to say it anyway.[47]

So softened up and stunned, the reader may breathe easier at the apparently innocent concession Machiavelli soon offers. Cruelties, he opines, can be well or badly used. "Those can be called well used (if it is permissible to speak well of evil) that are done at a stroke, out of the necessity to secure oneself, and then are not persisted in but are turned to as much utility for the subjects as one can." Badly used cruelties don't diminish but mount over time. The passage invites another defense of Machiavelli's tattered moral credentials. Concede that cruelty is politically inescapable and then say the wise prince economizes on it and turns it to his subjects'

---

[47] On *virtù* and the predatory relationship between *il principe* and *lo stato*, J. H. Hexter, *The Vision of Politics on the Eve of the Reformation: More, Machiavelli, and Seyssel* (New York: Basic Books, 1973), chaps. 3–4, remains unparalleled.

benefit.[48] There are two redemptive possibilities here. One: no prince can discard cruelty, so the good prince will be cruel only when he must, or as little as possible, or something like that. Two: the prince is not playing the game (solely) for his self-interest; he's (also) pursuing his subjects' welfare. That last is reminiscent of a trademark maneuver in many political theories. Instead of longing for altruistic saints to lead us, we can try to channel the tawdry ambitions of selfish politicians so that they can reward themselves only by serving others. (If we use the cunning, whose tactics are blameworthy?) So Machiavelli suggests that a prince seeking glory will not just win a new principality but will also give it "good laws, good arms, good friends, and good examples." Still, that worrisome parenthesis—"(if it is permissible to speak well of evil)"—lingers. Is it permissible? The question triggers an ominous afterthought. If cruelty can be well used, if it can redound to the people's welfare, is it a vice?

Machiavelli leaves cruelty and his poor perplexed reader hanging for dozens of pages. Then he unveils a chapter entitled, "Of Cruelty and Mercy, and Whether It Is Better to Be Loved Than Feared, or the Contrary." His rhetoric is more sizzling, more subversive, than ever:

> Each prince should desire to be held merciful and not cruel;
> nonetheless he should take care not to use this mercy badly. Cesare
> Borgia was held to be cruel; nonetheless his cruelty restored
> the Romagna, united it, and reduced it to peace and to faith. If one
> considers this well, one will see that he was much more merciful
> than the Florentine people, who so as to escape a name for cruelty,
> allowed Pistoia to be destroyed. A prince, therefore, so as to keep his
> subjects united and faithful, should not care about the infamy of
> cruelty, because with very few examples he will be more merciful
> than those who for the sake of too much mercy allow disorders to
> continue, from which come killings or robberies; for these
> customarily hurt a whole community, but the executions that
> come from the prince hurt one particular person. And of all princes,
> it is impossible for the new prince to escape a name for cruelty
> because new states are full of dangers.

---

[48] Sheldon S. Wolin, *Politics and Vision: Continuity and Innovation in Western Political Thought* (Boston: Little, Brown, and Company, 1960), chap. 7.

If you "desire to be held merciful," not to be merciful, you want to have a reputation for mercy. But reputation isn't always deserved. Cesare Borgia was thought cruel, but because he used cruelty well, he was actually merciful. If you use mercy badly, as did the Florentines, you're actually cruel. Anyway, new princes are going to earn a reputation for cruelty. Which is the vice, which the virtue? Once again Machiavelli leaves the implicit query and the reader hanging, this time only briefly, and turns to his query about love and fear, surely provoked by Cicero's plaintive sigh that Rome's misfortunes arose from relying on fear instead of love.[49] Best would be both fear and love, retorts Machiavelli, "but because it is difficult to put them together, it is much safer to be feared than loved, if one has to lack one of the two." (So too Machiavelli thumbs his nose at Cicero's sentiment that the lion's force and the fox's cunning are beneath man.[50] No, avers Machiavelli, a prince must know how to be bestial, must be ready to ape the lion and the fox by turns.) Now the reader is ready, if he's ever going to be ready, for the knockout blow.

> But when the prince is with his armies and has a multitude of soldiers under his government, then it is above all necessary not to care about a name for cruelty, because without this name he never holds his army united, or disposed to any action. Among the admirable actions of Hannibal is numbered this one: that when he had a very large army, mixed with infinite kinds of men, and had led it to fight in alien lands, no dissension ever arose in it, neither among themselves nor against the prince, in bad as well as in his good fortune. This could not have arisen from anything other than his inhuman cruelty which, together with his infinite virtues [*sua inumana crudeltà, la quale, insieme con infinite sua virtù*], always made him venerable and terrible in the sight of his soldiers; and without it, his other virtues would not have sufficed to bring about this effect [*e sanza quella, a fare quello effetto, le altre sua virtù non li bastavano*]. And the writers, having considered little in this, on the one hand admire this action of his but on the other condemn the principal cause of it.[51]

---

[49] *De officiis*, bk. II, viii.

[50] *De officiis*, bk. I, xiii.

[51] I've inserted the Italian from *Machiavelli's The Prince: A Bilingual Edition*, trans. and ed. Mark Musa (New York: St. Martin's Press, 1964), p. 140, to show that the following argument doesn't hang on an artifact of translation.

A prince commanding an army must be cruel. Damn the reputation.

Now inspect the complex sentence applauding Hannibal's inhuman cruelty. In the first clause, Machiavelli antiseptically pares away his cruelty from "his infinite virtues," implying that cruelty is a vice or at least no virtue. In the second, he refers to cruelty and "his other virtues," forcibly implying that Hannibal's cruelty was itself a virtue. That's the blow the reader was not yet ready for when he encountered Agathocles. Battering away, Machiavelli ridicules the nameless writers applauding the prized end, that is, keeping his diverse army unified, but condemning the necessary means, that is, his cruelty. Their contradictory commitments lead them to unwitting, say rather witless, self-contradiction. Who wills the ends, wills the means, right? If virtue's three features won't cohere, the sensible move is to jettison the list stipulating the virtues. A manly man eager to succeed must learn that mercy may be a vice, cruelty a virtue, more generally that the received wisdom about the virtues is all wrong. Don't blame Machiavelli if the three features don't cohere. At least he has the searing intellectual honesty to force the reader to confront these troubling contradictions.

So we might wonder about the alleged horrible Satanism of it all. Who is the audience of *The Prince*? It's dedicated to the august Lorenzo de' Medici and looks like a bid by Machiavelli to claw his way back from dusty obscurity. That motive aside, we might construe the book as addressed to ordinary people, lowly subjects, instead of exalted princes. It invites subjects to eavesdrop on the chilling conversations of the corridors of power, to ponder the seamy currency of the realm. Then it's a bracing wake-up call. Beware, it warns, these are the rules your leaders play by. Yes, Machiavelli insists repeatedly that princes ought to imitate Borgia's tactics. Like a whispered aside onstage, though, the comment might not really be directed to its official dedicatee. Despite the deafening chorus of Satan denouncers, some seventeenth-century writers are already defending Machiavelli in this way.[52] The moralisms heaved up by the mirror-of-princes

---

[52] For instance, *The Atheisticall Politition or a Breife Discourse Concerning Ni. Machiavell.* [London, 1642]; *Nicholas Machiavel's Prince. Also, The Life of Castruccio Castracani of Lucca. and The Meanes Duke Valentine Us'd to Put to Death Vitellozzo Vitelli, Oliverotto of Fermo, Paul, and the Duke of Gravina*, trans. E[dward] D[acres] (London, 1661), Epistle to the Reader, sig. Z recto; James Boevey, "The Vindication of That Hero of Political Learning, Nicholas Machiavel, the Second Tacitus," unpublished ms. from 1692, in *The Harleian Miscellany*, 11 vols. (London, 1808–11), 10:183–87.

literature hadn't domesticated princely rule. But they might have lulled subjects into believing politics a kinder, gentler enterprise than it is. That's why, to recur to Marlowe's preface, princes would strenuously disavow Machiavelli's advice even while following it. It's easier to rule subjects when they're drowsy.

Those inclined to defend Machiavelli can also seize on the opening chapters of *The Prince*. There Machiavelli declares that he will consider neither republics nor hereditary principalities. Instead he will focus on the special perils of consolidating control over a new principality. That suggests that not everyone needs to master the arts of cruelty well used or have enough fiendish imagination and resolve to slice his advisers in two. Yet this suggestion domesticates Machiavellian strategies, which can't be readily cabined. Recent political theorists anguishing over this problem of dirty hands have cast it as generally applicable to politics.[53] Not only new princes, but democratically elected leaders entrusted with the welfare of their citizens may find that lying, cheating, even killing are helpful, even required tactics. They may fool themselves or try to fool us about these matters. Caught with their ballot boxes stuffed, their Swiss bank accounts laden with bribes, their henchmen in the other party's headquarters, they may invite us to lament the agonies of their dirty hands when all they really are is selfish scoundrels. But it would be starry-eyed to insist that any politician can keep his hands clean and do a good job. So we've enlarged the apparent domain of Machiavellian tactics from the new principality to all of politics—and we can press on. Not only politicians are entrusted with what lawyers call fiduciary obligations to attend to others' interests. So are parents, teachers, priests, coaches, doctors, all kinds of authority figures. Machiavellian tactics beckon them all. May or must they do wrong for their charges?

That cunning is distinctively the new prince's, even politician's, is then a bit of fatuous complacency. The Roman Catholic Church forbade the faithful to read or even possess Machiavelli's works, but it has its own inglorious history of pious frauds.[54] Some are delicious. About a century after

---

[53] Michael Walzer, "Political Action: The Problem of Dirty Hands," *Philosophy & Public Affairs* 2:2 (Winter 1973):160–80; Thomas Nagel, "Ruthlessness in Public Life," in Nagel, *Mortal Questions* (Cambridge: Cambridge University Press, 1979); Martin Hollis, "Dirty Hands," *British Journal of Political Science* 12:4 (October 1982):385–98.

[54] For a bruising polemic on the modern Church, see Garry Wills, *Papal Sin: Structures of Deceit* (New York: Doubleday, 2000).

the Spanish army threw out the Moors, overindustrious forgers in Granada staged spelunking expeditions of prodigious fecundity. They surfaced half a handkerchief of the Virgin Mary and twenty-two lead books with sayings of the Virgin, Saints Peter and James, and others, all recorded by two Arab brothers converted by Jesus Himself. It took the Church almost a century to disavow these relics. In the meantime they'd helped secure a Christian identity for the region.[55] A whopping lie advanced the true Church and saved countless souls: Machiavelli would have applauded the tactics, even if he'd have guffawed at the goal. Or again: Constantine became the first Christian emperor of Rome in 324. Church father Eusebius extolled the man and the miracles he witnessed, such as the cross obscuring the sun accompanied with the words, "By this conquer."[56] (Discreetly, he didn't mention that Constantine had his eldest son executed and then forced his wife to commit suicide.)[57] Some four or five centuries later, a crucial document emerged. The Constantine Donation recognized the papacy as supreme. Lest anyone doubt what sort of supremacy was intended, Constantine assigned Pope Sylvester the emperor's crown, tiara, tunic, and other trappings of earthly rule. The pope demurring, Constantine himself placed a tiara on the pope's head and deferentially held the pope's horse as if he were his groom. For some six centuries the document meant that the emperor owed his authority to the Church. Yet the document was forged, as a humanist scholar demonstrated ferociously in 1440.[58] Dostoevsky's parable of the Grand Inquisitor,[59] who tells an imprisoned Jesus there is no room for Him in the Church, is exquisitely Machiavellian. After all, a newly returned Jesus is a threat not just to the Church's power but to Christians' welfare. The Grand Inquisitor is no scoundrel clinging to power and perquisites. He's nobly sacrificing himself, dirtying his hands to

[55] A. Katie Harris, "Forging History: The *Plomos* of the Sacromonte of Granada in Francisco Bermúdez de Pedraza's *Historia Eclesiástica,*" *Sixteenth Century Journal* 30:4 (1999):945–66.

[56] Eusebius, *Life of Constantine,* trans. Averil Cameron and Stuart G. Hall (Oxford: Clarendon Press, 1999), bk. 1, chap. 28, p. 81.

[57] Timothy D. Barnes, *Constantine and Eusebius* (Cambridge, MA: Harvard University Press, 1981), pp. 220–21; compare the more speculative account in Michael Grant, *Constantine the Great: The Man and His Times* (New York: Charles Scribner's Sons, 1993), pp. 110–14.

[58] For the primary texts, see Christopher B. Coleman, *The Treatise of Lorenzo Valla on the Donation of Constantine* (New Haven: Yale University Press, 1922). For the episode's political significance, see Walter Ullmann, *The Growth of Papal Government in the Middle Ages: A Study in the Ideological Relation of Clerical to Lay Power,* 3rd ed. (London: Methuen & Co. Ltd, 1970), pp. 74–86.

[59] *The Brothers Karamazov,* pt. 2, bk. 5.

serve the people. The poor, weak faithful must be crammed full of nonsense in order to limp along happily.

I've taken a detour from *The Prince*. Even there, we can see that the domain of cunning sprawls across social life. Machiavelli (in)famously affirms that the prince must learn how not to be good. But his defense of that pithy slogan isn't tethered to the menacing landscape of the new prince:

> And many have imagined republics and principalities that have never been seen or known to exist in truth; for it is so far from how one lives to how one should live that he who lets go of what is done for what should be done learns his ruin rather than his preservation. For a man who wants to make a profession of good in all regards must come to ruin among so many who are not good. Hence it is necessary to a prince, if he wants to maintain himself, to learn to be able not to be good, and to use this and not use it according to necessity.

Machiavelli clearly grasps the thought that what's prudent or morally attractive may depend on what others are doing. While here he again stresses the prince's own interests, we can add the link between the prince's interest and the people's welfare. A credulous prince willing to trust others' goodness will sacrifice not just himself but his people, and to a new prince who's already demonstrated his lack of scruples. Machiavelli wasn't the first to notice the point. One medieval Burmese text, mostly as smarmy as the mirror-of-princes literature that Machiavelli so gleefully subverts, notices the logic of what game theorists call security dilemmas: "He who, having elephants, horses, wealth, and forces, is satisfied, does not engage in war, another subjugates him."[60] Nor was he the last. Around 1605, Thomas Middleton placed onstage a mother defending her plan to marry off her courtesan daughter as a virgin:

> Every part of the world shoots up daily into more subtlety.
> The very spider weaves her cauls with more art and cunning to
>   entrap the fly.
> The shallow ploughman can distinguish now

---

[60] *Râjaniti*, in James Gray, *Ancient Proverbs and Maxims from Burmese Sources; or, The Niti Literature of Burma* (London, 1886), p. 137.

'Twixt simple truth and a dissembling brow.
Your base mechanic fellow can spy out
A weakness in a lord, and learns to flout.
How does't behoove us then that live by sleight,
To have our wits wound up to their stretched height![61]

In one of La Fontaine's verse fables, a dog attacks another dog fetching dinner for his master. Their fight attracts still more dogs; soon they're all devouring a pie. The moral:

The image of a town is what I think I make out here,
Where public funds are liable to fraud and conversion.
    Judges, merchants practice subversion,
    Everyone has a free hand. A quite clear
Example is set by the cleverest one, and it's a genuine diversion
To see a whole heap of pistoles cleaned out in any season.
If someone who's got scruples, for some very frivolous reason,
Wants to protect the money and invokes the slightest rule,
    The rest all oblige him to see he's a fool.
    With no qualms he concedes his mistake,
    And he soon becomes the first one to take.[62]

Hume presses the same point when he ponders the unraveling of schemes of social cooperation: "I should be the cully of my integrity, if I alone shou'd impose on myself a severe restraint amidst the licentiousness of others."[63] A *cully* is a dupe, someone easily ripped off. There's no point, the thought is, doing your fair share if others aren't doing theirs. Take one of Hume's celebrated examples: promising, a practice magically enabling us to cooperate with strangers over long stretches of time. Ordinarily you're obliged to keep your promises. But now imagine a world where the practice is falling apart, where increasingly people make promises but don't keep them. If you continue faithfully to keep your promises, you shouldn't flatter yourself on your scrupulous integrity. You should notice that you're a chump stupidly inviting others to exploit you. I assume the

[61] *A Mad World, My Masters*, act 1, sc. 1.

[62] *The Complete Fables of Jean de la Fontaine*, ed. and trans. Norman B. Spector (Evanston, IL: Northwestern University Press, 1988), pp. 368–71.

[63] *Treatise*, bk. 3, pt. 2, sec. 7.

same thought underlies a Mexican proverb: "He who does not cheat does not advance."[64]

No wonder we use *politics* not just narrowly to refer to the actions of government officials or candidates for office, but broadly to refer, roughly speaking, to manipulative schemes of questionable legitimacy. In 1606, Thomas Dekker sketched the politician, not a member of parliament but a nimble social climber and unsavory hypocrite. "In words, is he circumspect: in looks, grave: in attire, civil: in diet, temperate: in company affable; in his affairs, serious: and so cunningly does he lay on these colours, that in the end he is welcome to, and familiar with the best."[65] In 1745, Henry Fielding indicted "those great arts which the vulgar call treachery, dissembling, promising, lying, falsehood, etc., but which are by great men summed up in the collective name of policy, or politics, or rather *pollitrics*," and everything in his indictment urges that we align ourselves with the vulgar and reject the sophisticated nonsense of the great.[66] In 1779, we find *politics* defined as "a cunning science regulated by interest."[67] In this mood, we chortle at the thought that politics is a noble pursuit. It's political, we say disapprovingly, when the job goes not to the best qualified candidate but to the candidate who flattered the interviewer or knew some stupid secret handshake from a college eating club. Then the one who lands the job marvels at our colossal simplicity in believing the job market a meritocracy. It's not as if the other applicants just send in résumés and dutifully wait by the phone. Many other candidates are busy working the system, finding connections, calling in favors. Among so many who aren't good, won't he come to ruin if he plays by merit's rules? If he doesn't cheat, he won't advance. His grungy ascent accomplished, he takes his place as meritocracy's high-minded defender, sounding the mendacious tones Dekker might expect. Then he plots his next victory.

In other writings, Machiavelli himself delights in tales of cunning, some in narrowly political settings, some not. Sometimes he underlines the connection to princely politics. The dying Facino Cane left his states to his wife Beatrice and arranged that she marry Filippo Visconti. Filippo used

---

[64] *The Economist* (28 October 2000), survey on Mexico, p. 11.

[65] *The Seuen Deadly Sinnes of London* (London, 1606), in *The Non-Dramatic Works of Thomas Dekker*, 5 vols. (New York: Russell & Russell, 1963), 2:20–21.

[66] *Jonathan Wild*, bk. 2, chap. 5.

[67] *Lucubrations, Civil, Moral, and Historical* (London, 1779), p. 37.

the states as a springboard to further power and then, with what Machiavelli describes as ordinary princely gratitude, accused Beatrice of adultery and had her executed.[68] In *Mandragola*—Machiavelli was also a comic playwright—he portrays Callimaco, a lusty protagonist panting with desire for Donna Lucrezia, the most beautiful woman he's ever seen. There are just a few problems. She's married, her insipid husband Nicia is insanely possessive, she never socializes or even admits merchants into her home, and she's a devout Christian. Lesser men would be discouraged, but Callimaco's hopeful. Not exactly enlivened by the thrill of the chase, he knows that Nicia is an idiot and that the couple have been unable to have children for six years and desperately want to. He has also employed the shadowy Ligurio, once a marriage broker, now Callimaco's sometimes dinner companion and a close friend of Nicia.

Friendship enables treachery: Ligurio cooks up the perfect scheme. Posing as a doctor, Callimaco persuades the husband that his wife can bear him a child after she consumes a potion made with mandrake. The herb's aphrodisiac properties were known in antiquity,[69] but here it is dangerous medicine indeed: the next man to sleep with her will die within the week. Then she'll be gloriously fertile. So all they need is some poor wretch to drain off the poison. Next Callimaco drafts a corrupt friar and her free-spirited mother to persuade Donna Lucrezia that it is pious to go through with it. The friar's terse arguments, a pungent reminder of how casuistry fell into ill repute, leave her grudgingly willing to comply. Then Callimaco poses as a drunken stranger to get himself shoved into her bed. After their encounter, she announces—archly? ventriloquizing some male fantasy? because she has so enjoyed good sex?—that she will take the episode as God's will and welcome Callimaco back to her bed. (Or does she announce it? She's not even onstage. Vaunting in triumph, Callimaco reports that she talked this way.) Nicia, clueless to the bitter end, hails Callimaco as his savior and offers him a house key.

No scruples bar Callimaco from his end. The prince of private life, he boldly conquers a new terrain—a bedroom—and decisively reduces his

---

[68] Machiavelli, *Florentine Histories*, bk. 1, chap. 37. For the princely tactics urged by a guild member, see *Histories*, bk. 3, chap. 13.

[69] Theophrastus, *Enquiry into Plants*, IX.1. The episode of Reuben's mandrake in Genesis 30 raises different problems, on which see the magisterial David Daube, *Studies in Biblical Law* (Cambridge: Cambridge University Press, 1947), pp. 17–24.

new subject to loyalty. If the audience is snickering too much to think, the playwright doesn't mind being didactic about the parallel. Early on, tormented by sleepless foodless bootless sexual frustration, Callimaco declares, "I've got to try something, be it great, dangerous, harmful, scandalous. Better to die than to live like this. . . . I'm not afraid of anything, but will take any course—bestial, cruel, nefarious [*bestiale, crudele, nefando*]. . . ."[70] Bestial (brave as a lion, cunning as a fox), cruel (doubtless using his cruelty well), nefarious, unconcerned with hell, proudly conquering: princely indeed. Christianity may be a childish toy, but it sure comes in handy for bamboozling the believers. Callimaco gleefully enrolls not just a corrupt churchman but sacred principles themselves to serve his profane cause. Machiavelli conjures up the audience's vigorous approval. As Donna Lucrezia demands in the closing scene, "Who wouldn't be happy?"

Mandragola distills a literary tradition jauntily celebrating the sexual conquest of women—and women merrily giving voice to the same tactics against men, even fighting back. In the thirteenth-century French *Romance of the Rose*, Old Woman lectures Fair Seeming. "Briefly, all men betray and deceive women; all are sensualists, taking their pleasure anywhere. Therefore we should deceive them in return, not fix our hearts on one. Any woman who does so is a fool; she should have several friends and, if possible, act so as to delight them to the point where they are driven to distraction."[71] In the fourteenth century, Boccaccio's tales of sexual escapades include that of a man who poses as a deaf-mute to work as a gardener in a convent. Soon he's servicing one sister after another. "So, thanks to the cunning he had employed in his youth, Masetto became a father and a wealthy man without having, in his old age, to toil for the support of his children, and without having to pay for their upkeep. As he returned whence he had set out with an axe across his shoulder: 'This,' he asserted, 'is the way Christ treats the man who makes a cuckold of Him by making free with His brides.' "[72] One of Boccaccio's male characters tells that story.

---

[70] *Mandragola*, act 1, sc. 3. I quote from Machiavelli, *Mandragola*, trans. Mera J. Flaumenhaft (Prospect Heights, IL: Waveland Press, 1981), and I've added the Italian from Niccolò Machiavelli, *Mandragola*, a cura di Giorgio Inglese (Napoli: Società Editrice il Mulino, 1997), p. 45.

[71] Guillaume de Lorris and Jean de Meun, *The Romance of the Rose*, trans. Charles Dahlberg, 3rd ed. (Princeton, NJ: Princeton University Press, 1995), p. 229.

[72] *Decameron*, day 3, story 1; I quote from Giovanni Boccaccio, *The Decameron*, trans. Guido Waldman (Oxford: Oxford University Press, 1993), p. 177.

A woman soon fires back with one about a crafty woman who gets a stupid friar to serve unwittingly as her pander.[73] A couple of centuries later, Marguerite de Navarre has one of her male protagonists confess his tactics. Or boast about them: "If we were to bare our souls, and show ourselves in our true light, there's many a man usually well-received by the ladies whom they would no longer deign to consider. So we devise the most angelic appearances we can, to cover up the devil inside, and thus disguised, we receive a good few favours before we're found out, and perhaps even manage to draw the ladies on so far, that, thinking they're set on the road to virtue, it's too late for them to beat a retreat when they find themselves in the midst of vice!"[74]

Cunning here is what it takes for a man to bed a woman. Its structure is then gendered. Thus some of the tales in which women manage to bed men are still about images of masculinity, the men so bedded being feminine in their way—or just slobbering and hypnotized by the usual vistas of sexual allure. Defoe's Roxana is "not ignorant that I was very handsome"[75] and she plays that for all it's worth. Thackeray's Becky Sharp does her wily best to cash in on being a sexpot: one bit character chalks up her success to "famous frontal development."[76] Outside the novel and more recently, literary agent Lucianne Goldberg succinctly explained her own success years before she popped up on the fringes of the Clinton/Lewinsky scandal: "When you're tall, thin, blond and have big boobs, you can have any job you want."[77] There's room in the tradition for feminine wiles that are savvier than the lubricious and craven techniques for soliciting men craving curves and crevices. Moll Flanders has more arrows in her quiver than Roxana. Still, we shouldn't underplay sexual come-hither tactics. Call them cheesy or contemptible, tired or tragic, shake your head disapprovingly, pretend to be too high-minded to notice, no matter, the point remains: those tactics have motored a lot of literature and life—and camp. As I write, the news reports the impending arrival of a cartoon version of

[73] *Decameron*, day 3, story 3.

[74] Marguerite de Navarre, *The Heptameron*, trans. P. A. Chilton (London: Penguin, 1984), p. 165.

[75] Daniel Defoe, *Roxana, or The Fortunate Mistress*, ed. Jane Jack (London: Oxford University Press, 1964), p. 57.

[76] William Makepeace Thackeray, *Vanity Fair*, chap. 19.

[77] Kim Hubbard, "A Ghostwriter's Haunting Tale," *People* (27 April 1992), p. 112.

voluptuous blonde Pamela Anderson as nightclub dancer Erotica Jones and alter-ego superhero Stripperella (or Secret Agent 0069). When her belly-button pager beeps, she zips out of the nightclub and gets to work with her hi-tech superpowers. (Her lipstick is a laser, her nipples lie detectors.) Anderson's contract specifies no nudity, please: it's sweet if curious of her to evince a fastidious concern for her animated twin that never troubled her real self.[78] But are bedroom antics a sideshow? Is it an accident that Odysseus has a lot of sexual knowledge? that the author of *The Prince* also wrote *Mandragola*?

Sex and politics, politics and sex: they seem different, even antithetical. Sex seems quintessentially private, politics quintessentially public, however we construe that slippery distinction. Clinton was loathsome not just for adultery, not just for lying, not just for exploiting an intern, but for having oral sex in the Oval Office, "where," an irascible friend of mine fumed, "Lincoln gazed out at Lee's armies camped across the Potomac." But sex and politics are also twinned, sometimes identically. Callimaco and Machiavelli's prince prevail with the very same virtues. Politics is sexy, not least because of the famously aphrodisiac qualities of power supposed to explain what the ravishing young intern sees in the pot-bellied middle-aged pol. Sex is political, even military, with campaigns, conquests, battles between the sexes, and the like. I have no expertise in the idioms of sixteenth-century Italian, but consider our own locutions. In politics, you can screw someone or you can get fucked. We know which side the manly man or anyway the masculine actor wants to be on. Recall George Bush *père*, captured by a lurking boom microphone, boasting, "We tried to kick a little ass" in his 1984 vice-presidential debate with Geraldine Ferraro. Bush wasn't all that virile, but his dominance entitled him to strut. That comment got much more attention than the faltering afterthought we might think truer to sweet if feeble character: "Whoops, oh God, he heard me."[79]

Cunning, then, has a familiar if depressing structure: men on top, dominating, ruthless; women on bottom, submissive, exploited. With surpris-

---

[78] Vinay Menon, "The Silicone Doesn't Fall Far from Pamela's Tree," *Toronto Star* (3 July 2003), A26.

[79] Dale Russakoff, "Bush Boasts of Kicking 'A Little Ass' at Debate; Ferraro Will Understand 'Competitive' Nature of Overheard Remark, He Says," *Washington Post* (13 October 1984), A8; and see the further language on sex and gender in Hedrick Smith, "Rivals' Camps Doubt Big Shift After 2d Debate," *New York Times* (13 October 1984), 1:1.

ing frequency, this binary opposition provides the conceptual horizon of cunning. But like any other structure, it invites ironic play. It gets tweaked, subverted, even exploded. We can count on the cunning to assist in the demolition work when it advances their agendas.

KNAVES AND FOOLS

"Knaves and fools divide the world."[80] That's a seventeenth-century English proverb, but the sentiment seems perennially available. In some moods—mean-spirited, vaguely paranoid, the sort embraced by those who flatter themselves realists—we glimpse vistas populated only by those two types. Sometimes we add stern moralists and intrepid detectives, Sherlock Holmes figures guarding the sheepish fools against the foxy knaves. One such was Anthony Comstock, zealously tracking down not just purveyors of obscenity and (shudder) birth control but practitioners of mail fraud, and noticing another strand in the tangled skein of gender dynamics surrounding cunning: "The highwayman who boldly walks up to his victim and demands his money, makes a more manly show than the lying thief, who skulks behind some poor man as a tool, and prints his lies to deceive and defraud the credulous."[81] Sometimes we add people alert enough to guard themselves against the knaves, innocent or principled enough not to exploit the fools. Or just weak enough not to: "Ah," sighed Kierkegaard, "if a census of the human race is ever taken, there will be a far greater number under the rubric of the flabby than under the rubrics of thieves, robbers, and murderers reckoned together." Unwilling to let their flabby weakness pass as virtue, he condemned them to hell.[82] No wonder the cunning congratulate themselves on having the gumption to rip off others. But sometimes we cast the world austerely, with only knaves and fools. Then we wonder who's more admirable, or anyway less contemptible, which type we'd rather be. Literature and history are stuffed,

---

[80] J[ohn] Ray, *A Collection of English Proverbs* (Cambridge, 1670), p. 111, italics removed.

[81] Anthony Comstock, *Frauds Exposed; or, How the People Are Deceived and Robbed, and Youth Corrupted* (New York, 1880; reprint ed. Montclair, NJ: Patterson Smith, 1969), p. 194. For Comstock's ambivalence about protecting the fools, compare pp. 13, 160, 245.

[82] *Judge for Yourself!*, in Søren Kierkegaard, *For Self-Examination; Judge for Yourself!*, ed. and trans. Howard V. Hong and Edna H. Hong (Princeton, NJ: Princeton University Press, 1990), p. 99.

overstuffed, with tales—celebratory, condemnatory, mournful, quizzical—
of the face-off between knaves and fools. I'll briefly rehearse a few.

Lucian, that barbed writer of Roman antiquity, sketches a false prophet,
Alexander, active from about 150 to 170 A.D. and celebrated by a cult for
another century. His collaborators planted an oracle predicting the prophet's
arrival. The locals suitably expectant, Alexander emerged, his hair long, his
clothing exotic, his descent, as he explained, from Perseus. He faked attacks of madness or religious frenzy by chewing soapwort root, which let
him foam at the mouth. He planted a small snake inside a goose egg, summoned everyone, spewed gibberish, and announced the arrival of the god
Asclepius. A few days later, the little snake had grown magically into the
huge tame serpent Alexander had brought with him. He held sessions in a
dimly lit chamber, the serpent now sporting a human head actually made
of linen. The god, he explained, would deliver oracles—for a fee. All a sup-
plicant had to do was write down what he wanted to know on a scroll and
seal it. Alexander would resort to the usual tricks—it's sobering to contemplate how many have placed their trust in wax seals—to open the
scrolls, read them ahead of time, and reseal them. His responses were obscure in the ordinary oracular way, though he did permit himself concrete
answers to questions no one had posed. The show was good enough to cre-
ate a swell of business, Alexander greedy enough to send emissaries abroad
to drum up more, audacious enough to coax the serpent into speaking in
its own voice. (All that took was a speaking tube and a concealed confederate.) The credulous locals advertised for him. "Many women even boasted
that they had had children by Alexander, and their husbands bore witness
that they spoke the truth!"[83] Lucian himself submitted a taunting scroll
asking when Alexander would be exposed. The gibe earned the usual
opaque drivel and enough enmity that Alexander tried to have him thrown
overboard at sea.

On the domestic or even friendly side of witchcraft were the cunning
men and cunning women of early modern England. They predicted the
future, helped find lost objects, provided magic spells for lovesick lads and
lasses, and the like. (America had the same types, if not that label for

[83] "Alexander, the False Prophet," in *Lucian*, trans. A. M. Harmon et al., 8 vols., Loeb Classical
Library (Cambridge, MA: Harvard University Press; London: William Heinemann, 1913–67),
4:229.

them.[84]) But they weren't always so friendly, which is why we find church court proceedings in 1590s Essex against cunning men consulted about lost and stolen goods.[85] Judith Philips, a cunning woman winding her knavish way through the 1590s, was, warned the chronicler of her exploits, "the mirror and map of all cozenage and deceit, whereat all modest women may blush, and every true meaning man may smile at the folly of the world."[86] Learning of a miser pursuing a lawsuit, Philips showed up to predict that he would win—and to reveal that there was buried treasure on his land. (That much was true. She knew it was. She'd buried it herself.) She instructed the miser and his wife to set out a lavish display of linen and gold and then to lay prostrate outside in the cold for three hours while she summoned the Queen of Fairies. Philips could have briskly wrapped up the goods and gotten away in well under three hours. But she appeared before the couple garbed as the Queen and left them shivering before she took off. She got away with that stunt. Another time, though, her own insatiable greed tripped her up. She'd succeeded in swapping a purse with two stones for one full of gold. Gilding the lily, she asked the woman she'd just swindled to supply "a fat Turkey, and a couple of Capons" to help her friend win the acquaintance of (yes, you guessed it) the Queen of Fairies. Philips came back to try plucking this fool again, but this time the fool unleashed a constable. Philips was jailed in Newgate and sentenced to be whipped through the city streets.

Stock market scams are nothing new. The South Sea Bubble of 1720 triggered republican fretting about untrammeled commercial greed and the eclipse of virtue in modern society.[87] Lotteries, unsecured debt, gar-

---

[84] John Putnam Demos, *Entertaining Satan: Witchcraft and the Culture of Early New England* (New York: Oxford University Press, 1982), p. 81.

[85] *Lincoln Diocese Documents, 1450–1544*, ed. Andrew Clark (London: Kegan Paul, Trench, Trübner & Co. for the Early English Text Society, 1914), p. 108. Contrast the more serene account in Shaftesbury, "Sensus Communis," IV.iii, in *Characteristicks of Men, Manners, Opinions, Times*; and the more impish treatment in *The Cunning-Man, a Musical Entertainment, in Two Acts* (London, 1766), Charles Burney's musical setting of Rousseau's *Devin du village*.

[86] *The Brideling, Sadling and Ryding, of a Rich Churle in Hampshire, by the Subtill Practise of One Iudeth Philips, a Professed Cunning Woman, or Fortune Teller* (London, 1594), p. 4.

[87] John Carswell, *The South Sea Bubble*, rev. ed. (Dover, NH: Alan Sutton, 1993), is a first-rate financial history. For the fretting, see especially John Trenchard and Thomas Gordon, *Cato's Letters*, 4 vols. (London, 1723). For context, see Shelley Burtt, *Virtue Transformed: Political Argument in England, 1688–1740* (Cambridge: Cambridge University Press, 1992).

gantuan guaranteed returns, an official monopoly of trade with the Americas granted with blithe disregard of the actual trade conducted by Spain, a slippery corporate charter enabling a small committee to act secretly, share issues and annuity payments qualifying as a Ponzi scheme (in which primarily the accelerating rush of later cash investments, not the rivulets of actual business, pay off the earlier investors), and more: the South Sea Company wasn't just an unfortunate or unintended financial disaster waiting to happen; it was designed that way from the get-go. Intoxicating rewards were available to expert insiders. No dupes, they took care to safeguard their own finances. The setup promised to transfer a cool £1 or 2 million from the public to politicians.[88] One play staged in London that year had Mrs. Subtle arranging the sale of two shares of stock to Squire Pheasant, "a Soft-Head," at the inflated price of £260 apiece. Alone on stage, her soliloquy baring her sentiments for the audience's contemplation, Subtle crows, "Fare thee well, honest *Truepenny*, were it not for such rich Fools as thou art, the poor wise Part of the Nation must starve."[89]

Recollecting the debacle in 1776, Adam Smith commented that the Company's "knavery and extravagance" were well known.[90] Well known, but it's never too late to crank them up again. In the 1990s, Rumania and Albania nearly collapsed as people flocked to pure pyramid schemes, with no productive investment whatever in the works and only the feverish later investments supplying the funds to pay off the earlier ones. These schemes seemed the embodiment of magical get-rich-quick capitalism.[91] (Magic indeed: one Albanian scheme featured a woman reading the financial future in her crystal ball.)

Don't assume the sophisticated investors of the West are immune to such nonsense, and I don't mean the dot.com bubble.[92] Unmistakable scams succeed in the first world, too. In 1996, a couple of Australian lesbians in their fifties surfaced in London promising a return of 100 percent.

[88] Carswell, *Bubble*, pp. 153, 112.

[89] [William Chetwood,] *The Stock-Jobbers: or, The Humours of Exchange-Alley* (London, 1720), Dramatis Personæ, n.p., and p. 12.

[90] *The Wealth of Nations*, bk. 5, chap. 1, pt. 3, article 1.

[91] Compare the approaches of Katherine Verdery, *What Was Socialism, and What Comes Next?* (Princeton, NJ: Princeton University Press, 1996), chap. 7, and Dirk J. Bezemer, "Post-Socialist Financial Fragility: The Case of Albania," *Cambridge Journal of Economics* (2001) 25:1–23.

[92] For an amusing and detailed polemic, see John Cassidy, *dot.con: the greatest story ever sold* (New York: HarperCollins, 2002).

They racked up millions. The investors were puzzled—not by the astounding profits on offer, even though they scream out their incredibility, but by one's jamming hundreds of thousands of pounds into her bra and joking, "You just thought I had big tits, didn't you?" They didn't know that she'd picked up the habit of storing money that way when running a whorehouse, nor that her companion had done sadomasochistic work in a massage parlor. Before the scam came undone, the two had had tea with the queen.[93]

Famed Yorkshire witch Mary Bateman finally ascended the scaffold in 1809. For her crimes, not for witchcraft: by then the authorities were more secular and skeptical. Already in 1736, Parliament had repealed some older witchcraft statutes and instead prohibited "pretend[ing] to exercise or use any kind of witchcraft, sorcery, enchantment, or conjuration," adding for good measure the efforts of cunning folk to locate missing goods.[94] Bateman had pulled one scam after another. One of her hens, she announced, had laid an egg with the inscription, "Crist is coming." (Come on, the spelling isn't that bad for a hen.) To prove that she hadn't herself inscribed the egg, Bateman "had the cruelty to force up at different times, into the ovary of the poor hen, two other eggs bearing similar inscriptions, and these were of course deposited into the nest."[95] People rushed and paid admission to see the marvelous hen. Bateman may well have been trying to set herself up as one of the day's prophets. Fraud or not, Bateman's contemporary Joanna Southcott had been enjoying phenomenal success.[96] Again, Bateman's victims were not just pliable but complicit, even eager to be ripped off. Her champions roundly abused those daring to venture any skepticism.

It isn't a long way from Bateman to the ten-year-old grilled cheese sandwich imprinted with the face of the Virgin Mary, auctioned off on eBay in November 2004 for $28,000. (Me, I thought the face looked more like Jean Harlow.) Nor from Philips and the South Sea Bubble to today's Nigerian letter scam, written in someone's fantasy of semiliterate English. A friend or relative of some deposed politician or exploited businessman, or maybe a bureaucrat in a corrupt ministry, has tens of millions of dollars

[93] Christine Middap, "Lying High," *The Advertiser* (17 February 2001), M8.

[94] 9 Geo. II c. 5.

[95] *Extraordinary Life and Character of Mary Bateman, the Yorkshire Witch*, 4th ed. (Leeds, 1809), p. 14.

[96] For the milieu, see Susan Juster, *Doomsayers: Anglo-American Prophecy in the Age of Revolution* (Philadelphia: University of Pennsylvania Press, 2003).

to move out of the country. All he or she needs is a trivial fee of some thousands up front or the use of your bank account, for which—such generosity!—you'll get millions yourself. Working on this book, I permitted myself to voice reluctant concern about that risky advance fee and ask how they'd gotten my name. I can't paraphrase Christain Agor's startlingly eloquent email response or amend his grammar, though I can clean up his spelling errors:

> The answer to your question how I got your email address. To be sincere, we just came to this country about one week and two days now with reasons and rumors that this country might come to be a country of war and polities, so we decided to look for a foreign business investor and companies that will negotiate with me to invest this fund into a lucrative business area in abroad.
>
> Because this, we have went to the world trade center here, to find away of lifting this money out of this place to a safety account overseas, based on my late father Chief Henry C. Agor's instruction and his advice for me to look for reliable company in overseas where there's good stability and good economy.
>
> Please don't be offended, because we have never met each other before and have never been into any business relationship despite my proposal to you, which we must advise you not to be afraid that we was convinced with every humanity of truth that we are telling you now the truth that we got your name from the net when we were browsing website with international chambers of commerce to search for company and individual business area is where I got your mail, but cannot predict whom you are in person but only contacting you if interested, to help us provide your foreign account so that we can instruct the bank to transfer the $4m dollars into your account as our father's business partner and the owner of this fund. On the date of this deposit, my late father told that this money belongs to his business partner abroad in other to avoid any eye bruise towards his family fund. So that is why I, and my younger sister Mary have decided to ask you for help.
>
> We don't want to waste time here because this country is not safe so we need to do fast in other to lift this money out from here first before any other thing.

Uncle, do not worry, because the fund is in our hand and even
the code to access the account is here with us, so all we need from
you is your help and please don't be offended and try to give us
your full name address, telephone and fax number for our easy
communication. We will give you the account code for you to verify
and ask the Credit Union bank here how to transfer the money into
your account. But first of all, we will like you to tell us more about
you and your family background.

Samuel Kokou (would I make up a name like that?) beat me to the punch,
volunteering, "As it may interest you to know, your contact was given to me
by divine aspiration from a good friend of mine who lived and worked in
your country. . . ." I countered the request from Emmanuel Eze (would I
make up a name like that?) with an invitation to purchase some (swampy)
Florida real estate, but his entrepreneurial zeal flagged and he didn't get
back to me. Mukus Kendo (would I make up a name like that?), Auditor
General of a South African bank, wanted to move $26 million out of an
account no one was claiming. I saluted him: "Kendo, you rogue, I can't believe you've surfaced by email after all these years. Last I heard, you were
in Nigeria. And the terms we parted on were not, as you must remember,
the warmest: what made you think of me for this latest stunt?" Alas,
Mail-Delivery-Subsystem impassively reported that my pal's email account already had been canceled. When the Rev. Mark Okoye, aka
reverendmark@catholic.org, tried his own version of the scam, I felt duty-
bound to apprise the site he was using.

Cheap thrills? Maybe, but I found myself fretting that I might be
chump enough to get in over my head and find my money floating away.
The usual version of the scam is transparent enough, but people fall for it.
In 2002, some 16,000 people reported to the federal government that
they'd received such email. Seventy-four of them, overcoming the obvious
diffidence and shame, confessed that they'd lost money totaling a hefty
$1.6 million.[97] When the knaves ask for cash to lubricate the gears of fi-
nance, people send it. When the knaves come back and stammer, gosh,

---

[97] "IFCC 2002 Internet Fraud Report," p. 7, at www.ifccfbi.gov/strategy/2002_IFCCReport
.pdf. Check too the sorry parade at www.scamorama.com. But they also have a few cases of people
who managed to extract some money from the con artists.

problems have arisen, we need more cash, people send more. When the knaves seek bank account numbers and powers of attorney, people obligingly provide them. Instead of depositing money, the knaves withdraw it.

The advance fee fraud routinely elicits the enthusiastic cooperation of fools—even when they're warned. About a hundred years ago, Seth Savage, a poor farmer in Vermont, got a letter explaining that a lottery ticket sent to him a month before had won $3,000. All he had to do to collect his prize was send in $35. The postmaster patiently explained the fraud. So did a special postal agent. Not to be deterred, Savage sold his only cow and sent in the money. Asked why he threw his money away, Savage explained that he wouldn't let the post office men beat him to his prize.[98] He is the fool as would-be cagey operator, confused about who are his friends, who his enemies.

Today Canada has emerged as the international leader in telemarketing scams worth billions a year, not a bad haul for such stunts as asking people to pay fees to collect their already-approved loans. If you're astonished to learn that such a famously sweet country could harbor such wicked scoundrels, think again. It's precisely because of Canada's relaxed amiability: the Ontario detective who runs Phonebusters moans that the crooks don't fear the toothless criminal justice system.[99] Lots of these schemes are as transparent as the Nigerian letter scam. But even that infamous hoax has its translucent, maybe opaque, versions. In one, they offer to mail you a check to allay your suspicion.[100] So go ahead, deposit it, why not? All it can do is bounce, right? Yes, the check will bounce. But—rehearse what you and your bank do when you deposit it—it will leave the sender with your account information and signature. Then it's child's play and the minimal investment of a decent laser printer and paper to produce facsimiles of your checks and sign them. Those checks won't bounce. Not for a while, anyway, at which point somehow the ones you're writing will bounce, too.

The tricksters of world religion, mythology, and folklore, slippery

[98] P. H. Woodward, "Adventures in the Secret Service of the Post-Office Department," in *Classic Mystery and Detective Stories: Real Life*, ed. Julian Hawthorne (New York: Review of Reviews Co., 1909), pp. 44–46.

[99] Robert Cribb and Christian Cotroneo, "In Telemarketing World, Canada Is the Wild West," *Toronto Star* (4 November 2002), A8.

[100] Frank W. Abagnale, *The Art of the Steal: How to Protect Yourself and Your Business from Fraud—America's #1 Crime* (New York: Broadway Books, 2001), pp. 120–22.

rogues as different as Norse god Loki and Indian demon Bakasura, and as similar too, sometimes prance onstage as unassuming knaves.[101] In one Philippine tale, Juan turns a gaily painted straw hat into a fortune. He secretly prepays merchants at three stores twenty pesos apiece and explains that he'll take merchandise worth less than that and bow. Then, he adds, their clerks should thank him profusely. The merchants promise not to reveal the arrangement. All he has to do, Juan now tells his wide-eyed friends, is bow with his hat and storekeepers will give him whatever he wants. He works his sorcery twice in a row and auctions off the hat to one friend for five thousand pesos. The high bidder suddenly doubtful, Juan dutifully works his sorcery at the third store, closes the sale, and cruises off. The new owner invites some friends to a restaurant, but somehow his bow doesn't work: the host demands payment and has him arrested. "When the owner of the hat heard how Juan had played his trick by paying twenty pesos in advance, he fainted and became very sick. In the meantime Juan was performing other tricks in some different country."[102]

In a Navajo tale, Coyote, wily way before the fine folks at Looney Tunes snared him, enrolls the assistance of an initially stupid Skunk in slaughtering other animals. Coyote pretends to be dead—he's sprinkled with grass seeds supposed to look like fly larvae—and Skunk rounds up their targeted victims to celebrate. Prairie Dog is wary, but they all finally join in. Then Skunk urinates into the air and yells, "Look. Look. Look in the sky. There is something real pretty up there!" Blinded by the descending droplets, the animals succumb to Coyote's enthusiastic clubbing, leaving the two conspirators with a mouth-watering heap of freshly slaughtered meat. Coyote proposes that he and Skunk race to see who wins the meat. But Skunk outwits the trickster. Instead of running, he hides under some tumbleweed. While Coyote zips along, Skunk drags the meat to the top of a cliff. When Coyote tries to get him to share, he contemptuously throws down a

[101] For an introductory overview of the cross-cultural wealth of trickster tales, see Kimberly A. Christen, *Clowns & Tricksters: An Encyclopedia of Tradition and Culture* (Denver: ABC-CLIO, 1998). Less focused on the ethnography is Lewis Hyde, *Trickster Makes This World: Mischief, Myth, and Art* (New York: Farrar, Straus and Giroux, 1998). Still well worth reading is Paul Radin, *The Trickster: A Study in American Indian Mythology* (London: Routledge and Kegan Paul, 1956).

[102] *Philippine Folk Literature: The Folktales*, comp. and ed. Damiana L. Eugenio (Quenzon City: U.P. Folklorists, Inc., in cooperation with the Philippine National Science Society, 1989), pp. 377–79.

rat and some bones.[103] The knave outwitted by the fool, the biter bit, not just neat inversions but roiling ambiguities of who is using whom: the motif affords poignant pleasure, from *Double Indemnity* to *The Third Man* to *Conversation*, outside the movies, too. "You fancy a man your dupe," offers La Bruyère, "but if he only pretends to be so, who is the greatest dupe, you or he?"[104]

If you imagine the world as peopled solely by knaves and fools, which do you want to be? Why? Some will find it tempting to jeer at the fools, to think they get just what's coming to them; tempting too to flatter themselves they can join the ranks of the knaves, since some of these scams don't look difficult to run. Much of what passes for cunning, after all, is really the stupidity and cupidity of the victims. The knaves look strong, assertive, manly; the fools weak, spineless, feminine or effeminate. In a noir novel of the 1940s, Stanton Carlile flings his declaration of faith at Dr. Lilith Ritter, his sober psychoanalyst.

> "I'm a hustler, God damn it. Do you understand that, you frozen-faced bitch? I'm on the make. Nothing matters in this goddamned lunatic asylum of a world but dough. When you get that you're the boss. If you don't have it you're the end man on the daisy chain. I'm going to get it if I have to bust every bone in my head doing it. I'm going to milk it out of those chumps and take them for the gold in their teeth before I'm through. . . . They're all Johns. They're asking for it. Well, I'm here to give it out."[105]

Those ready to roll up their sleeves and plunge into knavery had better watch out. They don't want to become Coyotes who discover too late that the Skunks aren't quite as blank as they'd imagined. They should chasten their predatory ambitions with two other English proverbs: "None is so wise but the fool overtakes him"; "Every man hath a fool in his sleeve."[106]

---

[103] "Coyote and Skunk," in *Coming to Light: Contemporary Translations of the Native Literatures of North America*, ed. Brian Swann (New York: Random House, 1994), pp. 606–13.

[104] La Bruyère, *Characters*, trans. Henri van Laun (London: Oxford University Press, 1963), p. 76.

[105] William Lindsay Gresham, *Nightmare Alley* (New York: Rinehart and Company, 1946), card XII, p. 168.

[106] Ray, *Collection*, pp. 29, 91, italics removed. Here's Halifax: "No Man is so much a Fool as not to have Wit enough sometimes to be a Knave; nor any so cunning a Knave, as not to have the Weakness sometimes to play the Fool." George Savile, *A Character of King Charles the Second; and Political, Moral and Miscellaneous Thoughts and Reflections* (Dublin, 1750), p. 77.

Or they should notice that after her affair with Carlile, Ritter swindles him out of $150,000, uses her authority to impeach his ensuing complaint as a fantasy and has him institutionalized, marries his last plutocratic target, and sends him plunging down the greased pole of success until he's reduced to being a geek, the degraded buffoon in the circus who grabs live chickens and chews off their heads, his princely salary the alcohol in which he's stewing his sorrows and pickling his liver. (Should her devilish first name have put him on notice?) Still, if it's knaves and fools, some will do their damnedest to set up as knaves. They'll be gunning for the prize, whether it's blue-chip bonds or blue-eyed blondes.

It's a bleak vision. For relief and realism alike, why not deny that the world is composed only of knaves and fools? Why not add decent, upstanding people? Trustworthy, even models of probity, they are prudent enough to know that some deals are too good to be true, perceptive enough to pick out other upstanding people to cooperate with. Their consciousness of their own integrity enables them to stand tall, look others in the eye, deliver firm handshakes, greet their reflections in the mirror with calm approval. (Central casting routinely equips these guys with jutting jaws.) Others respect and fear them. Loath to cross or double-cross them, haunted by uneasy consciences, knaves shrink from their coolly appraising gazes. None of the nauseating minuet of knaves and fools for these upright men. Theirs are loftier pursuits.

Sermons and literature endlessly adumbrate some such picture. But it's suspect to the core; our mood in glimpsing the vista of knaves and fools isn't mean-spirited or paranoid enough. In the criminal lingo of Elizabethan England, the upright man is leader of a criminal gang, with the right to skim the others' earnings and sleep with their women.[107] There is more here, I'm afraid, than a mischievous inversion. And there's more to cunning than knaves, fools, and the consciousness of good intentions.

[107] [John Awdelay,] *The Fraternitye of Vacabondes* (London, 1575), n.p.; [Thomas Harman,] *The Groundworke of Conny-Catching* (London, 1592?), n.p. For the endurance of the language, see Richard Head, *The English Rogue Continued in the Life of Meriton Latroon, and Other Extravagants*, pt. 2 (London, 1680), p. 120.

APPEARANCES

✻ Etymology can be suggestive: the English *cunning* reveals knotty ties to knowledge. *Cunning* stems from a root of *can*, an irregular verb meaning *to know*. Indeed, *cunning* means *knowledge* for centuries before it gains its associations with sly deceit or artifice, which it has by the late 1500s. In the first edition of 1755 and still in the fourth edition of 1773, Samuel Johnson's *Dictionary* defines the adjective *cunning* as "Skilful; knowing; well instructed; learned" before turning to "Artfully deceitful; sly; designing; trickish; full of fetches and stratagems; subtle; crafty; subdolous." (But in both editions, Johnson's definition of the noun form opens with "Artifice; deceit; slyness; sleight; craft; subtilty; dissimulation; fraudulent dexterity" before turning to "Art; skill; knowledge.") I conjecture that repeated experiences of what the knowing do with their knowledge finally get built into the meaning of the word. The sole surprise is that it takes so long. *Canny*, with the same root, emerges in the 1600s with the same meaning it has today. A bridge between knowledge and deceit is provided by *cunning* as a craft, especially a magical art: the cunningly wrought device is skillfully done, intricate, ready to lend itself to deceit. Think here of Celtic knotwork or M. C. Escher's engravings. (*Con*, as a now archaic verb meaning to know or to learn something by repeatedly studying it, or more generally to scan, has the same root. But *con man* goes back to the French for *confidence*.) Occurrences of *know*, still from the same root, show up in the sense of carnal knowledge as early as 1200. The disguises of *Measure for Measure* allow Mariana, about to unveil, to confront Angelo, "Who thinks he knows that he ne'er knew my body, / But knows he thinks that he knows Isabel's."[1] Other languages display the same connection. More generally, we apprehend knowledge with the categories of sex and politics. Trying to figure out who to trust, who to believe, we look for a penetrating understanding or for someone who has mastered a subject.

Knowledge, sex, and power are realms open to the mastery and manipulation of the cunning, who get inside our heads and jerk us around. How do they do it? I'd like next to survey two connected problems: the

[1] *Measure for Measure*, act 5, sc. 1.

appearance/reality distinction and the rationality of belief. We need to beware deceptive appearance, to become expert in the arts of unmasking, to trust the right people on the right issues. If only it were easy to know how! Playwrights are merrily tinkering with the trope of unmasking before it's had an opportunity to become stultified. So Ben Jonson treats the audiences of *The Alchemist* and *Bartholomew Fair* to some enthusiastic rubbishing and unmasking of Tribulation Wholesome and Zeal-of-the-Land Busy, righteous Puritan saints with nasal whines, as worldly hypocrites. But Jonson knew this terrain was liberally mined with difficulties. In *Every Man out of His Humour*, Deliro solemnly thanks Macilente for unmasking Brisk: "Well, I repent me I e'er credited him so much: but (now I see what he is, and that his masking vizor is off) I'll forbear him no longer." The only problem is that Macilente, whose "judgment is dazzled and distasted" by "an envious *Apoplexy*," is lying.[2] Deliro believes he's just learned to see the world more clearly, but actually he's newly confused. Still, having seen what they've seen and prompted by some knowing asides from Fallace, the audience know perfectly well what's going on. Whatever confusions plague the actors don't cross the threshold of the stage.

Does real life offer spectators the same certitude? Outside the theater, we sometimes manage devastating unmaskings. One New England prophet of the 1790s kept announcing his immortality and physical invulnerability—until an annoyed skeptic gave him a bloody nose.[3] Yet it's sobering to notice how easy it can be to don a mask and get away with it. One American hobo recalled how belligerent detectives and policemen constantly hindered him from grabbing free rides on trains. A change of costume, he decided, would be just the thing. He prevailed on some railroad workers to give him a jacket, overalls, and a trademark striped cap. Later, when he had some cash to spare, he'd occasionally treat himself to a spanking new outfit. His camouflage gave him untrammeled access to railroad yards. "I even talked to a known bad dick in the yards in East Omaha, and he treated me like a brother while at the same time he was looking around for a hobo to arrest for trespassing on railroad property. I thought to my-

---

[2] Ben Jonson, *Every Man out of His Humour*, act 4, sc. 1; cast of characters.

[3] Stephen A. Marini, *Radical Sects of Revolutionary New England* (Cambridge, MA: Harvard University Press, 1982), p. 54.

self, Good old clothes, a little deception is a wonderful thing."[4] You might think the detective was a fool. Shouldn't he have asked for some identification? or seen if the other workers would vouch for the hobo? But what grounds did he have for suspicion? Wouldn't it be awkward, offensive, foolish to start grilling people who look just like railroad workers? The detective might unthinkingly have taken the hobo's new clothes at face value. Yet even if he thought through the possibilities, it's not clear he would or should have done anything different. Instant mask, instant success.

Now we see through a glass, darkly, a predicament from which only the afterlife, divine intervention, or necromancy could rescue us. Egypt's magicians matched Aaron for several rounds. They too turned rods into serpents. They too produced blood and frogs. But they couldn't produce lice. Looks like Aaron had God on his side, though it's possible he was just a better magician. (So why did Pharaoh's heart stay hardened? Because God hardened it, so that He could publicly certify His power and status.)[5] The church fathers vindicated the claims of Christianity by reporting the same kinds of contests—and by bravely challenging skeptics to them.[6] In every culture I've ever glanced at, some claim sixth senses, uncanny access to knowledge denied the rest of us. In 1624, one Englishwoman disclosed that she could detect whether another woman was a virgin simply by looking at her.[7] In daily life, alas, we've no such resources. In the meantime, what can we do?

APPEARANCE AND REALITY

Masks needn't mean malevolence. There's the innocent masquerade, great fun for one and all. These days no one expects any harmful pranks at Halloween. There's the mask of evil that disguises good. Take the undercover

---

[4] Charles Elmer Fox, *Tales of an American Hobo* (Iowa City: University of Iowa Press, 1989), p. 118.

[5] Exodus 7:3–11:10.

[6] For instance, Tertullian, *Apologeticus*, XXIII.4–7; Origen, *Contra Celsum*, III.36, VII.3. So too Bede, *Historia Ecclesiastica Gentis Anglorum*, I.18, I.21, II.2.

[7] Laura Gowing, "Language, Power, and the Law: Women's Slander Litigation in Early Modern London," in *Women, Crime and the Courts in Early Modern England*, ed. Jennifer Kermode and Garthine Walker (Chapel Hill: University of North Carolina Press, 1994), p. 31.

agent who infiltrates a terrorist cell. Then there's the masquerade enabling actors to take a discrete slice of time and play by holiday rules without suffering accountability when they return to their regular lives. In 1724, Lady Mary Wortley Montagu reported that the Duke of Wharton had organized a committee of twenty. "They call themselves Schemers, and meet regularly 3 times a week to consult on Gallant Schemes for the advancement of that branch of Happiness which the vulgar call Whoring," or what we'd call fornication. Masked lords and ladies would meet for gracious dinners and sex. Members were sworn not to attempt to see through any lady's disguise, and "if by Accident or the Lady's indiscretion her name should chance to be discover'd by one or more of the Schemers, that name should remain sacred and as unspeakable as the name of the Deity among the Jews."[8] (With a shrewd anthropological eye, Lady Mary also decided that the elaborate wrappings of Turkish women made them "the only free people in the Empire" because they could arrange whatever public meetings they liked with no fear of detection. "This perpetual Masquerade gives them entire Liberty of following their Inclinations without danger of Discovery," indeed without having even to identify themselves to their lovers.)[9] Their servants must have known what was going on, but these aristocrats weren't inclined to fret too much about downstairs chatter. Here the masked confederacy can greet those not privy to their Scheming evenings with composed faces; conduct straight-faced, straitlaced social intercourse with each other on ordinary, unmasked occasions; and thrill to being complicit, not just in the fornication but in the scheming itself.

Nor need masks mean mystery. Sometimes artifice deliberately calls attention to itself. When Tammy Faye Bakker plastered her face with makeup, she wasn't trying to fool anyone. Who was under the makeup? Suppose the Tammy Faye we all came to know and, um, love? revile? snicker at? pick a verb, any verb, but anyway, suppose she were to return to the style of her days at North Central Bible College, where she met Jim. She was slender—he says 83 pounds, she says 73—and didn't wear

---

[8] Lady Montagu to Lady Mar, [March 1724], in *The Complete Letters of Lady Mary Wortley Montagu*, ed. Robert Halsband, 3 vols. (Oxford: Clarendon Press, 1965–67), 2:38–39.

[9] Lady Montagu to Lady Mar, 1 April [1717], in *Letters*, 1:328–29. But Lady Mary also worried that "women are treated in Turkey as something between beasts and men": Robert Halsband, *The Life of Lady Mary Wortley Montagu* (Oxford: Clarendon Press, 1956), p. 85.

makeup.[10] In public, would she be hailed as the real Tammy Faye? Without her makeup, would she be herself? or painfully naked? Or after all those years, is she herself only with the cosmetic armor? Historically, many have thought the only successful makeup doesn't call attention to itself. It subtly enhances your appearance, but no one can tell whether you have it on.[11] So too with plastic surgery. Sometimes it calls attention to itself as phony. No one "really," as we'd say, has body parts shaped and sized and smoothed so perfectly. But those who have them do, they really do; caress or squeeze them as you like, they don't disappear, there are no trick mirrors in sight. They believe their surgery has genuinely made them more attractive and can point to ogling others as evidence. Are they desirable in spite of the fact that the artificiality is transparent? or somehow because of it? What about plastic itself? Sometimes it masquerades as marble or hardwood or gemstones. Sometimes it is unabashedly itself, plastic through and through. And we vacillate between seeing it as phony and seeing it as real, even indestructible.[12]

Nor need public virtue be the masked face of private vice. Consider the curmudgeon with a heart of gold who secretly dispenses charity by night while growling all day at the idle poor. Or if you doubt the existence of that time-honored character, take this episode. In the glory days of the papacy, with naked prostitutes sashaying through the Vatican, Pope Alexander VI wanted his son, Cesare Borgia—yes, the same scoundrel lionized by Machiavelli—to ascend to the rank of cardinal. There were daunting obstacles, not least Cesare's notorious status as illegitimate son of the pope. So in 1493 Alexander issued a papal bull declaring Cesare the legitimate son of his actual mother and her legal husband. That same day, he issued a second, secret bull testifying that Cesare was in fact his own son.[13] As it happens, we have good reason to be confident in the second: we have independent evidence for it. And the first served Alexander's in-

[10] Jim Bakker with Robert Paul Lamb, *Move That Mountain!* (Plainfield, NJ: Logos International, 1976), p. 21; Tammy Bakker with Cliff Dudley, *I Gotta Be Me* (Charlotte, NC: PTL Television Network, 1978), p. 43.

[11] Kathy Peiss, *Hope in a Jar: The Making of America's Beauty Culture* (New York: Henry Holt, 1998), esp. chap. 5.

[12] Jeffrey L. Meikle, *American Plastic: A Cultural History* (New Brunswick, NJ: Rutgers University Press, 1995).

[13] Sarah Bradford, *Cesare Borgia: His Life and Times* (London: Weidenfeld and Nicolson, 1976), p. 35.

terests of the moment. So far so good. But now suppose that Alexander issued the opposite bulls: a public one sadly acknowledging Cesare's illegitimacy and repenting for his own sinful affair, and a private one confirming Cesare's legitimacy. What would—what should—the locals have made of that? Suppose he issued a public bull certifying Cesare's legitimacy and a private bull insisting that the public bull was true. Suppose he deliberately leaked the actual private bull. Suppose he had it leaked and denied its authenticity. Suppose he leaked the fact of its existence and multiple rumors about its content, or no rumors at all. Suppose he grumbled about the actual public bull, muttering that it was extorted from him by the College of Cardinals, and sarcastically raised an eyebrow or snorted when asked about its veracity. And just what were the effects of the actual bulls? They enabled Cesare to ascend to the cardinalate. But it's not as though the public bull persuaded anyone who mattered that Cesare was legitimate. It provided a fig leaf of respectability, homage to legal form, the hypocritical tribute that vice pays to virtue. Was Cesare really a cardinal? Or did he merely seem to be a cardinal? Well, at the cost of whatever unblinking lies were required, he held the office and commanded its perquisites. Then again one can imagine—I know no canon law, but it would be surprising were there no such possibility—a straightforward legal argument that his title was wholly invalid, so he only seemed to be a cardinal all along.

The church has weathered other hurricanes of embarrassment. After the Great Schism of 1378, the Roman Catholic Church for decades had two popes, one installed at Avignon and one back in Rome, and for several heady years—someone must have misheard the passage in Genesis about being fruitful and multiplying—a third pope in Pisa.[14] These years included riots, looting, cardinals proceeding to the solemn duties of election under threats of coercion, and the slaughter of thousands. The popes in question were a miserably colorful lot, one insane, one near death at his election, another fond of butchering rich and poor alike before declaring himself pope. Their tenures were unhappily precarious, too. A couple abdicated, one was deposed, and another was poisoned, at least according to legend. (Recall Marlowe's Machiavelli: popes who "cast me off, / Are poi-

---

[14] For the basic narrative, see Marzieh Gail, *The Three Popes: An Account of the Great Schism—When Rival Popes in Rome, Avignon and Pisa Vied for the Rule of Christendom* (London: Robert Hale & Company, 1972).

soned by my climbing followers.") It's easy to describe the cardinals who donned disguises as laymen or pilgrims to slip past furious mobs as real cardinals who only appeared to be something else. But was Benedict XIII the real pope? When Pope Urban excommunicated Pope Clement, what really happened? The issues here are all about law and legitimacy, not what exists and what only seems to.

Then too, what exists plain as day, in front of your nose, might not be what it seems. Some decades ago, new Vermeers began turning up and commanding stratospheric prices. The only problem was that they were literally new, not merely previously undiscovered. Painstaking work went into them: finding and preparing seventeenth-century canvases, mixing the paints, and so on. Obviously, too, some serious artistic talent was required—though somehow it was easier to detect flaws after the works were exposed as forgeries. At the 1947 trial of forger Han van Meegeren, the prosecutor declared, "One begins to doubt the very essence of artistic evaluation."[15] He meant, I think, our ability to trust expert appraisals; but he could well have been wondering about what makes a painting valuable anyway. As Vermeers, the canvases were worth millions. As van Meegerens, they had mere curiosity value. But they were the very same canvases. "Real" here means "really from the hand of Vermeer."

Masking too is trickier than its ostensible grammar suggests. You can pretend to be masked. Some masks for Venetian carnival are full-scale imposing disguises, leaving observers no way of knowing who's inside short of forcibly ripping off the things. But others are slight, evanescent: you hold them up on a stick and they barely cover your eyes and part of your nose. They're as-if masks, reminders that it's carnival and you too want your slice of time out of everyday life. So others would be rude to notice who you are or remember what you're doing, even if they could. You can wear a mask that allows you to be sincere. In May 1945, Victor Klemperer, the magnificent diarist of Nazi Germany, took refuge with a Catholic family. He didn't know them yet and they'd no idea that he was Jewish, or anyway so tagged by the regime, but the father

---

[15] Lord Kilbracken, *Van Meegeren: A Case History* (London: Thomas Nelson and Sons, Ltd, 1967), p. 183. Well worth consulting are John F. Moffitt, *Art Forgery: The Case of the Lady of Elche* (Gainesville: University Press of Florida, 1995), on a famous piece of Iberian art, and Anthony Grafton, *Forgers and Critics: Creativity and Duplicity in Western Scholarship* (Princeton, NJ: Princeton University Press, 1990), on textual forgeries.

talked interestedly and sympathetically about politics, in a Catholic anti-Nazi sense, of course. On such occasions I am always the probably Catholic, at any rate strongly religious senior educationist, who regularly win hearts with the sentence: "Above all young people must once again learn the Ten Commandments." By saying that I really get to the heart of things and also express my own conviction (but at the same time nevertheless play hide-and-seek).[16]

You can wear a mask of evil to disguise some other evil. One recent currency counterfeiter in Britain scattered materials for producing soft pornography all over his workshop. That way, he figured, even a police raid would lead only to a fine, not to the seizure of his equipment.[17] You can double your masks, pretending to be someone else pretending to be you. When Bertie Wooster valiantly sails off to Deverill Hall to impersonate Gussie Fink-Nottle, will he then have to impersonate Fink-Nottle impersonating Wooster?[18] What can Bertie do when the endearingly inept Fink-Nottle shows up to impersonate him? What if Jeeves, in on the plot, for once slips up and refer to Bertie as Mr. Wooster in front of those supposed to be deceived? What if one of the formidable aunts, not in on the plot, addresses Bertie as Mr. Wooster? How can he decide if he's been unmasked or whether she's mistaken? And—slippery business—how could she be mistaken in addressing him by his correct name?

If this doubling seems too whimsical for words, consider the double agent and his easy turns on a dime. Spying for the USSR and the USA, he will sometimes let the USA know that he has relayed confidences to the USSR to gain his sources' trust. Sometimes, not always. He won't tell his American handlers if he reveals top-secret information. But he might tell the handlers with a straight face that Soviet spies believe he's one of their own. And the handlers might jubilantly seize on the fact as an opportunity to extract priceless information. Which it may in fact be. Minute by minute, syllable by syllable, what's going on here? What's under the spy's mask? That he's "really" a double agent isn't bedrock truth. It's just an innocent redescription of the shifting facets of this kaleidoscopic puzzle.

---

[16] Victor Klemperer, *I Will Bear Witness: A Diary of the Nazi Years*, trans. Martin Chalmers, 2 vols. (New York: Random House, 1998–99), 2:498 [26 May 1945].

[17] Charles Black with Michael Horsnell, *Counterfeiter: The Story of a Master Forger* (New York: St. Martin's Press, 1989), p. 76.

[18] P. G. Wodehouse, *The Mating Season*.

Or take masks you're not allowed to take off. The prospect sounds dehumanizing. Surveying the grim prospects of American blacks, W.E.B. Du Bois acknowledged "the present hopelessness of physical defence" and the limits of political and economic defense. "But there is a patent defence at hand,—the defence of deception and flattery, of cajoling and lying." Medieval Jews had adopted the same pose, he thought, and it "left its stamp on their characters for centuries." Worn long enough, the mask becomes the face.

> To-day the young Negro of the South who would succeed cannot be frank and outspoken, honest and self-assertive, but rather he is daily tempted to be silent and wary, politic and sly; he must flatter and be pleasant, endure petty insults with a smile, shut his eyes to wrong; in too many cases he sees positive personal advantage in deception and lying. His real thoughts, his real aspirations, must be guarded in whispers; he must not criticise, he must not complain.

Only such emasculating sacrifices win blacks a chance to advance. Du Bois's harrowing conclusion? "The price of culture is a Lie."[19]

No wonder so many rush headlong into embracing sincerity, authenticity, transparency. I'd rather hesitate. It all depends on the setting. We should recall Huizinga's pregnant concept, "cruel publicity."[20] There are facts about ourselves we'd rather not disclose. If it takes a lie, that's fine. If there's a routine mask we can slip on, that's fine too. And hypocrisy is often a political virtue.[21] There's ordinarily no point bemoaning masks when racists pretend to be egalitarians. Even obligatory masks can be wonderful, both personally and politically. Consider the longstanding worry that lawyers rise in court and vigorously press arguments they don't believe. The indefatigable Boswell, himself a lawyer, peppered Dr. Johnson with objections:

> I asked him whether, as a moralist, he did not think that the practice of the law, in some degree, hurt the nice feeling of honesty.
> JOHNSON. "Why no, Sir, if you act properly. You are not to deceive

---

[19] W.E.B. Du Bois, *The Souls of Black Folk*, chap. 10.

[20] J. Huizinga, *The Waning of the Middle Ages: A Study of the Forms of Life, Thought and Art in France and the Netherlands in the XIVth and XVth Centuries* (London: Edward Arnold, 1924), p. 1.

[21] Judith N. Shklar, *Ordinary Vices* (Cambridge, MA: Belknap Press, Harvard University Press, 1984), chap. 2.

your clients with false representations of your opinion: you are not to tell lies to a judge." BOSWELL. "But what do you think of supporting a cause which you know to be bad?" JOHNSON. "Sir, you do not know it to be good or bad till the Judge determines it. I have said that you are to state facts fairly; so that your thinking, or what you call knowing, a cause to be bad, must be from reasoning, must be from your supposing your arguments to be weak and inconclusive. But, Sir, that is not enough. An argument which does not convince yourself, may convince the Judge to whom you urge it: and if it does convince him, why, then, Sir, you are wrong, and he is right. It is his business to judge; and you are not to be confident in your own opinion that a cause is bad, but to say all you can for your client, and then hear the Judge's opinion." BOSWELL. "But, Sir, does not affecting a warmth when you have no warmth, and appearing to be clearly of one opinion when you are in reality of another opinion, does not such dissimulation impair one's honesty? Is there not some danger that a lawyer may put on the same mask in common life, in the intercourse with his friends?" JOHNSON. "Why no, Sir. Every body knows you are paid for affecting warmth for your client; and it is, therefore, properly no dissimulation: the moment you come from the bar you resume your usual behaviour. Sir, a man will no more carry the artifice of the bar into the common intercourse of society, than a man who is paid for tumbling upon his hands will continue to tumble upon his hands when he should walk on his feet."[22]

We can impeach Johnson's ready confidence in the superior judgment of the judge. The lawyer often knows crucial facts that never emerge in discovery or trial. She can leave court secure in the judgment that her victorious client should have lost—and she can take professional pride in the victory. Still, Johnson is onto something. Today American lawyers are not permitted, in trying a case, "to state a personal opinion as to the justness of a cause, the credibility of a witness, the culpability of a civil litigant or the guilt or innocence of an accused."[23] Their doing so can count as prejudicing

[22] James Boswell, *Life of Johnson*, Spring 1768.
[23] *Michigan Rules of Professional Conduct* (2002), Rule 3.4(e), echoing the parallel provision in the American Bar Association's Model Rules of Professional Conduct.

the jury and give the other side grounds for appealing an adverse result. So the lawyer's mask is glued on. Without the rule, many lawyers might well strenuously assert in every case that their clients and witnesses were right. Then some lawyer's silence on the matter would be taken as a confession that his clients and witnesses were wrong. Opposing counsel would obligingly draw the jury's attention to that silence. Better, surely, to adopt the gag rule and let the lawyers get on with the business of vigorously pressing lines of argument they might or might not believe. Here sincerity would be pernicious.

So again, the grammar of masks is complex. We inherit a vocabulary of cunning focusing on masks and unmasking, appearance and reality. But that vocabulary is not wholly trustworthy; we should use it with gingerly care. Still, sometimes masks are intended to conceal malevolence. Tacitus scornfully reveals that the emperor Nero would disguise himself and join his friends for rowdy, even criminal, evenings out on the town. They'd get drunk, visit whorehouses, shoplift, and beat people up.[24] Usually, rogues do not have the common decency or appalling honesty to tell you that they want to rip you off. They don't want you wary. They want you with your guard down. They don't want third parties noticing their peccadilloes or crimes, condemning them, seeking their punishment. So they strike poses, wear disguises, pretend to be what they are not. The literature of cunning revels in unmasking the scoundrels. Sometimes literally: I shudder to contemplate how many plays there must be, more flatfooted than Jonson's, where one character triumphantly rips the mask off another's face, leaving the rogue to his shamefaced confession or just truculent silence. More often, the unmasking is figurative. Then the spatial imagery is deceptive. The problem is not laying bare the underlying fact of the matter or stripping aside the superficial pretext. The problem is replacing an unhelpful description with an illuminating one. But how?

Earnest moralists have their clues about how to identify certain characters. The proud or great-souled man, Aristotle reveals, speaks with a deep voice and walks slowly.[25] Outdoing the master, the pseudo-Aristotelian *Physiognomonics* offers a detailed key to deciphering the body's meaning: well-defined ankles are a sign of a strong character, knock-knees of effeminacy, hairy legs of lasciviousness, but coarse hair of courage. The sly man

---

[24] *Annals*, bk. 13, xxv.
[25] *Nicomachean Ethics*, 1125a.

has a fat face, wrinkles around his eyes, and looks sleepy. Theophrastus announces that the ironic or dissembling man uses telltale phrases: he doesn't believe it, he doesn't think so, he's astonished.[26] And so it goes. Trust men (not people) who look you square in the eye and give you a firm handshake. Distrust men (not people) with slouching posture and beady little eyes. Those cartoonists knew what they were doing when they gave us Snidely Whiplash, with his top hat and his waxed mustachios, tying poor Nell Fenwick to the railroad tracks. Surely these injunctions, however time-honored, are laughable. How cunning is it to skulk around and squint out of your beady little eyes? You might as well brandish a sign saying

URGENT WARNING
CUNNING ROGUE APPROACHING
WATCH YOUR WALLET, YOUR CHASTITY, YOUR SOUL.

So something apparently has misfired when Dickens mentions "the earnest cunning of Fagin's looks": or is it that the criminal ringleader is in private with his hardened associates and helpless Oliver?[27] What about Trollope's abhorrent moneylender, Tom Tozer?

> Tom Tozer was a bull-necked, beetle-browed fellow, the expression of whose face was eloquent with acknowledged roguery. "I am a rogue," it seemed to say. "I know it; all the world knows it; but you're another. All the world don't know that, but I do. Men are all rogues, pretty nigh. Some are soft rogues, and some are 'cute rogues. I am a 'cute one; so mind your eye." It was with such words that Tom Tozer's face spoke out; and though a thorough liar in his heart, he was not a liar in his face.[28]

I can't help thinking that Trollope's usually deft way with moral psychology has failed him. These words read chillingly well in a novel, but what in the world do they refer to? Can you picture Tozer's face? or Fagin's face? What's the look of cunning or acute roguery when there's no need to wear a mask? Is it the look accompanying the sniggering nyaah-ha-ha of the grade-B movie villain?

Forget novels. An intrepid eighteenth-century physiognomist offers the

[26] *Characters*, 1.

[27] *Oliver Twist*, chap. 20.

[28] *Framley Parsonage*, chap. 32.

face of "a crafty, designing man, who will make a bad use of his skill and address, instead of employing them for the benefit of society." For real? "The forehead and the nose," we learn, "announce so much capacity, so much reason, such a spirit of reflection, that, to consider them separately, you could expect nothing but good from them." So where does the guy's face go wrong? "A man who knows the world would pronounce, on the first glance, that it is the face of a knave.—It is only upon the lips,—or rather between the lips, that the depravity lurks."[29] Apparently I should confess that I do not know the world. Ability plus depravity equals cunning: that I understand. That this forehead, nose, and pair of lips (or space between them!) reveal the telltale traits: that I find absurd.

Forget novels and art: what about history? The overheated history of Catholic-bashing boils over with polemics against the Jesuits, infamous for their equivocations and silent mental reservations, their skulking and lurking, their penetrating state affairs "in so subtle and so sly a manner, that as it is extremely hard to dive into, so 'tis almost impossible to explain it

[29] John Caspar Lavater, *Essays on Physiognomy, Designed to Promote the Knowledge and the Love of Mankind*, ed. Thomas Holloway, trans. Henry Hunter, 3 vols. (London, 1789–1810), 1:152. Reproduction courtesy of the Special Collections Library, University of Michigan.

well."[30] Anywhere, everywhere, up to no good, the Jesuits were "a pack of Arch-Machiavellian Gypsies," "the last *Crack-Fart* of a daring Devil."[31] So the anxious reader wants some help identifying them. Something surely has misfired when a Puritan divine, slamming these much maligned Jesuits in 1659, asks the obvious question but flubs the answer: "*How shall these Hiders be Detected?* . . . You have cause to *suspect* all that use a *Mask*, and purposely hide their minds."[32] But how can we tell the difference between face and mask? If we knew how to do that, masks would be less insidious, deception less nefarious.

The cunning will learn to mimic the virtuous. They'll do that whatever the local code suggests about how to identify the virtuous. That means you can't identify trustworthy or virtuous characters by reading off their characters from conspicuous cues. All due deference to Aristotle and the rest, but those taken with such visible signs will be taken. The real problem is flagged by a 1616 writer on witchcraft who warns his readers against "sly and masked Atheists, who overshadow their secret impiety, loose and dissolute behavior with some outward conformity and show of religion . . . and therefore pass uncensured, having a civil, but dissembled carriage."[33] As Defoe puts it in his ramshackle but charming *Political History of the Devil*, "The *Devil* is a true Posture-master, he assumes any Dress, appears in any Shape, counterfeits every Voice, acts upon every Stage." That makes the devil as rational as Odysseus—but not, thought Defoe, "a politician at all: Our old friend *Matchiavel* outdid him in many things," the devil all too prone to exposing himself.[34] When Plutarch wondered how to distinguish a flatterer from a friend, the strategic indeterminacies drove him to a baffling and inadvertently hilarious conclusion: beware the one who never seems to flatter you and denies that he's a flatterer.[35] Sure, the cunning rogue learns

---

[30] *The Jesuits Unmasked: or Politick Observations upon the Ambitious Pretentions and Subtle Intreagues of That Cunning Society* (London, 1679), p. 3.

[31] *Jesuits Unmasked*, p. 27; *Jesuita Vapulans: or A Whip for the Fool's Back, and a Gag for His Foul Mouth, in a Just Vindication of Sixteen Noble Peers of the Realm, Petitioning His Majesty* (London, 1681), p. 1.

[32] Richard Baxter, *A Key for Catholicks, to Open the Jugling of the Jesuits* (London, 1659), p. 342.

[33] Alexander Roberts, *A Treatise of Witchcraft* (London, 1616), Epistle Dedicatory, sig. A3 verso.

[34] [Daniel Defoe,] *The Political History of the Devil, as Well Ancient as Modern* (London, 1726), pp. 236, 2.

[35] "How to Tell a Flatterer from a Friend," in *Moralia*.

how to mimic your friend. But then how is your admiring friend supposed to persuade you that he's a real friend? Are your friends only those who gush flattery? Plutarch's advice is no better than that of Aristotle and Theophrastus, but no worse. We're stuck. I prefer the immortal moment in *Duck Soup* when Groucho, as Firefly, addresses the court. "Gentlemen," he intones, "Chicolini here may talk like an idiot, and look like an idiot, but don't let that fool you. He really is an idiot."

Let's be more concrete about who might want to deceive others. Take the fellow who wants to hustle money playing dice and who isn't too terribly fussy about honesty—less euphemistically, he's willing to cheat. That drearily familiar English verb stems from *escheat*, a legal term indicating property reverting to the lord of the estate when no one else could prove a rightful claim to it. The nobility, rightly dubbed by one historian fur-collar criminals,[36] proved rapacious in ambiguous cases, so *escheat* came to mean booty or plunder. In 1555, Gilbert Walker explained the "new found name" of "Cheaters" and its legal derivation in apprising gentlemen of the perils awaiting them. (Don't imagine a golden age of honesty prior to the sixteenth century. Loaded dice go back to antiquity.)[37] There you are, a traveling gentleman alighting in a London inn, hoping to while away the hours over a beer or three with some merry strangers. They propose a game of dice. You'd relish a fair game. But rousing with a hangover and an empty purse is not your idea of a good time, so you falter. Rummaging through your bag, you yank out Walker's pamphlet. "The first & original ground of Cheating," he warns, "is a counterfeit countenance in all things: a study to seem to be, & not to be in deed. And because no great deceit can be wrought but where special trust goeth before, therefore the cheater when he pitcheth his hay to purchase his profit enforceth all his wits to win credit & opinion of honesty, and uprightness."[38]

You look warily at the strangers. They lean forward inquisitively. Those solicitous looks must be genuine concern, right? You're about to accede to their proposal when suspicion freezes you in your tracks. "Oh," says one genially, softly, a little sadly, "I see. You fear we would cheat you." This tid-

---

[36] Barbara Hanawalt, "Fur-Collar Crime: The Pattern of Crime among the Fourteenth-Century English Nobility," *Journal of Social History* 8 (Summer 1975):1–17.

[37] Ricky Jay, *Dice: Deception, Fate & Rotten Luck* (New York: Quantuck Lane Press, 2003).

[38] [Gilbert Walker,] *A Manifest Detection of the Moste Vyle and Detestable Use of Diceplay*, 2nd ed. (London, 1555), n.p.

bit of conversational extortion makes you assure them that you're not worried about that, no, certainly not, they are trustworthy men and enjoy your implicit confidence. "Excellent!" cries another, "let's to it, then!" Now you have a choice. You can plead a throbbing headache or travel fatigue and beat a hasty retreat to your room. (How secure is that latch, anyway?) Or you can offer the same plea but agree to a few rounds for conviviality's sake. You impulsively opt for the latter—the game looks intriguing and you can use a tankard of that fragrant warm beer—so the play begins. For low stakes, you all easily agree. Too easily? you wonder, so you hesitate, but they don't notice, or maybe they do? but anyway the dice clatter, the game is underway, one of the others out already, and a speedy three minutes later you've won. The next round offers more of the same. The third round, too, and now they propose quadrupling the stakes. Ooh, there's another bit of social pressure: only a boor cuts the game short when he's ahead. You may want to win money when you gamble, but you shouldn't be too blatantly instrumental about it. After protracted legal investigations into allegations they had cheated, two seasoned gamblers insisted, "It is as good to lose as to win. There is only a shadow of difference between them, and that shadow is insignificant. Winning is better than losing, but neither one is the goal of gambling, which is *playing*. Losing never feels like the worst part of gambling. Quitting often does."[39]

You know how this narrative ends: with you groaning upstairs late next morning, clutching your head, rifling feverishly through your purse, and wondering how all that money skipped away; and with the innkeeper's daughter telling you that your three dear friends departed abruptly just before dawn and declared that you'd be happy to pay their bill. Yet they had behaved just as honest friends would have. Plutarch's bleakly paradoxical wisdom beckons: that's how you were supposed to know they weren't your honest friends, right? You've been betrayed by deceptive appearance. You sucker! And now which is worse, the loss of the money or the gut-wrenching sensation that you're a chump? A prudent man would have found some guarded if not entirely graceful way of spurning the game and, while he was at it, made sure his room was secure. You could have shoved the dresser in front of the door, couldn't you?

[39] Frederick and Steven Barthelme, *Double Down: Reflections on Gambling and Loss* (Boston: Houghton Mifflin, 1999), p. 121.

Can you ever afford to play dice with strangers in an inn? Win some, lose some, you might think. I don't mean that when you play, you can win or lose cash. The more fateful stakes are the fair and enjoyable social interactions on one side, the manipulative ones whose enjoyment is shattered the moment you realize you were cheated on the other. That remains the structure of the problem even if you refuse to make a wholesale commitment (always play or never play) but instead adopt a retail strategy (don't play when you're most confident that the strangers are cheating). After all, you'll make mistakes, so even if you're pretty good at detecting cheats you'll still sometimes get ripped off. Are you willing to suffer that in order to enjoy the fraternal pleasures of fair play? Should you be? If you are, can you write off the cheats not just financially but also emotionally? That is, instead of floundering in remorse, can you maintain your equanimity? You can always skip the dice, barricade your room, and stay secure. But it sounds desperately lonely.

It looks like the price of playing dice with strangers is being cheated now and again. Worse, it looks like there's nothing special about dice or gambling, inns or traveling: whenever you deal with strangers, you risk being cheated. But can you get through a day without trusting strangers? You walk into the coffee shop to pick up a mocha. The employee takes your $20 bill, sticks it in the register, thanks you cheerfully—no, saucily, as you'll realize in a moment—and turns to the next customer. "Wait!" you protest, "what about my change?" She smiles sweetly. "I'm sorry, but you paid exact change." "No," you insist, "I gave you a twenty." But the customer behind you is visibly irritated. Audibly irritated, too: his smirk is accompanied by a "sheesh!" He thinks you're a crank and he's in a hurry. The other employees are scurrying around and wouldn't have seen anything anyway. So now what? Well, you could summon the manager. Or the police. It would be your word against hers. Maybe the manager would give you the money to safeguard the shop's reputation. Maybe not. You could insist they cash out the register, that is, compare the money in the till to what the day's receipts say should be there. But if she's any good she lifted the extra money from the register before you ever walked in. Then everything will balance perfectly and your story about her audacity will seem ludicrous—or like an attempt to bilk the shop! Ponder the mortifying phone call from the manager. Or, worse, the laconic report from the cop. Can you face the mortifying prospect of going back for more coffee?

What if she's there again? What will you do if she pockets another twenty?

None of this ever happens. And you never think about it. (If you do think about it, you're paranoid. Or doing theory.) Is your failure to contemplate the possibility a lamentable oversight? Those crisp heads of lettuce at the grocery might be poisoned, you know. You don't know who put them on the shelf. You don't know who trucked them in, who put them in the shipping crate, who picked them in the fields of California. If any of them wanted to kill a stranger and get away with it, a dab of poison would be just the thing. You can rinse the lettuce off when you get home, right? But that water coming out of the faucet, wow! wait a minute, where's it been? and who's had a chance to tamper with it? And so on, and on, and on. Wondering at every juncture whether it's rational to trust the strangers you're relying on isn't prudent, isn't a recipe for self-preservation. It would drive you batty. So you casually rely on ordinary appearances. The cashier looks friendly, or anyway, not pathologically dishonest. The pimply teenager shelving the lettuce looks fine, too.

But this looks hopeless. If the cashier intends to supplement her salary with your twenty, she's going to do her best to look friendly, or anyway, not pathologically dishonest. (Grab Plutarch in a time machine and zip him into the shop with you. If the employee looks friendly, he whispers, don't trust her.) Again, the cunning are going to be adept in the arts of appearance. There are social actors who are amusingly or ominously incompetent in the arts of self-presentation.[40] In small but significant ways, they get the scripts wrong. They walk too fast or too slowly. They check their watches too often or gaze at them two seconds too long. They aggressively pick their noses in public without any propitiatory gestures. But there is no significant mapping between those social incompetents and cunning rogues up to no good. We can enjoy lampooning the would-be crooks expert only in bumbling. Take the bank robber who scribbled his holdup note on the back of his résumé and left it at the bank. What a dolt! but he did tape strips of black construction paper over his personal information.[41] Never

---

[40] "Normal Appearances," in Erving Goffman, *Relations in Public: Microstudies of the Public Order* (New York: Basic Books, 1971), remains priceless; see too Goffman, *The Presentation of Self in Everyday Life* (Garden City, NY: Doubleday, 1959).

[41] "Robber's Holdup Note on Back of His Résumé," *Houston Chronicle* (24 July 2003), A20.

has the refrain of reuse and recycle been more rebarbative. But for every such crook, there's a klutz of a Keystone Kop. Some good guys look good, some good guys look bad; some bad guys look good, some bad guys look bad. Enjoy scrutinizing their appearances. Are you expert in detecting deception? Are you even competent? Experimental psychologists, mostly skeptical about our skills, do turn up evidence that cops, judges, and parole officers might get pretty good at detecting lies.[42] And Iraqis play a curious game called *mahabis*.[43] Two teams of up to 250 players apiece square off. One team hides one ring in one player's fist. The other team's leader can dismiss as many opponents as he likes, but he has only one guess to identify who's clutching the ring. Here's the startling thing: *mahabis* is a game of skill. So it's possible to learn to read faces. But it's difficult, and anyway you don't even lay eyes on many of the strangers you're trusting. They aren't even Odyssean nobodies. They're invisible. Want to inspect or interview the migrant laborer who picked the precise head of lettuce you decide to purchase? Good luck.

Then too—a nasty thought which can worm its way into the happiest among us on our sunniest days, but it's got to be faced—can you be wholly secure about your friends and loved ones? Strangers can cheat you, but only intimates can betray you. Leaf through your Bible in search of consolation and you might light upon these verses: "Trust ye not in a friend, put ye not confidence in a guide: keep the doors of thy mouth from her that lieth in thy bosom. For the son dishonoreth the father, the daughter riseth up against her mother, the daughter in law against her mother in law; a man's enemies are the men of his own house." Or these: "Take ye heed every one of his neighbor, and trust ye not in any brother: for every brother will utterly supplant, and every neighbor will walk with slanders. And they

---

[42] Compare Stephen Porter, Mike Woodworth, and Angela R. Birt, "Truth, Lies, and Videotape: An Investigation of the Ability of Federal Parole Officers to Detect Deception," *Law & Human Behavior* 24:6 (December 2000):643–58, and Paul Ekman, Maureen O'Sullivan, and Mark G. Frank, "A Few Can Catch a Liar," *Psychological Science* 10:3 (May 1999):263–66, with Aldert Vrij, "Credibility Judgments of Detectives: The Impact of Nonverbal Behavior, Social Skills, and Physical Characteristics on Impression Formation," *Journal of Social Psychology* 133:5 (October 1993):601–10. For an overview of the experimental literature, see Paul Ekman, *Telling Lies: Clues to Deceit in the Marketplace, Politics, and Marriage* (New York: W. W. Norton & Company, 1985).

[43] "The Ancient Art of Deception," *The Economist* (29 November 2003), p. 43.

will deceive every one his neighbor, and will not speak the truth: they have taught their tongue to speak lies, and weary themselves to commit iniquity."[44] The sentiment is as realistic as it is jaundiced. Like it or not, sometimes the world is like that. Can you tell when? How?

Years of sustained contact may not strip away masks. It looks like newscaster Charles Kuralt's wife didn't know about the mistress he kept for thirty years until an explosive contest over his will.[45] (But that appearance too might not be trustworthy.) Would you have suspected that cherubic teddy bear? Or again: it is dispiriting to contemplate how many happily married Americans, as they'd thought of themselves anyway, awoke one day to have their spouses come out as gay or lesbian ("no, not bisexual, not at all, and no, this isn't a recent development, I've always been that way, I've been wearing a mask imposed by homophobia"); just as it is dispiriting to contemplate how many gays and lesbians have felt compelled to wear that mask; just as it is dispiriting to contemplate how many such marriages silently, sadly endure without any coming out.

I've been probing ways in which the distinction between appearance and reality teeters. Sometimes it looks like it will collapse, jumbling appearance and reality together. Some try to (and some have to) live up to, or down to, their reputations. Sartre's crack about his grandfather is instructive: "He was a man of the nineteenth century who took himself for Victor Hugo, as did so many others, including Victor Hugo himself."[46] In on his own grandiose joke or not, Hugo sure was busy being Victor Hugo. He managed to live and write ostentatiously enough to deserve a fabulous funeral attended by some two million—and, his own choice, a pauper's hearse, yet another gesture of cloying, melodramatic virtue.[47] But the convergence of appearance and reality can be social and political, not just individual and psychological. Sometimes society is a house of mirrors, everyone reflecting what he thinks others expect him to do or want him to do or think he should do—and everyone could be wrong about that. In this way, lynchings could linger on long past the time anyone was racist enough to

---

[44] Micah 7:5–6; Jeremiah 9:4–5. I've quoted throughout from the King James Bible and eliminated occasional italics.

[45] Paige Williams, "Charles Kuralt's Other Life," *Charlotte Observer* (28 May 1998), E1.

[46] Jean-Paul Sartre, *The Words*, trans. Bernard Frechtman (New York: George Braziller, 1964), p. 24.

[47] Graham Robb, *Victor Hugo* (London: Picador, 1997), chap. 24.

want them. (That explains why such practices can grind to a halt so suddenly.) Take Václav Havel's diagnosis of the lies of everyday life. The grocer displays a sign saying, "Workers of the world, unite!" Havel comments that "the greengrocer declares his loyalty (and he can do no other if his declaration is to be accepted) in the only way the regime is capable of hearing; that is, by accepting the prescribed ritual, by accepting appearances as reality, by accepting the given rules of the game. In doing so, however, he has himself become a player in the game, thus making it possible for the game to go on, for it to exist in the first place." Everyday private cynicism coexists with public enthusiasm for the sublime joys of communist rule. The grocer doesn't want to be punished. Then too, individuals don't know whom it's safe to confide in. Spies are everywhere, betrayal all too frequent. One might think that the more people mutter these obligatory Marxist catechisms, the more they will believe them, the more they will act on them, and the more the catechisms will become true. Havel, though, insists that the grocer and his ilk are "living a lie" and could and should instead be "living the truth." He goes metaphysical in a way I'm afraid I can't make sense of. We need "authentic existence," "a new experience of being, a renewed rootedness in the universe," "a profound respect . . . for the order of Being."[48] These opaque categories helped provide the solace Havel and other dissidents needed, so they were politically useful, even indispensable. That doesn't make them intelligible. So how else might we describe the difference between the grocer's life and that of a Charter 77 member? How ghastly is it to wonder whether the member, too, lives in a house of mirrors where he answers to the imagined demands of others? whether the crucial difference is not replacing lies with truth, alienation with authenticity, but rather a thuggish community with a humane one?[49]

Sometimes the distinction between appearance and reality really does collapse. Really. "Reputation of power, is Power," notices Hobbes.[50] If others believe you're powerful, they'll do what you say so you won't exercise your power and punish them. But that makes the belief in your power self-

---

[48] "The Power of the Powerless," in Havel, *Open Letters: Selected Prose 1965–1990*, ed. Paul Wilson (London: Faber and Faber, 1991). That last phrase is from "Thinking about František K.," in *Open Letters*, p. 365.

[49] Compare "Solidarity or Objectivity?" in Richard Rorty, *Objectivity, Relativism, and Truth* (Cambridge: Cambridge University Press, 1991).

[50] *Leviathan*, chap. 10.

fulfilling. On this reading, Hobbes's pithy claim isn't exactly true. In the nearby counterfactual world in which they decide anyway not to obey you, you still can't do anything about it. Still, close enough for government work. Hobbes suggests a different explanation: "because it draweth with it the adherence of those that need protection." This reason draws appearance and reality even more closely together. Fearful subjects look for a leader who can protect them. Now if someone disobeys him, he can do something about it. Once they band together to support him, he can command them; able to dispose of a horde, he's powerful. That remains true even if the subjects' initial judgment is mistaken and the alleged leader they seize on is a nobody. (Not the Odyssean kind.)

Here a false belief causes actions that render it true. Collections of false beliefs, or false beliefs mixed with true ones, can trigger the same dynamic. If you wrongly believe your well water is polluted and wrongly believe DDT in large doses an anti-pollutant, you will conscientiously pollute your well water, making your first false belief true. Wars can have the same structure. If Ruritania wrongly believes that neighboring Grand Fenwick is going to invade and rightly believes bigger armies are good for defense, Ruritania will start to build up its army. That looks hostile even if it isn't, so Grand Fenwick, till then the incarnation of benevolent peace, will launch a preemptive strike.[51] Appearance becomes reality. False beliefs make themselves true.

Call it the Arabella effect, after the heroine of Charlotte Lennox's incandescent 1752 novel, *The Female Quixote*. (The counter-Arabella effect, in which true beliefs cause actions that make the beliefs false, is worth noting. Once word gets out about that pristine beach, it promptly becomes littered and congested.) Beautiful and bright, consigned to her father's secluded country home, Arabella has gobbled up too many romances and believes that society faithfully adheres to the intricate rules of chivalry. Her principal suitor realizes her language is eccentric. At first, though, he doesn't realize what he's up against, so he's forever blundering. For instance, he doesn't wait silently for years before tremblingly declaring his love at his lady's feet. So she imperiously commands him never to see her again—and he thinks she's joking. Readmitted at her father's command,

---

[51] Compare Robert Jervis, *Perception and Misperception in International Politics* (Princeton, NJ: Princeton University Press, 1976).

he begins to catch on. To humor her, he starts acting the properly courtly part, even while he "silently curse[s] his ill Fate, to make him in Love with a Woman so ridiculous."[52] So do others dealing with her. She is a beautiful woman set to inherit a fortune, and there's no point upsetting her. As the locals play-act their archaic parts, as they strike chivalric poses and speak inflated language, the environs of the country home become a miniature social landscape straight out of her romances. Not completely: when she's not around they lapse, the law wouldn't enforce any feudal claims, and so on. But partly: as far as everyday social interactions in Arabella's presence go, her once deluded beliefs become true. What is appearance, what reality? What could it possibly mean to strip away the locals' confused beliefs and reveal the underlying truth?

Let's return to the dice cheaters but this time set out in a different direction. The cheaters, up to no good, need to disguise themselves. Now consider the converse problem. Some people, utterly fair and decent, find themselves thrust into social roles where others will suspect everything they do or say. For centuries, Jews were forbidden to hold real estate and Christians were forbidden to charge interest. No surprise that many Jews ended up as financiers and merchants; no surprise that any number of writers indicted Jews as conniving rascals and griped that Christians entering business were themselves turning into Jews.[53] Henry James charted "the extent of the Hebrew conquest of New York," the city's transformation into a garish New Jerusalem devoted to business, studded with tenements, white marble, and "the blaze of the shops addressed to the New Jerusalem wants and the splendour with which these were taken for granted. . . ." The kicker is James's arch confusion over the spectacle's significance: "the only thing indeed a little too ambiguous was just this look of the trap too brilliantly, too candidly baited for the wary side of Israel itself. It is not *for* Israel, in general, that Israel so artfully shines—yet its being moved to do so, at last, in that luxurious style, might be precisely the grand side of the city of redemption. Who can ever tell, moreover, in any conditions and in presence of any apparent anomaly, what the genius of Israel may, or may not, really be 'up to'?"[54] Jewish merchants apparently

---

[52] *The Female Quixote*, bk. 2, chap. 11.

[53] For the discussion in England after the French Revolution, see my *Poisoning the Minds of the Lower Orders* (Princeton, NJ: Princeton University Press, 1998), pt. 2.

[54] *The American Scene*, III.iii.

making no bones about their desire to close sales with Jewish customers: the cultivated mind reels in nauseated disbelief—or it would without the consolations of its own sumptuous syntax.

We may wriggle in discomfort at what might seem the unabashed anti-Semitism of it all. But when today's pieties don't forbid it, we stew in much the same anxieties. The used car salesman knows which cars on the lot are okay, which lemons. But why should he tell you? Suppose now that some decent soul takes a job as a used car salesman. How can he communicate honestly with you? "I wouldn't buy that Dodge," he tells you, conspiratorially it seems, after he looks around to make sure his manager isn't in earshot. "The drive shaft is going to need work quite soon. You're looking at thousands of dollars. This Ford is in much better shape." What should you make of this? If the Ford costs more, you'll think he's trying to push you into spending more money so he can make more commission. Are you indelicate enough to say so? He looks slightly pained and patiently explains that the Ford should cost more because it's a better car, adding that it's much better, more than you'd expect from the price differential. "I'm not in the market for a car right now," he adds, "but if I were, I'd grab this one for my own family." Checkmate or stalemate? If the Ford costs less, will you trust him? Maybe he's trying to save the Dodge for his buddy and it's much better than the Ford. Maybe he's trying to persuade you that he's trustworthy—just what any rascal in his role would do! You'll be on guard regardless. There might be idiosyncratic ways in which particular used car salesmen can persuade particular customers that they're honest. But there can't be anything general or structured about eliciting trust here. If there were such reliable tactics, the cunning would seize on them and deploy them relentlessly until word got out to consumers. Then the tactics wouldn't work any more.

True story—honest, trust me: I go to buy a new car. The salesmen aren't as stereotypically dishonest as used car salesmen, but we don't enshrine them as icons of probity, either. Bargaining makes me uneasy. Not—and this must be true of most of us who aren't living on the economic edge—because of what economists call opportunity cost: that is, I don't walk out thinking, oh, if only I'd paid $500 less, I would have had enough money to buy. . . . Rather it's the prospect of being taken, of having the salesman double over laughing, or worse, just smirk, after I leave. Just knowing that he might prompts a queasy feeling in my gut. A couple of other explanatory devices from economics don't work here, either. That isn't any kind of reputational effect. I don't fret that the salesman will tell someone else that I've been had. Nor is it the opening move of a repeat game. I don't worry that he will write down my name and will flash a shark-toothed grin or restrained smile, ready to pounce, when I reappear some years later. I just don't want to be a wimp who can't hold his own in this setting. (Wimp? Yup, this is all about gender, and no, the gendered strands of it don't disappear, they merely change, when women buy cars or when the salesman is a woman.) Okay, so actually I am a wimp. But I don't want to seem like a wimp. I could try on a pose of aristocratic largesse, thinking it beneath me to fret about $500 here, $2,000 there, and in my turn showering down contempt at the small-minded salesman occupied with such trivia. Could I make the pose stick? It would take more than sheer force of will. Salesmen too are exhilarated and anxious in ways that have nothing to do with their paychecks. Take this thought from a 1921 newsletter sent out to American salesmen: "The contest is what makes it interesting to us all and the glory of being victorious often means as much as the sordid remuneration represented by our stipends."[55]

Now again the salesman is saddled with the wearying knowledge that anyone coming in suspects him of being a ripoff artist. How is he to deal with it? Mine jovially beams, firmly shakes my hand, looks me right in the eye, and says, I kid thee not, "I pride myself on being a straight shooter." Right, I think dourly, sure, you bet. Courtesy of the AAA, I am clutching an invoice with the dealer's cost of my model. Glancing at it, he immediately says in his frank manly way, "Oh, those are entirely unreliable." I declare my intention nonetheless to rely on it, to bargain up from their cost, or anyway what my invoice claims is their cost, instead of down from a meaningless sticker price. I announce what I am willing to pay for the car. He wants to bargain. I decline. Laughing—well, forcing a chuckle; it is hard to laugh when your hands are a trifle clammy: oh, is that why he shook my hand? to find out?—I say, "I'm not going to bargain with you. You have tons of experience. I have none. This is what I'm willing to pay. If you like it, I'll pay right now. If not, I'll go buy a Taurus." Does he find my threat credible? I assure him the Taurus is $3,000 cheaper than what I'm offering for the Camry wagon. Does he know that I'm an academic

[55] "Kissing 'Em out the Door," *Salesmen's Letters* (Chicago: Stevens-Davis Co., 1921), no. 3.

and that the local social code for folks like me, while not flatly prohibiting a Taurus, would vigorously approve the Camry? No, I've not told him what I do for a living, not least because I don't want him to look up my salary, which is published. But people in his situation are discerning readers of the relevant cues. After wondering aloud if he should call the Ford dealer to complain about their predatory pricing policies—an icily polite way of reminding me that he can check my assurance—he sighs. "I'd really love to sell you this car. Between you and me, I haven't sold any cars for two weeks and my monthly paycheck is going to be a disaster. But I can't possibly sell it at that price. I'm sorry." Between him and me? I'll bet his manager knows. Is he paid by the month? Is he sorry? Do I care?

I thank him for his time, shrug nonchalantly (or was it flippantly?), and stride out of the dealership. One step, two steps, three steps, four—and I manage to profess surprise at his reappearance. He cordially invites me back inside. I join him. He begins bargaining. The monotony of his recidivism is tiresome. "I'm sorry," I say firmly. "I guess I wasn't clear enough. I won't bargain with you. Goodbye." Out I march again. One step, two steps, three—and this time I get to meet the dealer. He is clad in plaid and mirrored wrap-around sunglasses, despite the usual grey Michigan day, and is, to be only mildly hyperbolic, half my height and twice my weight. He gives me a bear hug. (Does the manual say, "If the customer is leaving before you close the sale, crush his spine"?) "You know what?" he booms out. "I like you." Funny coincidence: he is my new best friend. I manage to resist the temptation to give him a smooch, perhaps because I am beginning to suffer acute battle fatigue. We traipse back inside. "I'm Monty Hall!" he exclaims. "Let's make a deal!" No, I demur, I don't want to make a deal, I just want to buy the car, here's the money I'm offering. . . .

I bought the car at my price, not theirs. I don't mean to vaunt in my victory; somehow it never felt like a triumph. Along the way, I practiced some deception of my own. Confidentially, I never would have bought the Taurus. (But there was a real Taurus and it really did cost $3,000 less. I even test-drove it. Was I using the Ford salesman as a prop in my little game of combat with Toyota? I did tell him I was leaning toward the Camry: does that absolve me?) I had the minimal good sense to avoid other shopworn tactics, like having my wife show up to denounce the Camry as overpriced and wring her hands about our parlous domestic finances. Had the sales-

man unmasked me, would he have held out for a higher price? Or did he
see right through my amateur's pose and decide further negotiations weren't
worth his time? After all, there were other people in the showroom wait-
ing to be helped. (Or hindered.) Was my deception justified? I wouldn't be
the cully of my integrity. I suppose—the supposition seems profoundly
charitable—that scads of other customers play by the same rules I did.
Why then do these experiences leave so many of us feeling ritually un-
clean, as if we need a ten-mile run and a long shower? When car salesmen
slather us with their unctuous dishonesties, can they justify themselves by
fuming that their customers are inveterate liars? In this sleazy pas de deux,
who goes first? Is there a culprit? Maybe we shouldn't think of the car
salesmen as villainous liars. The right question might be not, who's responsible? but, what's responsible? It might be those weird sticker prices cou-
pled with the uncertainties of bargaining, something our culture offers
perilously scarce training in. Yes, there is in turn a who behind that what:
whoever is responsible for deciding car dealerships should sell cars that
way. But then why don't we excuse the salesmen and blame whichever
fiendish managers are backing them into this sordid corner? Can the managers complain that they're caught in a prisoners' dilemma, that no firm
can afford to change its practices while the other firms are still having
dealers use sticker prices? But Saturns are sold for the sticker price, no bargaining permitted. Do Saturn dealerships attract salesmen of unyielding
integrity, or laggards who can't cut it hustling in traditional dealerships? If
you buy a Saturn, should you be relieved to avoid the sordid bargaining?
Or should you fear that you're being ripped off and haven't got even a
chance to secure a halfway decent deal?

Even salesmen not selling cars are haunted by more than faint disre-
pute. How are they to deal with it? Consider more advice from a salesman's newsletter:

> Every salesman knows the necessity of neatness, cleanliness,
> simplicity and good taste in dress.
> Personal appearance is only the minting which indicates the
> character of the coin—but there are thousands of counterfeits in
> circulation and a man's "full value" is measured by what he carries
> within his breast and brain rather than by the style of his clothes.

This full value is what enables you to give those you meet that warm sense of *friendliness* and *sincerity*. "Your attitude" toward others—your look of heartiness, interest and good will is what determines the first attitude of others toward you. It is displayed in your manner, your expression and the light that shines in your eyes.

It is that attitude which makes men glad to see you and always willing to give you an attentive ear.

The buyer's first impression of a salesman—whatever that impression may be—is invariably the reflection in the mirror of the buyer's mind of the salesman's own attitude toward him.[56]

How curious! Shower and dress well, but any cunning rogue can learn to do that, too. So, the letter solemnly continues, you need a good character. But what's the alchemy by which the sterling contents of your breast and brain make themselves manifest in the world? The anonymous adviser can't describe that alchemy without lapsing into the language of appearance. No accident that *attitude* can mean physical posture, nor that *posture* can mean pose. Nothing is easier to adopt. A little attention and practice will emancipate you from that limp handshake and lackadaisical greeting: clench hard, jut that jaw, make direct eye contact; got it? Even if *attitude* is a sentiment, a psychological posture, is it much harder to adopt than a shower, a shave, or a nice trim suit? Aren't those counterfeit salesmen worrisome because they too know how to strike the "look" of heartiness? Doesn't that then become the very look that makes cautious customers shrink away instinctively? One princessa of the cosmetics realm bubbles over about the psychology of masks. "The funny thing about putting on a happy face is that if you do it again and again, pretty soon that happy face is there to stay. It becomes *the real you.*"[57] But it's stretching it to think that once a salesman learns to fake sincerity, he becomes sincere. Even if he does have it made.

Others counseling salesmen have embraced manipulation. "Almost everyone is susceptible to flattery," reports one writer, "if it has a ring of sincerity about it." A ring of sincerity, not sincerity, and it's easy to attain: "We all have a basic wish for recognition by society; to be considered im-

---

[56] "First Impressions and Final Results," *Salesmen's Letters* (Chicago: Stevens-Davis Co., 1920), no. 15.

[57] Mary Kay Ash, *Mary Kay* (New York: Harper & Row, 1981), p. 51.

portant. And because we wish to believe the nice things that people say about us, we are pleased and have kindly feelings toward the salesman whose approach seems to place us on a higher plane." (You don't have to be a salesman to exploit others' insatiable vanity. One of Dale Carnegie's leading principles was, "Remember that a person's name is to that person the sweetest and most important sound in any language.")[58] One shoe salesman broke into a new market by telling one farmer after another that his firm wished leading members of the community to sport their wares and would let him have a pair at cost if he bought another at the regular price.[59] What a deal, eh? Some salesmen themselves have embraced not just manipulation but shapeshifting. Take the wholesaler of groceries who ridiculed the thought that he was caught in a rut. "One minute I'm a merchandiser, teaching a new store owner how to build sales through display. The next I'm a management engineer, helping an owner build a better trade through higher-class merchandise." He builds customer goodwill, handles complaints, and more. "I'm as many different salesmen as I have prospects and customers. How could that be a grind?"[60] No mechanical drudgery, no one-size-fits-all strategies for this Proteus. He is uncannily adept at sizing up his customers, rapidly figuring out what pose to strike, what attitude to adopt, with each one; uncannily plastic, too, in molding himself to the demands of the moment. No Odysseus, no prince, no politician could do better. He can read his customers better than they can read him: he has more practice. But don't doubt that the occasional cagey customer, Skunk to his Coyote, outwits him.

So if salesmen are cunning or if we think they're cunning, it's not because they have bad characters. (Since labor markets are tight, it seems churlish to wonder what kind of people become salesmen in the first place.) You don't need to know anything at all about the individual salesman you're dealing with to distrust him. The logic of the social setting—his superior knowledge of the quality of merchandise, the pricing structure, and so on—creates your dilemma. And his. So salesmen have cunning thrust upon them. Even if they do their best to behave decently, we will second-

[58] Dale Carnegie, *How to Win Friends & Influence People*, rev. ed. (New York: Pocket Books, 1982), p. 112.

[59] David Seltz, *215 Successful Door Openers for Salesmen* (Englewood Cliffs, NJ: Prentice-Hall, 1956), pp. 65–67.

[60] A. L. Harris, "The Same Old Grind," *Men Who Sell* (Chicago: n.p., 1950?), no. 24, p. 8.

guess their every move, wonder whether their occasional generosity is set-ting us up for a catastrophic fall, implicitly encourage them to distrust us and to become the cunning rogues we imagine they already are. They may decide anyway that it's in their interests to be shabby and deceptive.

Salesmen aren't alone in this predicament. Those who have won our distrust may find it impossible to climb back into our good graces. Once Richard Nixon earned the sobriquet Tricky Dick, what could he have done to show that he wasn't sneaky? So he was dead wrong in announcing we wouldn't have him to kick around any more. Even if he hadn't reentered politics, kicks would always have been there for the taking, Nixon a peren-nial target for malicious nostalgia and wry chuckles over his conniving ways. If you're powerful, you may not even need to earn a reputation for trickiness. Others know that, dirty hands aside, you have favors to dispense or refuse, your own agendas to pursue too; that they might be pawns in games they don't fully understand, let alone control. Stendhal's Marchesa Balbi, young and attractive, profits from the constant attendance of the prince. The narrator confides in us that her smile, constant, malicious, cun-ning, is also meaningless. But it makes her look like she's up to something. So she manages to pocket a bribe every time even a paltry public contract is negotiated.[61] Placed by her side, a servant, even another aristocrat, could smile the same way. She could even accompany the smile not with the Marchesa's blank serenity but with furious internal plotting and intrigue. Nothing would happen.

So cunning can reside in social settings just as well as in devious minds. I don't mean to overplay the point. Some people do have bad char-acters. Beady-eyed or not, they survey their surroundings searching for corners to cut, chumps to cheat. They don't have cunning thrust upon them, they achieve it. (Or, for those smitten by sociobiological fantasies, they're born to it.) Surely, you'd think, that must have been the case for the snake-oil salesmen hawking patent medicine in America a century ago. Savor the cadences of this 1886 entry cum advertisement in a popu-lar medical textbook:

> *Dr. Pierce's Pleasant Purgative Pellets.* These pellets combine the pure, concentrated, active principles of several vegetable alteratives,

---

[61] *The Charterhouse of Parma*, chap. 6.

and the result is, that within the small compass of a few grains he has most happily blended and chemically condensed these properties, so that their action upon the animal economy is sanative and universal. They awaken the latent powers, quicken the tardy functions, check morbid deposits, dissolve hard concretions, remove obstructions, promote depuration, harmonize and restore the functions, equalize the circulation, and encourage the action of the nervous system. They stimulate the glands, increase the peristaltic movement of the intestines, tone the nutritive processes, while aiding in evacuating the bowels. All this they accomplish without corroding the tissues or vitiating the fluids. Their assistance is genial, helping the system to expel worn out materials, which would become noxious if retained. Having expended their remedial powers upon the various functions of the body, they are themselves expelled along with other waste matter, leaving behind them no traces of irritation. This cannot be said of mercurials, or of other harsh, mineral alteratives. These Pellets may be safely employed when the system is feeble, frail, and delicate, by giving them in less quantities.[62]

Dr. Pierce hypes his pellets as if they're more than a mere laxative. Could he conceivably have believed that his medicine was both wholly benign and wondrously effective? That's got to be a lot of tripe, right? (But couldn't it be homeopathy?) What about Hamlin, a former magician who promoted his Wizard Oil with music?[63] Or Dr. Johnson, whose 1911 ads promised his "Mild Combination Treatment" would cure cancer at home? No shrinking violet he:

I will gladly furnish to every sufferer positive and indisputable proofs that my treatment Does Cure Cancer. I will furnish ample evidence of my integrity, honesty, financial and professional ability. No matter how serious your case may be—no matter how many

---

[62] R. V. Pierce, *The People's Common Sense Medical Adviser in Plain English: or Medicine Simplified* (Buffalo, 1886), pp. 308–9.

[63] James Harvey Young, *The Toadstool Millionaires: A Social History of Patent Medicines in America before Federal Regulation* (Princeton, NJ: Princeton University Press, 1961), plate 15 (between pp. 122–23) and pp. 193–94.

operations you have had—no matter what treatments you have tried, do not give up hope, but write for my book, "Cancer and the Cure." It will cost you nothing.[64]

Aren't these texts precisely what they seem to be? Don't they trumpet their authors' mocking duplicity? (I bet you've already figured out what Dr. Johnson's boasted financial ability was: an unflinching knack for extracting gobs of money from the pitiful dying.) Don't they compel us to imagine that their consumers are so stupid that they're irrational stooges? (Or so desperate that they prudently calculate it worth squandering money on the scant probability that these ludicrous frauds can actually help? Or so hypersophisticated in the arts of self-deception that they swallow the snake oil thinking, "I take it for the placebo effect"?)

No.

THE RATIONALITY OF BELIEF; OR, THE CUNNING OF REASON

"Every man can educate himself. It's shameful to put one's mind into the hands of those whom you wouldn't entrust with your money. Dare to think for yourself."[65] So Voltaire's Boldmind, his protagonist in a dialogue on freedom of thought. This enlightenment rhetoric is familiar but somehow not hackneyed. Many still find it stirring. I recall one of my junior high school English teachers getting enthusiastic about it, heatedly celebrating stone-cold sobriety. So you don't need a dog-eared copy of Voltaire in your hip pocket, you don't need any grasp of the ferocious attack on priestcraft and statecraft, the attempt to rouse deferential subjects from their dogmatic slumbers, to know the mantra. Don't take things on faith; don't be credulous; trust your senses, not what others tell you. But you might pause before following this advice. It seems like patent rubbish.

You are ineluctably dependent on others for your knowledge. You know that the Soviet Union's evil empire started crumbling in 1989, after Mikhail

---

[64] James Harvey Young, *The Medical Messiahs: A Social History of Health Quackery in Twentieth-Century America* (Princeton, NJ: Princeton University Press, 1967), between pp. 240–41. For many more reproductions of such advertisements, see James Harvey Young, *American Health Quackery: Collected Essays* (Princeton, NJ: Princeton University Press, 1992).

[65] Voltaire, *Philosophical Dictionary*, s.v. "Liberté de pensée," ed. and trans. Theodore Besterman (London: Penguin, 1972), pp. 280–81.

Gorbachev signaled that there would be no dreary repeats of Hungary in 1956, Czechoslovakia in 1968, that the newly docile Red Army would be staying home. You know that because other people—Peter Jennings, the writers of the *New York Times* or the *Wall Street Journal*, your sister who's constantly tuned into National Public Radio, or whoever you got your news from in those days—told you it was true. You believed them. You trusted them. You had no reason to doubt them. Were you relying only on the evidence of your own senses? Maybe you glimpsed pictures of some graffiti-daubed concrete barricades getting knocked over with jubilant people carousing. And you heard the announcer's honeyed reminders that that was the Berlin Wall and that Reagan had challenged Gorbachev to tear down the wretched thing. You believed the announcer, too. You believed the follow-up stories about Yeltsin in that tank, Chechen terrorists and suicide bombers, all sorts of dizzying anecdotes about the roller-coaster ride the former subjects of the USSR have been on since the stodgy days of Brezhnev. You were right to believe them, too.

Could you have checked? Suppose you wanted to see for yourself. You could have boarded an airplane and flown to a place other people would have told you was Moscow or Berlin. You could have interviewed the locals. They'd have vigorously agreed: yes, absolutely, Gorbachev, huge changes, oh, there's still a Communist Party, maybe even they vote for it, but absolutely, the USSR is no more. You'd have believed them, too, and you'd have been right to do so. But still you'd have been trusting others. Even if you were an eyewitness, right there when the wall started tumbling, you'd still be massively dependent on what others told you. Just how could you check the claim, "This is Berlin"? How could you check, "That's the wall that separates East and West Berlin"? It's tempting to press the point to extremes. How do you know what your own name is? If a name is what other people usually call you to your face, you don't have to trust others to get that right. But if a name is what's on your birth certificate, you're stuck: how do you know it's your birth certificate? And if a name is how others refer to you when you're not around, you're stuck again.

The point here is not that none of your knowledge is strictly speaking certain, though that's true too. You could always be mistaken in trusting others. Plenty of news reports turn out to be false. Insiders are forever appalled by how journalists botch the story. I suppose that plenty of news reports that pass for true are actually false, that newspapers and history books alike are stuffed, maybe all too liberally, with mistakes if not outright lies. But you can be wrong in relying on your own senses, too. Lurking here is a version of the appearance/reality problem that has tortured hapless generations of philosophy students. "See that table? How do you know it's really a table? Maybe it's a 3-D holographic projection of a table." "What do you mean, the table is brown? Colors are secondary qualities, just tricks of our brains. Colors aren't in the world, only light wavelengths are, and our brain happens to interpret a particular range of wavelengths this way. Other animals respond to a different color spectrum. And you know those things we both call red? Maybe I see them the way everyone else sees red, but your subjective experiences, your private *qualia*, are yellow. You've just got your yellow and red perceptual wires crossed. How would you know?" These lines of questioning attempt to enlist the audience's sympathies with skepticism. The skeptic trades on familiar experiences: the shimmering water on the road that disappears as you drive closer, the oar that's bent where it goes into the water, the headphones that play monaural music from the middle of your skull. Then he generalizes like mad, wondering if all our experiences are misleading, and how—or whether—we know they're not.

In this realm, generalizing like mad is, well, mad. I have no guarantee that our ordinary claims of knowledge are true. The trick to shelving skepticism doesn't lie in trying to show that everyday knowledge claims are unimpeachable. It lies instead in denying that knowledge entails certainty. It's enough if your beliefs track reality, so that you wouldn't believe something if it weren't true and you would go on believing it if it remained true in nearby possible worlds.[66]

So first-hand sensory evidence and others' reports are both fallible. But we still need to sort out when others' reports are trustworthy. Others can offer competing, even contradictory, accounts on topics that we care about, even matters of life and death. Your partner nags you to have that annoying pain in your abdomen checked out, so you finally mention it to your doctor at your annual physical. You get an alarming diagnosis and head off for a second opinion. The second doctor avers that the pain will come and go but the underlying condition endures for decades with no ill effects.

---

[66] Robert Nozick, *Philosophical Explanations* (Cambridge, MA: Belknap Press, Harvard University Press, 1981), chap. 3.

The first responds that you need to act quickly before the problem blows up on you. Whom shall you trust? You can scour the internet or try to decipher the repellent jargon of the medical journals. Maybe those sources agree, maybe they don't, and anyway none of them is actually examining you. Worse, a friend of yours with expertise in statistics—or so you think—disdains epidemiology and tells you that academic doctors make so many elementary mistakes that you shouldn't believe anything they say. Should you seek a third opinion? Then what? Should you go with majority rule? Or side with whichever doctor seems to speak with the most gravity? Or whichever seems most likable? Should you investigate where each one went to medical school? Or what their other patients say about them?

What you believe depends on who you believe. And who you believe depends on what you believe. Your beliefs, your knowledge, your experience, your assignments of what I'll call epistemic authority, that is, who or what sources are trustworthy on what issues: all are caught up in each other.[67] (Why call it epistemic authority? It's not that others have a right to tell you what to believe. But that's a clumsy gloss on authority. We routinely describe others as authorities on their subjects and we mean we should believe what they say.) There's no priority relationship here, but an unfolding history. If you trust Al Sharpton, you'll believe that in 1987 Tawana Brawley was kidnapped and raped by six white policemen. (The claim went nowhere legally and Sharpton paid to settle a libel suit. Running for president sixteen years later, the unflappable reverend was sticking to his story. "Juries can be wrong," he noted.)[68] If you trust mainstream white news media, you'll believe that Brawley was lying and you'll dismiss Sharpton as a blustering scoundrel. Then again, if you know who the Scottsboro Boys were and what happened in the Tuskegee experiments, you will be more likely to scorn the mainstream media as propagandists, subscribe to the *Amsterdam News*, and admire Sharpton as a man brave

[67] For a relatively detached, sociological approach to these matters, see Patrick Wilson, *Second-Hand Knowledge: An Inquiry into Cognitive Authority* (Westport, CT: Greenwood Press, 1983). For a vivid historical study, see Steven Shapin, *A Social History of Truth: Civility and Science in Seventeenth-Century England* (Chicago: University of Chicago Press, 1994). For a useful philosophical survey and discussion, see C.A.J. Coady, *Testimony: A Philosophical Study* (Oxford: Clarendon Press, 1992). Russell Hardin, *Trust and Trustworthiness* (New York: Russell Sage Foundation, 2002), chap. 5, misses how dependent we are on what complete strangers tell us, I assume because of his focus on our assessing how compatible others' interests are with our own.

[68] *Face the Nation* (6 July 2003).

enough to speak truth to power. Then in turn you may well believe that O. J. Simpson was framed by the infamously racist Los Angeles Police Department. But if you grew up with parents and teachers assuring you that the policeman is your friend; if the cops, on your rare encounters with them, treated you amiably enough; if your American history textbooks glossed over the long-standing incestuous relations between American criminal justice and racism; then you will likely marvel that someone as flagrantly guilty as Simpson could have gotten off.

I've said nothing about whether any of these beliefs is rational. There is a specific sense in which the rationality of belief is relative. Whether it's rational for you to believe something depends on how it fits in with what you already believe, not least about the credibility of those reporting it. Joan confides in Fred and Sara that Paul has lapsed back into drinking heavily. Fred has always found Joan trustworthy, and what she says seems sensible: he saw Paul looking bleary-eyed the other day, and anyway, he's long been skeptical of those gimmicky twelve-step programs. Then it's rational for Fred to believe Joan. Sara doesn't know Joan, but Sara's good friend Bobby has told her that Joan is gratuitously malicious. And Sara knows people who have successfully overcome addictions and has heard that Paul just got an excellent performance review at work. Then it's rational for Sara not to believe Joan. Other versions of relativism here seem exotically implausible. There's no reason to say that Joan's claim is true for Fred but not true for Sara, unless we just mean elliptically to repeat that Fred will believe it and Sara won't. Either the claim is true or it's not, period. But that doesn't mean it's rational for everyone to believe it. So it can be rational to believe something that's actually false. (The point threatens efforts to draw close connections between truth and warranted assertability or between fact and what's rational to believe.) Not that you somehow believe it while knowing it to be false, say because it's reassuring. That thought does some violence to the concept of belief, though it may anyway be empirically possible: some people seem to have this stance about religious belief. Rather, you believe it in the familiar sense that you think it true, but are just mistaken.

We can rescue Voltaire's claim. Don't take him as proposing some radical experiment in first-person empiricism, as if you could work out everything for yourself. Take him instead as urging that you think critically about how you assign epistemic authority—more generally, about what maxims you use to evaluate new candidates for belief. Some maxims we use are risible. So: "Anything repeated often enough is true." "Anything said by a tall white man with a deep voice and a well-tailored business suit is true." Or, in the nuanced version more hilarious for its would-be moderation, "Anything said by such a man is more likely to be true than something said by a short, fat woman with a shrill voice." "Anything my husband says about household repair is false." The sullen adolescent's credo: "Anything my parents say is false and anything my friends say is true." When you appraise your principles of epistemic authority, you won't bootstrap yourself out of your contingent history and escape your current beliefs. How attractive different maxims seem will depend on what you already believe. But still you can make progress.

There is no bright-line distinction between epistemic virtues and political virtues, or, put differently, no priority of rationality over politics—and no priority the other way, either.[69] Sometimes we can tell them apart. Contrast "Theories should be simple" and "The marginal income tax rate on high earners should be lowered." But sometimes rationality and politics are coextensive. Think about the problems politicians face in learning what's going on and the solutions they adopt. Tacitus reports on another disguised leader besides loathsome Nero: Germanicus needed to learn his own troops' morale. How? No point asking his associates, a motley assortment of sycophantic flatterers, upbeat officers, and cringing former slaves. No point mustering the troops: a minority would speak up and the rest would sheepishly fall in line. Best would be eavesdropping on the unsupervised chatter of the troops as they ate. And it would have to be eavesdropping: what lowly soldier would dare speak his mind to a military leader and close relative of the emperor? So one night Germanicus, dressed in an animal skin, slipped out of camp and mingled unannounced with his troops.[70] Compare the epistemic predicament of monarchs in early modern courts, where stealthy plotting was decked out in ornate etiquette and no one dared deliver bad news to the king. One solution was the court jester, licensed to snitch on anyone and everyone, even to humiliate the king himself, and (at least officially) to suffer no reprisals.

[69] Compare "The Priority of Democracy to Philosophy," in Rorty, *Objectivity, Relativism, and Truth.*

[70] *Annals*, bk. 2, xii–xiii. Compare the contemptibly maudlin self-indulgence of the once valiant Prince Hal in Shakespeare, *Henry V*, act 4, sc. 1.

Next, marry the thoughts that rationality must involve assessing competing claims to epistemic authority and that politics is the realm of controversies over legitimate authority. Consider: "It's rational to believe whatever consensus emerges from the social practice of free speech, especially if the community discussing the matter includes people with different points of view, some of them partisan enough to leave no stone unturned in the pursuit of their views, others relatively disinterested." The proposal simultaneously tells you what to believe, what's trustworthy, and describes a choiceworthy social practice, implicitly condemns censorship and state promulgation of allegedly correct views, and so on. Now consider: "The community of American historians becomes more diverse and so more trustworthy when it comes to include more radicals and conservatives, blacks and Chicanos, gays, lesbians, and women, and so on, or when it becomes less of a preserve of middle-aged moderately liberal white men." (On its face this proposal is less plausible for physicists.) If or insofar as this diversity is epistemically unproductive—suppose the community suffocates in new ideological orthodoxies or is riven by overheated conflicts with no relatively disinterested observers—then affirmative action is an epistemic loser. But if or insofar as this diversity is epistemically productive—suppose the added perspectives and experiences lead to insights otherwise unavailable—then affirmative action isn't the politicized enemy of the academic pursuit of truth. It's a strategy for improving our knowledge.

Nor is there any bright-line distinction between epistemic virtues and gender. Again they are sometimes coextensive, and not because of the bedraggled old refrain that reason is masculine, emotion feminine. Consider: "Don't trust the outcome of debates that are too conflictual. When the conversational game is king of the hill, when everyone wants to vindicate his claim to be the smartest person in the room, when hesitating or reformulating your position is taken not as thoughtfulness but as defeat, you learn only how quick and combative people are, not what views are sensible. Instead trust the outcome of discussions whose participants cooperate to advance their collective understanding." The proposal simultaneously tells you what (not) to believe, what's trustworthy, and describes styles of conversation we recognize as gendered. If or insofar as the proposal is right, femininity is rational and rationality, on our current best construction of it, is feminine. If or insofar as the proposal is wrong—suppose conclusions blur in discussions where no one wants to be brash lest another's feelings are hurt—it isn't. But rationality might then be masculine.

I suggested before that practical rationality, that is, deciding what to do, isn't the colorless business of efficiently attaining ends. We can always ask not just whether an agent has realized her goals, nor for that matter whether her goals are good ones, but all kinds of questions about her means. Was she considerate or rude? Noble or base? Honorable or contemptible? Moral or immoral? So too with theoretical rationality, that is, deciding what's sensible to believe. We can always ask not just whether some epistemic stance or procedure leads to true beliefs, but how it does so. We don't want to bulldoze our way through the world, maximizing our true beliefs (or true beliefs on subjects that we care about or subjects that matter or something like that) with no regard to the damage we leave behind. Sometimes our concerns are aesthetic. Mathematicians prize elegant proofs, chemists neat experiments, over and above the truth of the results. Sometimes our concerns are morally and politically charged. Grueling examinations of hostile witnesses are one thing when a criminal defendant's life or liberty hangs in the balance, another when you want to sort out something inconsequential. But mustn't theoretical rationality be devoted to truth? Isn't truth the constitutive aim of the rationality of belief? So don't those ancillary concerns—gender, elegance, morality, and so on—just fall out as a result of whatever independent decisions we make about how to obtain true beliefs? No. One could press similar (mis)leading questions about practical rationality: mustn't practical rationality be devoted to what's good or choiceworthy? Isn't goodness the constitutive aim of the rationality of action? In some very general way, yes. But we know that it doesn't follow, it can't follow, that a conception of practical rationality must focus solely on the good. We can say, for instance, that a conception is defective if it pays no heed to being rude or cruel in the pursuit of good ends. So too for theoretical rationality and truth. Our ancillary concerns can help shape a conception of theoretical rationality.

Scoffing at honor and justice, Odysseus is willing to do whatever it takes to prevail. He needs that willingness every bit as much as he needs to be resourceful to be such a consummately cunning actor. Machiavelli, I suggested, stands for the thought that we can't cabin the apparent appeal of cunning to political emergencies, new principalities, or anything of the sort. Cunning tactics beckon us everywhere. Now I can add, so too in the realm of knowledge: we can be ruthless and tricky in figuring out what to believe. And—recall our massive epistemic dependence—others can manipulate our beliefs. If we trust them, they can get us to believe stuff that is useful for them. Scrutinize Fielding's language again: "those great arts which the vulgar call treachery, dissembling, promising, lying, falsehood, etc., but which are by great men summed up in the collective name of policy, or politics, or rather *pollitrics*." Here politics is centrally the manipulation of belief. Through the protracted closing years of the Vietnam War, Nixon wove webs of deceit. It's startling to compare what his administration said was going on with what we now know was going on—what they knew then, too.[71] Sometimes, though, it's exceedingly hard to figure out who knows what, who's using whom, what is appearance, what reality. Beyond flagrant lying are temporizing, insinuating, misleading by silence, all the artful and artless dishonesties of everyday life.

I want to explore an example from the heyday of political astrology. Today believers in astrology profess varying degrees of faith. Some find it amusing, even helpful, to learn others' zodiac signs. ("I'm sorry, darling, but I can't marry you. It would never work out. You're an Aries.") Some pay to have their charts drawn up. But they have to know the culture is telling them something when they open their newspapers and find their horoscopes right next to Beetle Bailey. The something in question is dismissive, even demeaning. It wasn't always so. William Lilly was a prominent, one might say infamous, astrologer of seventeenth-century England.[72] Lilly advised key members of the Rump Parliament of radical Puritans which declared a republic, put Charles I on trial for his life, and presided over a stormy interregnum before the triumphant restoration of Charles II in 1660. (Some twenty years ago, to show how exotic this historical period

[71] Jonathan Schell, *The Time of Illusion* (New York: Alfred A. Knopf, 1976), remains masterful on this topic, despite its accompanying loopy argument on nuclear arms and the credibility gap that Schell pursued in his *The Fate of the Earth* (New York: Alfred A. Knopf, 1982).

[72] For general background, see Keith Thomas, *Religion and the Decline of Magic: Studies in Popular Beliefs in Sixteenth and Seventeenth Century England* (London: Wiedenfeld and Nicolson, 1971), chaps. 10–12, with the usual cautions about his affection for functionalist explanations; Bernard Capp, *English Almanacs 1500–1800: Astrology and the Popular Press* (Ithaca, NY: Cornell University Press, 1979); and especially Harry Rusche, "Merlini Anglici: Astrology and Propaganda from 1644 to 1651," *English Historical Review* 80 (April 1965):322–33. For a painstaking intellectual reconstruction of contemporary astrology, see Ann Geneva, *Astrology and the Seventeenth-Century Mind: William Lilly and the Language of the Stars* (Manchester: Manchester University Press, 1995).

was, I reported that Cromwell, Charles I, and other notables consulted astrologers to advise them on timing and even measures.[73] My colleagues were suitably impressed. Then Nancy Reagan had to get into the act.[74]) When three suns appeared over London on Charles I's birthday in 1644, Lilly published an interpretation—and some crushingly obvious prophecies: "nothing but Fraud, Cozenage, Dissimulation, Hypocrisy, will be used amongst some pretended-Reformers both of Church and Commonwealth."[75] (Don't reject the tale of three suns. Modern astronomers call the extras parhelia or sundogs and explain that aligned plate crystals in clouds can refract sunlight and produce sharply defined images.) In a 1647 work, Lilly let one chapter trail off with a delicious taunt: "For Kings are earth, and no more than men; and the time is coming, &c. when."[76] The passage forcibly insinuates that like the rest of us, Charles would return to dust, as indeed he did in 1649 with a jolting assist from the hangman. (It may too be taking a swipe at the distinguished tradition of the king's two bodies, one the mortal flesh of the throne's current occupant and the other the mystic body politic supporting the ongoing institution of monarchy,[77] and so be declaring that monarchy itself was doomed.) We must then score this passage as a successful prediction. In a 1651 work, conceding that astrology was plagued with ambiguity,[78] Lilly reeled off what he styled unequivocal prophecies that would help consolidate the republic. These prophecies, I'm afraid, we would see as preposterously obscure. He closed that volume with sixteen pages of tantalizing pictures with no captions, no connected text, only the following modestly apologetic—defiant—introduction:

> Had the courtesy of the present Times deserved it at my hands,
> thou hadst seen an Explanation of the sixteen Pages following,
> which in Enigmatical Types, Forms, Figures, Shapes, doth
> perfectly represent the future condition of the *English* Nation and

---

[73] Thomas, *Religion*, pp. 312–13, 373–74.

[74] "Not the Storefront Type, Says Reagans' Astrologer," *New York Times* (9 May 1988), B7; Donald T. Regan, *For the Record: From Wall Street to Washington* (San Diego, CA: Harcourt Brace Jovanovich, 1988), pp. 3–4, 28, 73–74, 300–301, 344, 359, 367–68, 369–70.

[75] William Lilly, *The Starry Messenger; or, An Interpretation of That Strange Apparition of Three Suns Seene in London, 19 Novemb. 1644. Being the Birth Day of King Charles* (London, 1645), p. 17.

[76] William Lilly, *Christian Astrology Modestly Treated of in Three Books* (London, 1647), p. 128.

[77] The standard source remains Ernst H. Kantorowicz, *The King's Two Bodies: A Study in Mediaeval Political Theology* (Princeton, NJ: Princeton University Press, 1957).

[78] William Lilly, *Monarchy or No Monarchy in England* (London, 1651), pp. 33–34.

Commonwealth for many hundred of years yet to come. I have borrowed so much time from my Morning sleep, as hath brought forth these Conceptions. You that read these Lines must know I do no new thing, I do herein but imitate the *Ancients*, who so often as they resolved to conceal their intentions from profane hands, used *Hieroglyphics, Images, &c.*[79]

Punters and prognosticators, lurking under cover of a polite interest in the history of engraving or anyway craving some artistic verisimilitude, can consider these samples of the pictures. Are you deriding the thought that anyone could have been gullible enough to deem such scribbles prophetic? Well, Gemini had long been associated with London, and the engraving on the next page boosted Lilly's stock after London's Great Fire of September 1666. No wonder a Parliamentary committee summoned him to testify.[80]

Still, in 1651 he remained sternly silent about those engravings. Wouldn't it be great had Lilly vouchsafed us some of his pinpoint predictions? Might Tony Blair and Michael Howard—privately, of course; niceties and ceremonies must always be observed—bid on them? You may be leaping to the conclusion that Lilly knew he was a phony. (If you think that about all astrologers, you must be wrong.) You may be thinking that he was parading his fraudulence, chuckling in print at the staggering gullibility of the rubes. He wouldn't be the first—or the last. There's something painfully

---

[79] Lilly, *Monarchy*, p. 120, italics reversed and small capitals removed. The engravings are reproduced by permission of *The Huntington Library, San Marino, California*.

[80] Patrick Curry, *Prophecy and Power: Astrology in Early Modern England* (Princeton, NJ: Princeton University Press, 1989), p. 52.

accurate in the dramatic portrayal of the country wench eager to buy a
magic spell to enlarge her breasts. For what it's worth, I pass along the
cunning woman's advice: "for a Charm to make 'em grow, you must stroke
'em every morning before you get up, and say three times fasting, Grow
Breasts, grow; Rise Bubbies rise. . . ." The credulous wench recites the
charm and exclaims, "Methinks they begin to swell a little already."[81] There's
something painfully accurate, too, in Jonson's rendition of Fitzdottrel—the
name means "son of a fool"—salivating madly as Merecraft dangles untold

[81] Edward Ravenscroft, *Dame Dobson: or, The Cunning Woman* (London, 1684), p. 15.

millions and a dukedom in front of his nose.[82] But maybe your reactions to these scattered passages are anachronistic. What did contemporaries make of Lilly's performances? Could it have been rational for them to believe him?

One pamphleteer defended his skill and integrity.[83] Ah, but that pamphlet was published anonymously. Think it was written by Lilly? by a paid confederate? Knowing that Lilly was his bitter opponent, Charles I himself grudgingly acknowledged the astrologer's expertise: "Lilly understands astrology as well as any man in Europe."[84] Or so Lilly reported. Do you believe him? Should you write off the claim as arrant self-promotion? Or accept it on the theory that no one could hope to get away with such an outrageous lie? Some of the day's cunning folk boasted that he'd trained them.[85] The boast indicates not just their own ascriptions of epistemic authority, but also their beliefs about what might attract clients. Aubrey, that pithy biographer, approvingly noted that Lilly had successfully predicted the appearance of a comet.[86] The boundaries between astronomy and astrology, meteorology and magic, biblical interpretation and ancient philosophy, were fuzzy. Contemporaries knew to defer to "the incomparable Mr. Newton," as no less a writer than John Locke dubbed him.[87] But Isaac Newton didn't just write the *Principia*; he diligently pursued biblical interpretation and alchemy, too.[88] His account of comets was aimed in part at corrupt astrologists, but whatever his vaunted mechanist philosophy amounted to, he didn't strip comets of prophetic meaning.[89] For him all these

[82] *The Devil Is an Ass*, act 2, sc. 1.

[83] *The Late Story of Mr. William Lilly* (London, 1648).

[84] Derek Parker, *Familiar to All: William Lilly and Astrology in the Seventeenth Century* (London: Jonathan Cape, 1975), p. 151.

[85] Owen Davies, *Cunning-Folk: Popular Magic in English History* (London: Hambledon and London, 2003), pp. 73, 95.

[86] *"Brief Lives," Chiefly of Contemporaries, Set Down by John Aubrey, between the Years 1669 & 1696*, ed. Andrew Clark, 2 vols. (Oxford: Clarendon Press, 1898), 2:33.

[87] *An Essay Concerning Human Understanding*, Epistle to the Reader.

[88] On Newton's biblical work, see Maurizio Mamiani, "Newton on Prophecy and the Apocalypse," in *The Cambridge Companion to Newton*, ed. I. Bernard Cohen and George E. Smith (Cambridge: Cambridge University Press, 2002). For context on magic and science, see Charles Webster, *From Paracelsus to Newton: Magic and the Making of Modern Science* (Cambridge: Cambridge University Press, 1982); see too Michael White, *Isaac Newton: The Last Sorcerer* (London: Fourth Estate, 1997).

[89] Simon Schaffer, "Newton's Comets and the Transformation of Astrology," in *Astrology Science and Society: Historical Essays*, ed. Patrick Curry (Woodbridge: Boydell Press, 1987).

studies comprised a unified research program, as they did for the minister addressing the Society of Astrologers in 1649, for whom the story of the three magi locating Christ by the stars showed the seamless connections between religion and astrology.[90] True, the future first Astronomer Royal tried to shred the idea that the stars shed any light on human affairs.[91] So that skeptical view, which we now rationally adopt as true, was available. But that doesn't mean it was by contemporary lights the best available view or even a good one. It could have been rational for people to trust Lilly, a leading representative of an abstruse field producing real knowledge.

But Lilly faced caustic attacks, too. A solar eclipse panicked London on March 29, 1652.[92] One pamphleteer called it a natural phenomenon, a reminder of God's great power, and ridiculed the thought that astrologers could interpret it. Indeed he mischievously predicted the imminent downfall of astrology itself.[93] Another conceded that Lilly and other "insipid Astrologers" had predicted horrible darkness for that date. "But I think in the darkest night a man may spy such *Astrologic knaves* as they are, among a thousand: who by their knavery have cozened the whole Nation." Only the government's mercy, he sneered, left them their financial assets and their lives.[94] A fellow astrologer mocked Lilly's false predictions and reliance on devils.[95] Another pamphleteer wrote a poem lampooning astrology and singling out Lilly's 1651 book for special abuse.[96] Yet another vehemently urged that astrology was satanic and that its predictions were false anyway.[97]

[90] Robert Gell, *Stella Nova, A New Starre, Leading Wisemen unto Christ* (London, 1649).

[91] Michael Hunter, "Science and Astrology in Seventeenth-Century England: An Unpublished Polemic by John Flamsteed," in *Astrology Science and Society.*

[92] *On Bugbear Black-Monday, March 29. 1652; or, The London-Fright at the Eclipse Proceeding from a Natural Cause* (London, 1652). See William E. Burns, "'The Terriblest Eclipse that Hath Been Seen in Our Days': Black Monday and the Debate on Astrology during the Interregnum," in *Rethinking the Scientific Revolution*, ed. Margaret J. Osler (Cambridge: Cambridge University Press, 2000).

[93] L[awrence] P[rice], *The Astrologers Bugg-Beare* (London, 1653).

[94] William Brommerton, *Confidence Dismounted; or The Astronomers Knavery Anatomized* (London, 1652).

[95] H. Johnsen, *Anti-Merlinus: or, A Confutation of Mr. William Lillies Predictions for This Year 1648* (London?, 1648).

[96] J. B., Gent., *A Faire in Spittle Fields, Where All the Knick Knacks of Astrology Are Exposed to Open Sale, to All That Will See for Their Love, and Buy for Their Money* (London, 1652), pp. 5–6 on Lilly's *Monarchy.*

[97] *The Wizard Unvizor'd: or, A Clear Display of the Madnesse of Judicial Astrologie* (London?, 1652).

A minister ransacked the Bible for evidence that astrology was blasphemous.[98] One of Lilly's competitors in the trade tried "to take off the ugly and deformed vizard from the face of Astrology," that "fair and beautiful Virgin," and rescue the distressed damsel from Lilly's pawing affronts: "It is Astrology's greatest unhappiness, that her *pretended favorites* are her *greatest enemies.*"[99] Another writer tried to unmask him as a Papist or a lunatic: "is not the man, think we, not staring, but stark mad?"[100] Upon Charles II's restoration in 1660, an angry pamphleteer charged that Lilly had prostituted himself, supporting the outrageous claims of the republic for a whopping £200 a year, and urged the new parliament to attach his estate and have him "kept in such security as the *good people* of *England* may be secured from his *infernal Actings.*"[101]

The appeal of astrology seems to have declined around the Restoration. Its professional society's annual feasts lapsed in 1658.[102] Some later pamphlets appearing under Lilly's name—I'm not confident he wrote them—descend to the laughably pedestrian. If you dream of broken eggs, announces one, it means others were angry with you. But if a woman dreams of whole eggs, she and her neighbors will bicker the next day.[103] Elias Ashmole turned from his pursuit of the philosopher's stone to penning a huge and hugely enervating history of the Order of the Garter.[104] Samuel Butler's rapier wit punctured the "*Juggle, Cant* and *Cheat*" of Sidrophel's astrology.[105] But decline isn't death or even morbidity. Right through to the end

---

[98] John Geree, *Astrologo-Mastix, or A Discovery of the Vanity and Iniquity of Judiciall Astrology* (London, 1646).

[99] John Gadbury, *Neophuto-Astrologos: The Novice-Astrologer Instructed: in a New-Years-Gift to Mr. William Lilly; Occasioned by the Scurrility, Scandal, Ignorance, and Flattery of His Merlin for the Ensuing Year* (London, 1660), sig. A3 verso.

[100] Tho. Gataker, *A Discours Apologetical; Wherein Lilies Lewd and Lowd Lies in His Merlin or Pasquil for the Year 1654 Are Cleerly Laid Open; His Shameful Desertion of His Own Cause Is Further Discovered; His Shameless Slanders Fullie Refuted; And His Malicious and Murtherous Mind, Inciting to a General Massacre of Gods Ministers, from His Own Pen, Evidentlie Evinced* (London, 1654), p. 86.

[101] *A Declaration of the Several Treasons, Blasphemies and Misdemeanors Acted, Spoken and Published against God, the Late King, His Present Majesty, the Nobility, Clergy, City, Commonalty, &c. by that Grand Wizard and Impostor William Lilly* (London, 1660), pp. 1, 7.

[102] Patrick Curry, "The Astrologers' Feasts," *History Today* 38:4 (April 1988):17–22.

[103] William Lilly, *A Groatsworth of Wit for a Penny, or, The Interpretation of Dreams* (London, 1670), p. 6.

[104] Elias Ashmole, *The Way to Bliss* (London, 1658), bk. 3; Ashmole, *The Institution, Laws & Ceremonies of the Most Noble Order of the Garter* (London, 1672).

[105] *Hudibras*, pt. 2, canto 3; the quotation is from l. 218.

of the 1600s, Samuel Jeake kept an astrological diary. Had he avoided falling down the stairs? It must have been "the opposition of Mercury out of an airy sign both to the Radical & Transiting Ascendant & the square of Jupiter to them & Mercury."[106]

So it could have been rational to trust Lilly and it could have been rational to snub him. We have here not just the brute fact that contemporaries disagreed, but also their ability to produce good reasons on both sides of the debate. His certification as an expert by the community of practitioners, his mastery of learned sources, his successful predictions of events in the starry skies and the streets of London: all spoke in his favor. The availability of less ambitious explanations, the conjecture that his accurate predictions were just the remembered lucky guesses amidst swarms of false prophecies, his penchant for serving his own interests, the longstanding fear that no good Christian should traffic with pagan superstition or, worse yet, satanic sorcery: all spoke against. What about one's love of Puritan regicides or one's battle fatigue and relief at the Restoration? Do these properly count as reasons in evaluating Lilly's claims? They could. It's not unreasonable to take character as an indicator of epistemic authority, to reject what Puritans and their supporters say on the grounds that they've shown themselves irresponsible, corrupt, prisoners of poor judgment. That narrowly political point aside, whether to believe Lilly or to believe more generally in astrology is still a profoundly political question. It poses questions about the legitimacy of (epistemic) authority. And it invites cunning operators to swarm the terrain. Some years later, two men complained to one Dick Morris that the women they loved slighted them. Morris assured them that he'd lived with an astrologer and magician and knew charms that would render these women splendidly pliable. He told the men to bring him some of the women's hair and a sack, cord, knife, chain, and brush. They dutifully showed up equipped, and Morris took them for a nocturnal ride two miles outside town. Morris's potent charms left them naked and tied up, with Morris commanding their clothes and horses.[107] Who says astrology and magic don't work?

---

[106] *An Astrological Diary of the Seventeenth Century: Samuel Jeake of Rye 1652–1699*, ed. Michael Hunter and Annabel Gregory (Oxford: Clarendon Press, 1988), 8 January 1686, p. 176.

[107] Capt. Alexander Smith [Daniel Defoe], *The History of the Lives of the Most Noted Highway-Men, Foot-Pads, House-Breakers, Shop-Lifts, and Cheats, of Both Sexes, in and about London, and Other Places of Great-Britain, for above Fifty Years Last Past* (London, 1714), pp. 171–76.

Will the real William Lilly please stand up? The question seems irre-
sistible, but it can't be exhausted by Lilly's self-understanding. Lilly of
course may have been tortured with doubts about his abilities, like many
another prophet, magician, and astrologer before and after him. Even if he
was convinced of his astrological powers, he could have had nothing to offer. Maybe his learning was faulty, his charts bollixed; or maybe the astrological muse didn't speak to him; or maybe there is no sound astrological
knowledge, period. The converse is every bit as true and important. Even if
he was sure he was a fraud, even if he disdained the yokels he was fleecing,
he could have been purveying genuine astrological insights. There is some
linguistic pressure to describe Lilly as cunning if and only if he was self-
consciously strategic and deceptive. But now imagine a sincere Lilly who
does the very same things your self-consciously plotting Lilly does. He
publishes the same words (but doesn't believe they're pishtosh), he receives
the same cash subsidies from Parliament (but doesn't snicker, any more
than any other hard-working public servant does on receipt of a paycheck),
and so on. Is he not cunning? What if we add that there's nothing to
astrology, it's all cosmically, comically false? What if we add that he is
patently self-deceiving? Wouldn't it be cunning to trick yourself, too, so
you could work your scams with utmost sincerity? How good are people
at wearing poker faces? A man who'd done brutal work building the railroad in Burma as a war prisoner of the Japanese and who'd endured tor-
ture to boot was damned good at it. His psychiatrist "once told me that I
was the only patient he had ever met whose face was so inscrutable that
he could not tell what I was thinking. I had never heard my mask-like expression described so objectively; it must have slipped on whenever I
wanted to hide from his questions for a moment."[108] But maybe the psychiatrist was conceited. I doubt that trauma is the price we have to pay for
opacity.

Or try this: was William Lilly an astrologer? Yes, in that he performed
credibly in the role, at least for many contemporaries. His predictions and
advice, however weird or silly, influenced others and so changed the world.
(Reputation of astrology is astrology? A few decades later, freethinker Pierre

---

[108] Eric Lomax, *The Railway Man: A True Story of War, Remembrance, and Forgiveness* (New
York: Ballantine Books, 1995), p. 237.

Bayle heaped scorn on astrology but noticed that self-fulfilling prophecies made astrological predictions come true.)[109] In that sense, planets, constellations, and zodiac signs did indeed govern human life. No, if no one can deliver the goods that astrologers claim to, or anyway if Lilly didn't. So there's a sense in which he was a real astrologer and a sense in which he only appeared to be an astrologer. And some of our worries—their worries, too—about his being a cunning rogue are caught up in navigating that distinction. It's easiest to see him as a rogue if we imagine that he knew that astrology was bogus, that all his celebrated learning was nothing but a criminal toolkit for stealing wealth and power. But it may not be only the fools who are credulous, blank, unaware of the real significance of their own actions. The rogues may join them.

Here's one last example of the difficulties posed by appearance and reality and by the rationality of belief. Michael Cleary, a rural Irishman, apparently realized at the end of the nineteenth century that a fairy changeling had replaced his wife Bridget.[110] Bridget doggedly maintained that she was his true wife. She did so under duress, while swearing oaths to God, three times in a row. Just what a fairy changeling would do, right? Plutarch again: if she looks like your wife and acts like your wife, she must be a fairy changeling. Michael's belief wasn't idiosyncratic. He drew on long-held shared beliefs, surely arguable in his day, respectable enough in his social circle. In his community, it could be rational to believe in fairies; in principle it could even be irrational not to. (By the time educated circles in London got hold of the ghastly story, the belief underlined how appallingly backward, how in need of benevolently civilizing imperialism, Ireland really was.) Even the landscape boasted physical signs of fairies in ring forts, large circular elevations in the land. Today we think these raths, as they're now called, are the remnants of medieval dwelling places; Cleary and his contemporaries had another theory. Ten years younger than Michael, Bridget was pretty, childless, gutsier than many other women of her day, a skilled dressmaker who may have been having an extramarital affair. She

---

[109] Pierre Bayle, *Various Thoughts on the Occasion of a Comet*, trans. Robert C. Bartlett (Albany: State University of New York Press, 2000), pp. 30, 133.

[110] Angela Bourke, *The Burning of Bridget Cleary: A True Story* (London: Pimlico, 1999), is more compelling if worse written than Joan Hoff and Marian Yeates, *The Cooper's Wife Is Missing: The Trials of Bridget Cleary* (New York: Basic Books, 2000). For the key events, see Bourke, *Burning*, chap. 6.

took sick after exposure to the cold. Her concerned husband took two four-mile hikes to get a doctor, then ignored his prescription. But he did listen to the recommendations of some traditional herbalists. We shouldn't infer that he intended to neglect her by administering powdered plant of no medicinal value. Again it's not merely the brute fact that his world took herbalists seriously. It's that they had good reason to do so, not least the apparent success of many herbal treatments. Some herbs have beneficent impact; and some maladies get better anyway, but those suffering them and gulping down herbs might well attribute their cure to the herbs. And they had good reason to distrust the newfangled doctors, who charged more money for harsher treatments of uncertain value—medicine a century ago was not the stuff of miracles, and the doctor making the rounds in rural Ireland couldn't have been the most accomplished practitioner—and who might well have seemed like ripoff artists themselves. So Michael doused Bridget with urine from the chamber pot and, in a gruesome oral rape, he and others forced her to drink a bitter herbal potion made with new milk. They seemed satisfied the real Bridget had returned. She seemed better and left bed and dressed for the first time in a while. For good measure he had a priest perform a mass in his house, apparently to exorcise the changeling.

But gnawing suspicion is hard to defeat. Still dissatisfied, Michael decided to burn the changeling in accordance with folklore. "For the love of God," his friend implored, "don't burn your wife!" "She's not my wife," he snapped. "She's an old deceiver sent in place of my wife. She's after deceiving me the last seven or eight days, and deceived the priest today too, but she won't deceive anyone any more." He added, "You'll soon see her go up the chimney." He doused her with paraffin oil and burned her. Was he guilty of murder? Criminal law junkies will want to know that when he buried the body, Michael discussed pretending to be mad, emigrating to America, and killing himself. But again deferring to folklore, after her death he also spent three nights at the ring fort waiting for Bridget to ride by on horseback so he could wrest her away from the fairies.

The dizzying possibilities here outstrip the threadbare scheme of knaves and fools. Michael may have been knave to the core, seizing on an atrocious pretext to do away with his wife, though this would make him one foolish knave if he imagined he'd get away with it. But he may have been a fool who inadvertently acted knavishly. He may have been as anguished, as ambivalent, as the story suggests. Maybe he flitted between believing Bridget had been replaced by a fairy changeling and worrying that the creature he was torturing was still in fact Bridget. Maybe he harbored all kinds of hostility to Bridget without being fully aware of it. Maybe he was all too aware of it and distrusted his motivations. And we can imagine scenarios in which Bridget honestly believed she was a fairy changeling, even if there's no evidence that she did. Or suppose she believed that seeming to traffic in fairy lore would help protect her. Suppose she wasn't sure herself whether there was anything to fairy magic, but hoped there was. There is no point for us, today, in intimating that perhaps she really was a fairy changeling. But it's crucial to think about what she and Michael and their friends and family could have believed and did believe. Those beliefs, however contradictory or murky or false, are not mere illusions or pretexts. They are part of the reality of the tiny dismal smokey house where Bridget met her death.

Step back a minute. You can be forgiven for fearing that mine is a bleak counsel of despair. (Actually, you can be blamed if you're not worrying about that.) Cunning, I've argued, can't be cabined to the treacherous landscape of a new prince or even to politics. It sprawls across social life. There are no reliable tactics for unmasking cunning rogues. Worse, the appearance/reality distinction is bankrupt. We rely on others for our knowledge and they can deceive us. The way seems clear for cunning scoundrels to sprint to tawdry victories—clear, too, for deciding that we should strive to join them. So our grounds for despair seem ample.

DESPAIR?

The late music of Morton Feldman might be described as nothing but harmony. Sometimes the rhythms are notated but impossibly complex. In some chamber pieces Feldman allows the different players to play at their own rates, leaving to chance how their lines coalesce. To the listener the music floats, elongates, contracts; no cranky music teacher with a thudding metronome or baton could pound it into a refractory student. "I am not a clockmaker," sniffed the composer.[1] Feldman stacks up dissonances, even five half-steps in a row, sometimes arpeggiating them over different octaves, sometimes bunching them together. Somehow—it is one mystery of his work—they can sound painfully pretty, so luscious that it is surprising that they're also beautiful. Sometimes they are biting, even astringent. The instrumentation is often spare, severe—much of "For Bunita Marcus," a deliriously slow solo piano piece, unfolds one note at a time—and the dynamics routinely pianissimo. Much of the music is delicate, even fragile, but it isn't minimalist in the sense made familiar by the work of Philip Glass, Steve Reich, and Terry Riley, and anyway it has its moments of resilience, strength, triumph. The pieces lack any conventional structure. They don't do the grand theme-and-development thing; they don't develop motifs, though "modules" bubble up now and again; they aren't based on twelve-tone rows. Some are marathons imposing strenuous demands on performers and listeners alike: the second string quartet runs six hours. You might think Feldman's music must then be unlistenable. You'd be wrong. It's magnificent.

So how did Feldman compose? We know that Stefan Wolpe taught him; that Jackson Pollock and Philip Guston, John Cage and Christian Wolff, were associates, maybe co-conspirators; that he collaborated with Samuel Beckett and with pianists David Tudor and Aki Takahashi. We know that Feldman immersed himself in the irregular patterns of Oriental rugs. We know that the man who composed such frail and fetching music was tall, fat, funny, a boisterous chain-smoking New York Jew, though one

---

[1] *Give My Regards to Eighth Street: Collected Writings of Morton Feldman*, ed. B. H. Friedman (Cambridge, MA: Exact Change, 2000), p. 87.

stellar pianist and passionate champion of twentieth-century music confided in me that Feldman was "an asshole." But such facts are only hazily
evocative in explaining the music, let alone helping the listener approach
it. It lives in a serene and austere musical space of its own. "Stockhausen
asked for my secret," reported Feldman. "And I said, 'I don't have any secret, but if I do have a point of view, it's that sounds are very much like
people. And if you do push them, they push you back. So, if I have a secret:
don't push the sounds around.' Karlheinz leans over to me and says: 'Not
even a little bit?' "[2] Feldman showed John Cage the score for a string quartet. Cage examined it, asked him how he'd made it, and rejected Feldman's
initial stumbling reply as unintelligible. "And so, in a very weak voice I answered John, 'I don't know how I made it.'" Cage was delighted.[3] "One
evening Morton Feldman said that when he composed he was dead," reported Cage of another encounter.[4]

Feldman wasn't idiosyncratic. Plenty of composers, through one figure of speech or another—the muse speaks to them, or music does, or
God does; all they have to do is get out of the way, try not to interfere,
avoid fussing and imposing their stylistic mannerisms—deny that they
are consciously working. They testify too that if they try to force the
work, what they write is dull and mechanical or they can't write anything. But the compositions are theirs anyway, right? They're responsible for them, aren't they? Who else could be? Besides, it would be mistaken to conflate Feldman's intuitive way of working with the apparent
lack of structure of his pieces. When jazz musicians improvise badly,
they recycle preconceived licks. When they improvise well, they can
produce extended statements of impeccable musical logic—and not necessarily by design. Tenor saxophonist Sonny Rollins was surprised to
learn that his own improvisations were models of architectural clarity.[5]
Performing the longer tunes his quartet of the early '60s played in concert, John Coltrane knew there'd be "given landmarks" but not how he'd

    [2] *Give My Regards*, pp. 157–58. Compare the account of the exchange in Morton Feldman,
Essays (Kerpen, Germany: Beginner Press, 1985), p. 131.

    [3] *Give My Regards*, p. 4.

    [4] John Cage, *Silence* (Middletown, CT: Wesleyan University Press, 1961), p. 37.

    [5] Eric Nisenson, *Open Sky: Sonny Rollins and His World of Improvisation* (New York: St. Mar-
tin's Press, 2000), pp. 91–95.

get from one to the next.[6] Paul Bley memorably disses most jazz com-posers as "inept pianists," adding, "a composer is just somebody who can't play in real time." If improvisation is composition in real time, it looks like the player needs to be thinking hard and quickly. Bley declares that he's tried to extend Charlie Parker's ability to think ahead. "I've gotten to the point where I can hear a whole solo in advance—not note for note, but structurally." He thinks too about how logically to continue the previ-ous phrase and its closing note, how to avoid territory other jazz musicians have explored, and his destination. "All that in a split second during a pause in my phrasing."[7] Assuming we're unwilling to discard that claim as colossal hubris, it's hard to figure out what thinking ahead might mean here. Whatever's going on in their heads, however painstakingly conscious they are or aren't, Newk, Trane, and Bley are all stunning improvisers.

Meanwhile, consider these tantalizing sentences:

1. The coercion of some things is remarkable, as bread and molasses.
2. The stomach contains nausea.
3. Man is an animal that stands up. He is not very big and he has to work for a living.
4. Sugar is not a vegetable.
5. Edgar A. Poe was a very curdling writer.
6. The body is mostly composed of water and about one half is avaricious tissue.
7. We called our hippopotamus It's Toasted.
8. In the stomach starch is changed to cane-sugar and cane-sugar to sugar-cane.

What do these cryptic gems mean?

There are some vexing chestnuts about the connections among a speaker's intentions, audience interpretations, context, and meaning. We can imagine settings in which any of these lines might be sensible enough.

---

[6] Lewis Porter, *John Coltrane: His Life and Music* (Ann Arbor, MI: University of Michigan Press, 1998), pp. 229–30.

[7] Paul Bley with David Lee, *Stopping Time: Paul Bley and the Transformation of Jazz* (n.p.: Véhicule Press, 1999), pp. 24, 35. See too Norman Meehan, *Time Will Tell: Conversations with Paul Bley* (Berkeley, CA: Berkeley Hill Books, 2003), pp. 7–9, 89, 127.

Imagine a pediatrician ironically reproving indulgent parents about their obese seven-year-old: there the fourth sentence might be fine. Imagine a snide moralist trying to reopen an older debate about human nature with others enthusiastic about biology: there the sixth. Confronted with these puzzling sentences, we effortlessly look for contexts that would make sense of why speakers would say such things. I didn't write these sentences; their provenance might help. The fourth is from the opening of Gertrude Stein's *Tender Buttons* of 1912. The seventh is the opening line of E. E. Cummings's 1923 play *Him*. If you know something about literary modernism and experimental drama, or for that matter if you read what the three weird sisters are up to in the rest of Cummings's opening scene, you can begin to parse his line. If you assume the authors are savvy, you look for purposeful meaning in the admittedly odd ways they're stringing their words together. Then again, if you think that Stein and Cummings wrote hifalutin nonsense that only literary critics could fool themselves into perusing, you may refuse to find meaning in them. And if told that the pursuit of meaning here is philistine, that, say, you should luxuriate in the sheer phonetics of it all or permit yourself to free-associate, you may feel vindicated. (As you may on learning that at his 1915 Harvard commencement address, Cummings threw up his hands at how radically this very work of Stein had extended recent literary trends: "While we must admit that it is logic, must we admit that it is art?"[8])

The other sentences are from examinations written by American public school students—in the nineteenth century, so don't blame telephones and television.[9] Those student howlers are mistakes, but are they meaningless? Surely not. Regardless of what their authors were aiming at, we can always set their words in context and interpret them. At a cocktail party, Tina salutes Carol: "I haven't seen you looking so nice in years!" Carol flushes because she thinks that Tina is insulting her: what, she thinks, am I usually ugly? Tina blushes because she suddenly realizes that Carol will make that inference, but she stammers through an apology and emphasizes that she really meant only to flatter Carol on how especially nice she looks this evening. Carol would rightly be annoyed if Tina didn't apologize, if she

---

[8] *AnOther E. E. Cummings*, selected by Richard Kostelanetz with John Rocco (New York: Liveright, 1998), p. 249.

[9] Caroline B. Le Row, *English as She Is Taught: Genuine Answers to Examination Questions in Our Public Schools* (New York, 1887), pp. 9, 11, 32, 70, 94, 96, italics removed.

said airily, "I never intended to insult you, I didn't mean it, you're wrong to take offense, so there." Carol would think that that just redoubled the insult. Carol's flush, Tina's blush, and the ensuing apology suggest that what have been dubbed sentence meaning (roughly, what the audience actually does or should make of the speaker's language) and utterer meaning (roughly, what the speaker intended to convey in using it) are both crucial parts of everyday social life.[10] And Tina's apology is a reminder that she can be blameworthy for something she never intended to say or do.

We can even find meaning in strings of sentences cobbled together from different sources—and, trust me, I didn't put much thought into how I chose and ordered the sentences, so I don't deserve credit for a prose remix. (Not, anyway, if you want to reward only conscious effort.) Take the numbers off those eight sentences and it would be easy to read them as a poem in free verse. No, not a good one, but aesthetic merit and meaning aren't the same. Something treacly about the perils of life's sweets, the horrors of its seriousness, that sort of thing. Now try these:

1. It's a little cooler tonight.
2. SJL&P pr pfd 7% closed at 117.
3. I love you.
4. Torii are Japanese gateways or archways.
5. It is now eleven-twenty-nine P.M., Pacific Standard Time.

You can easily invent contexts to make sense of any one of these. Can you drop the numbers and read them together as a coherent assembly? At best, with difficulty. But these sentences were written in that order and without numbers by one author. They're the closing paragraph of one of Dashiell Hammett's early letters to Lillian Hellman.[11] Given Hammett's no-nonsense prose and persona, it's difficult to imagine any literary hijinks here. Unless you imagine him as a deadpan newscaster responding to specific idiosyncratic queries from Hellman, it's hard to find more in these sentences than a whimsical nod to the ineffable sentiment of that overworked third sentence. So this time we have one conscious author, a celebratedly gifted writer to boot, but that doesn't guarantee that we can find meaning

[10] Paul Grice, *Studies in the Way of Words* (Cambridge, MA: Harvard University Press, 1989), esp. pt. 1, remains crucial.

[11] Hammett to Hellman, [10 April 1931], in *Selected Letters of Dashiell Hammett 1921–1960*, ed. Richard Layman with Julie M. Rivett (Washington, DC: Counterpoint, 2000), p. 69.

in his words. Once again, we can prise apart meaning from author's intentions. Intention and meaning can be synonymous—"I didn't mean that!"
you cry after you trample on your hostess's formal evening gown and flinch
at the unmistakable buzz saw of the ripping seam—but they needn't even
be connected.

Meanwhile, consider the weird intricacies of animal behavior, at which
people have long marveled. Intent on erasing the apocalyptic divide between man and other animals, Darwin gladly reported on the "almost incredible amount of sagacity, caution and cunning" that American fur-
bearing animals displayed in avoiding traps.[12] A century ago, *Scientific
American* ran a piece on "The Cunning of Criminal Animals."[13] We can go
back many centuries more, not just to Aesop's fables but to sober studies.
Philo of Alexandria, a contemporary of Jesus, held that foxes deserved
their reputation for witty scheming, and added that even stupid monkeys
were clever enough to outwit others—and laugh at them. The male
Egyptian crocodile, he noted, flips the female over for copulation and then
flips her back. Now that she's impregnated, he continued, she gets mean—
so she sneakily flips herself over to invite more sex. The male sizes her up
to see if it's a sincere offer or if she's just hoping to eat him. "When the intent of the action is truly established by their looking into each other's
eyes"—do they scuttle to Aristotle and Theophrastus as reference books?—
"he claws her guts and consumes them, for they are tender."[14] With the
rudiments of evolutionary biology under our belts, we might wince at the
stupidity. The poor critter has just thrown away the chance to pass on his
genes. For Philo, though, the crafty male gets to top off the pleasures of
sex with a tasty meal. Whether he's cunning depends then on what ends
we attribute to him.

No wonder the fox has long been the emblem of cunning. You can't
capture one by ambush or with nets, cautioned Oppian sometime around
200 A.D. He added that the fox can cut through a rope and even untie a
knot. But other animals too, he explained, have their sly tricks. Craft or

---

[12] Charles Darwin, *The Descent of Man and Selection in Relation to Sex*, 2nd ed. rev., chap. 3.

[13] *Scientific American Supplement*, no. 1208 (25 February 1899). The piece reports the lightly
fictionalized incidents of Ernest Seton Thompson, *Wild Animals I Have Known* (New York,
1898).

[14] *Philonis Alexandrini De Animalibus*, trans. Abraham Terian (Chico, CA: Scholars Press,
1981), pp. 88, 90.

cunning, a weapon of the weak, is the divine inheritance of fish with no more obvious means of defense. The "cramp-fish" or electric ray may be slow and soft, but the predator that touches one of its rays immediately succumbs to paralytic languor. Then the cramp-fish devours the would-be predator: another biter bit. The crab cleverly sticks a pebble into the open oyster shell, waits for the helpless thing to die, and gluts himself. Fish deceive even seasoned fishermen. They wriggle off hooks and slip out of trawls. No wonder that it's so tempting to anthropomorphize other animals. The lobster, reported Oppian, bitterly resists leaving home and eagerly returns. Why not? It's just crustacean patriotism. Men, too, adore their birthplaces and bitterly rue their dishonored lives abroad as exiles.[15]

Are these animals cunning? Aristotle volunteered that the cuttlefish, which squirts its pigment when it wants to hide, is more cunning than the stupid octopus, which squirts pigment only out of fear.[16] Fair enough, but it's hard to think of any of these fish as plotting. Theirs are awfully small brains. But what about Philo's chuckling monkeys? What about the chimp who noticed but blithely ignored the grapefruits all the other chimps were frantically searching for and then returned to munch the treats at his leisure while the others were napping?[17] Surely he knew exactly what he was up to. We are not inclined to attribute any conscious strivings to the chameleon with its camouflage routines. But we do attribute plans to the canny Confederate general who managed with just six hundred troops to secure the surrender of almost seventeen hundred Union troops. He instructed men to bob up and down here and there shouldering his remaining two artillery pieces; eventually the Union colonel believed he had fifteen. He instructed other troops similarly to produce the phantom image of swarming extra units.[18] Between fish and primates, lizards and generals, are troubling cases where we're unsure what kind of consciousness, if any, is in play. If your cat saunters in clutching a half-dead mouse and lays the latent cadaver at your feet, is it deliberately reminding you of its lethal

---

[15] *Cynegetica*, IV.448–53; *Halieutica*, II.56–74, 167–80, III.92–97, I.273–79.

[16] *History of Animals*, bk. 9, 621b29.

[17] Frans de Waal, *Chimpanzee Politics: Power and Sex among Apes*, rev. ed. (Baltimore: Johns Hopkins University Press, 1998), p. 62.

[18] Jack Hurst, *Nathan Bedford Forrest: A Biography* (New York: Alfred A. Knopf, 1993), pp. 117–24. On military deception, see the priceless photographs in Jon Latimer, *Deception in War* (Woodstock, NY: Overlook Press, 2001).

skill? If so, is that a gesture of affection or tribute? Or a sly threat about your failure to feed it yesterday?

WRINKLES ON INTENTION

The musical composer who's intuitive, unconscious, even dead; the sentences spinning off meanings their authors were unaware of; the dimwitted animals whose actions strategically serve their interests: these cautionary examples remind us that we don't need the conscious self to stand behind significant or purposive action. Feldman's work can be cunning in ways he never intended or even recognized. Even the sentences of oblivious authors can be shrewdly meaningful. It's fun to think about what mental states we attribute to what animals and how reasonable we are in so doing. Regardless, evolution supplies a powerful model for cunning without consciousness.[19] When a biologist describes the strategy of a slime mold, it's pointless to complain that there's no strategizing going on inside. So too for what some evolutionary theorists have dubbed Machiavellian intelligence, animals' skills in dealing with other members of their own species.[20] Their actions can be deceitful even if they're not bravely struggling to learn how not to be good.

One molluscan parasite lives inside sea cucumbers. Biologists had thought the parasite genuinely hermaphroditic, but it turns out that the male organs belong to a tiny dwarf creature that permanently attaches itself to the much larger female, at which point almost all its organs disappear—except its testes, hard at work. Better yet for the tiny male's genes, once it's attached the female closes off other males' access.[21] Clever,

[19] For early cautions about attributing higher-level mental processes to animals to explain cunning behavior, see for instance W. L. Calderwood, "Cunning in Animals," *Natural Science* (December 1896) 9:380–85.

[20] For an introduction, see Richard W. Byrne, "Machiavellian Intelligence," *Evolutionary Anthropology* 5:5 (1996):172–80. *Machiavellian Intelligence: Social Expertise and the Evolution of Intellect in Monkeys, Apes, and Humans*, eds. Richard W. Byrne and Andrew Whiten (Oxford: Clarendon Press, 1988), reprints the classic papers by Nicholas K. Humphrey and Allison Jolly. *Machiavellian Intelligence II: Extensions and Evaluations*, eds. Andrew Whiten and Richard W. Byrne (Cambridge: Cambridge University Press, 1997), has more straight-on theory and less work in primatology.

[21] Stephen Jay Gould, *Hen's Teeth and Horse's Toes* (New York: W. W. Norton & Company, 1983), p. 25.

eh? But we are talking enormously small brains here, just rudimentary ganglia. If a cartoonist sketched the dwarf male lighting on this plan of attack, we'd giggle—not just ruefully at the sight of a male happy to reduce himself to his sex organs, but also cheerfully at the thought that such a creature could be thinking. More generally, cunning can attach to action or actor. We can describe an action as cunning without making any commitments to what the actor doing it intended or understood. Even when we call an actor cunning, as with other dispositional predicates, there's room for two interpretations.[22] We might mean that the actor is the kind—clairvoyant, on the lookout for shifty ways to advance her ends—who does cunning things; that is, we might refer to her internal structure. Or we might mean only that she does more cunning things than the average ordinary bear; that is, we might refer to the frequency with which the trait is manifested.

I'm still happy to grant that it's easiest to talk about cunning when there's self-conscious scheming. Another snapshot of a villain: Mme Thérèse Humbert grew up the eldest daughter of a modest farming family, but the gift of gab and a fertile imagination turned her into an American billionaire's illegitimate daughter, comfortably installed in the Olympian echelons of Parisian wealth and power, numbering presidents and prime ministers among her friends, dazzling one creditor after another. A disputed fortune was supposed to reside in a strongbox. The fortune didn't exist. Neither did its disputants, even if they did appear in lawsuits, woo Madame's sister with splendid gifts, and show up in impersonated person to propose marriage. At least the strongbox was real. Alas, eventually the Humberts were forced to open it, revealing not millions in bonds but "an old newspaper, an Italian coin, and a trouser button." Breathtaking stories of Humbert's powers unfolded at the ensuing criminal trial in 1903. Rumor had it that after Paul Schotmann had refused to extend the Humberts a second loan, one of Madame's brother's thugs shot him. Schotmann's brother Jean resolved that she'd have no more money from him and traveled from Lille to Paris to confront Madame. He departed after lending her two million francs—and agreeing to masquerade as a nonexistent Humbert uncle. "I admit I was dumbfounded, but my surprise was so great that I did not

---

[22] J. L. Mackie, *Truth Probability and Paradox: Studies in Philosophical Logic* (Oxford: Clarendon Press, 1973), pp. 120–48.

protest. Since then I have come to realize that I was playing a part in a play, but I still can't explain how it happened."[23] The chump had a spine of butter, you might think. But Mme Humbert had taken a gaggle of other seasoned businessmen and politicians for a long, strange ride, too, all of them ensnared in a web of illusions they now found convenient to brush off. I don't doubt that her conversation was arresting. But we should think too about the careful steps she took to lead others rationally to believe her tales, also about the snowball effect that made it easier for each new arrival on the scene to defer to the judgments of the ever-increasing swarm of distinguished characters who had adopted Humbert as one of their own.[24]

What was going on in Mme Humbert's head? She could have been plotting from the start. "Up before dawn, milking, mucking, mending: none of this miserable farm life for me! I'm headed for Paris, by hook or by crook." She could size up different strategies. "Ah, yes, there's a promising one, I'm supposed to inherit fabulous sums but the will is tied up in litigation." Maybe she could practice an economy of violence—unfortunate about the Schotmann death, but no way around it. Or maybe all that would register in such matters was the odds of her getting caught; maybe she wouldn't pause over murder's being wrong. When one does something for gain, one need not blush. If we picture Humbert as cool, methodical, we'll have no problems describing her as cunning.

But Humbert could have been sincere. Administer sodium pentothal or a Vulcan mind meld, ask a discerning crocodile to peer into her eyes, consult classical texts or early modern English pamphlets, deploy whatever fantastic technology you like to elicit her deepest convictions, and you'd find that she believed in the will and the wealth. She was more astonished than anyone else to see the coin and the button keeping one another meager company in her strongbox. Reeling in consternation, she wondered how one of the dastardly relatives contesting the will had managed to break open the lock and seal the strongbox shut again. Like the version of Lilly who believed in astrology, this sincere Humbert would do the same things the conniving one did. Why wouldn't she? If you had millions coming to you, you might live on credit and claw your way into high society,

[23] Hilary Spurling, *La Grande Thérèse: The Greatest Scandal of the Century* (New York: Harper-Collins, 2000), pp. 98, 119.

[24] For another way of bootstrapping yourself into epistemic authority, consider *The Life and Character of Harvey, the Famous Conjurer of Dublin* (Dublin, 1728).

too. So sincere Humbert's actions are cunning. Is sincere Humbert herself cunning? Then she's the cunning actor as artless dodger.

Now we want to know why she believed such a bunch of malarkey. Try a psychopathological account. Downtrodden by the hard routines of farm-work, sensitive young Humbert comforted herself with a dream world. These weren't her real parents, these filthy peasants reeking of leeks and swilling cheap red wine; oh no, her real father was absent but loving and powerful, in a word divine, enchantingly wealthy too, and he was looking after her—why, he'd bequeathed her millions. Someday she'd claim her in-heritance. Challenged, Thérèse would go glassy-eyed or mumble some-thing evasive. Her family learned to ignore her babbling. Their failure to discipline her, to force her to dwell in cold hard reality, gave her elastic room to elaborate on her fantasies in the otherwise taut domestic econ-omy. So now we have a sincere but delusional Humbert. Once we invoke the clinical categories, it's harder to hold her responsible. (Harder, not im-possible. Exasperated by the celebrity's antics, Hume indicted Rousseau as mad, cunning—"nothing so cunning as a Madman"—and still responsible for his actions.[25]) Some will say that she was lucky, not cunning. It's a fur-ther question whether her luck was good or bad even before her house of cards collapsed.

But Humbert's sincerity might not be delusional. It might be self-deceptive. It's difficult to explain how self-deception works, easy to lapse into a homunculus model, where a teeny you is sitting in front of some giant control panel, with all the parts of your body and many parts of your mind firing in signals and the teeny you slamming levers, pushing but-tons, making split-second decisions. The problem of course is the teeny you. If it's a smaller version of all of you, we have the usual regress: is there a teeny-tiny you sitting at a control panel inside teeny you? If it's not all of you, who or what is it? What's the part of yourself that decides to conceal something from another part of yourself? How does it manage the trick?

But it would be rash to deny the existence of self-deception just be-cause we don't command a cogent explanatory account. The phenomenon seems real enough. Nietzsche's example should make us wince in self-

[25] Hume to Anne-Robert-Jacques Turgot, [late September 1766], in *The Letters of David Hume*, ed. J.Y.T. Greig, 2 vols. (Oxford: Clarendon Press, 1932), 2:88–95.

recognition: memory testifies that you did it; pride stubbornly insists you couldn't have done it; memory capitulates.[26] Here belief is motivated by self-image. We can make sense of that without teeny you adjudicating between the claims of memory and pride.

In Humbert's case, self-deception could arise from a mix of repetition and experience. The repetition effect is an instance of the psychology of masks: embellish your lie with colorful details, tell it frequently enough, vigorously enough, and you start believing it yourself. Sound implausible? A more modest version has to be true: if you're given to filigree touches of hyperbole in recounting your favorite true stories, you'll lose the ability to distinguish what actually happened from your embroidery. The experience effect is another instance of what's slippery in the appearance/reality distinction. It follows on the heels of the Arabella effect. As Mme Humbert spins her fictions of untold riches, those around her start treating her accordingly. Next thing you know, she is wealthy. There's the Arabella effect—their false beliefs cause them to act in ways that make their beliefs true—but this time with a twist: Arabella's interlocutors were humoring her, but these people are dead serious. What a coup for Humbert! It is the tongue that wins and not the deed. Now Humbert, originator of the fantasy, looks out and sees it mirrored back at her as real. So shouldn't she too believe in it? There's the experience effect: a good empiricist, she trusts the evidence of her own senses. She may hear a shrill small voice within: "Thérèse, honestly, you know very well who your real father is and what's in that strongbox." Mustn't that voice have enough authority to push aside the weighty integuments of her posh life, the massive tapestries, the elaborate hats she became famous for? Here we can invoke Nietzsche's suggestion. Humbert's self-righteous conviction of her inability to commit such a pernicious fraud can silence memory's scolding.

So now we have three Humberts to appraise. Self-consciously scheming Humbert? Unambiguously cunning. Sincere and delusional Humbert? Probably not. Sincere and self-deceived Humbert? For reasons I've glanced at already, I'm inclined to say she's even more cunning than the self-conscious schemer. It has to be easier for her to lie convincingly when she believes the lies herself. Then, too, there is the extra layer of crookedness, of indirection, that we associate with cunning: no straight and obvious

---

[26] *Beyond Good and Evil*, pt. 4, §68.

approaches for any cunning operator, unless others expect crookedness, which makes straight crooked. Yet I'm also inclined to think she's less blameworthy than the self-conscious schemer. Is it invidiously paradoxical to describe her as more cunning but less blameworthy?

We can press further by asking, how does Humbert launch her career of self-deception? Suppose there were some arcane process she could voluntarily trigger to induce self-deception. (Recall the image of Odysseus deliberately whipping himself into a berserk frenzy, rationally plunging into irrationality, the better to seem the purely vindictive or backward-looking avenger.) Carefully weighing the costs and benefits, she decides that the most promising strategy for realizing her illicit ends is to pull the trigger, so she does. Now we have the most lethal Humbert of all, a witch's brew of blameworthy intentions and virtuoso cunning performance. Suppose instead that Humbert doesn't know that she's triggering the process, but she should know. In such cases, we ordinarily affix blame. We wouldn't blame her if it just happened to her, by surprise, and she couldn't reasonably anticipate and protect herself against it. Now we have three versions of the sincere but self-deceiving Humbert: the one who knows she's launching a career of self-deception, the one who doesn't know but should know, and the one who couldn't reasonably be expected to know. All of them, remember, perform cunning actions. Are they all cunning actors?

What's at stake in the question? If it's just the meaning of the word, nothing worth sneezing at. Peer behind the linguistic question and ask what we might care about, what might be troubling, in assessing Humbert and her deeds. First, we might be wondering whether to blame Humbert. If she has behaved wrongly but it is hard to locate any moment when she could and should have acted differently, it will be hard to blame her. She'll look like a tragic victim. Still, we might want to hold her responsible in the sense of punishing her. (If—another linguistic hiccup—you balk at calling it punishment if she isn't blameworthy, say instead we might want to incapacitate her.) We might think it too dangerous to allow such a woman to prowl the streets. Second, we might be wondering whether she's a trustworthy partner. Obviously she's not. We should steer clear regardless of which version of Humbert she actually is. Here our worries about her responsibility are irrelevant. We don't take in rabid dogs and we don't waste time investigating how they contracted their rabies. Well, but you can try to cure the rabid dog, right? So third, we might be sizing up strategies for reforming her. Which strategies are sensible will depend on what causes her cunning behavior.

Certain plays and novels are supposed to render others' motivations transparent to us. It's one thing for me to offer a gallery of splintered Humberts and invite your assessment of each. But the actual Humbert didn't come with a name tag guaranteeing just which splinter she was. So sweep up the splinters, remind me that they all perform the same hideous escapades, and decree that cunning is as cunning does, that every one of them is cunning. If you like. But then, too, it is an embarrassing mistake to imagine that our own mental states are transparent. We can be deeply confused about what we're up to and why. Cartesian dogma aside, we can even have better insight into others' mental states than we have into our own. Our friend thinks he's in love, but we know it's nothing but lust. At the same time, we're sure we're in love, but we're wrong. We're just melodramatically making our humdrum lives more interesting than they actually are.

That suggests another problem with the time-honored story about knaves and fools. You can play the part of a rogue while steadfastly convinced of your good intentions. It overstates the case to say that every upright man has a knave in his sleeve. Still, think about all the times when your decent, honorable, principled pursuits turned out to redound to your interests, even in surprising ways. Not that anything that redounds to your interests is objectionable. Rather think about the possibility that all that decent, honorable, principled stuff is purely pretextual, that you've pulled the wool over your own eyes, and that were it not for the obscure links to your own interests, you'd never have pursued those courses of action in the first place. Don't let yourself off the hook here any more easily than you do your enemies. Remember how you marvel at their apparent obliviousness to what rogues they are? how you fume contemplating their confidently meeting others' eyes? Maybe you're not immune to such fatuous self-satisfaction. Think about how genuinely shocked you would be to hear others indict your actions as shabby, unseemly, cutting corners. Your being shocked is no guarantee that they'd be wrong. Blundering knave and confused fool at once, you'd have managed to deceive yourself but not them.

The core case of cunning, the nyaah-ha-ha villain well aware of both his elaborate plots and how nasty they are, is much rarer than we think. So claims George Eliot, and I think she's right:

There is nothing more widely misleading than sagacity if it happens to get on a wrong scent, and sagacity persuaded that men usually act and speak from distinct motives, with a consciously proposed end in view, is certain to waste its energies on imaginary game. Plotting covetousness and deliberate contrivance in order to compass a selfish end, are nowhere abundant but in the world of the dramatist: they demand too intense a mental action for many of our fellow-parishioners to be guilty of them. It is easy enough to spoil the lives of our neighbors without taking so much trouble: we can do it by lazy acquiescence and lazy omission, by trivial falsities for which we hardly know a reason, by small frauds neutralized by small extravagances, by maladroit flatteries and clumsily improvised insinuations. We live from hand to mouth, most of us, with a small family of immediate desires—we do little else than snatch a morsel to satisfy the hungry brood, rarely thinking of seed-corn or the next year's crop.[27]

Eliot is not charitably letting us off the hook. Hers is a sly but somber moralism. Too lazy to rise or stoop to calculating roguery, we still spray a lot of harm in our wake, harm arguably all the more momentous for our dispensing it callously, sleepily, unawares. We're blameworthy if we could and should summon up the energies to see ourselves more clearly and behave better. If we're portioning out blame and praise, shouldn't we award those stage villains bonus points for their own integrity, a relentless honesty about themselves? Or should we blame them or their playwrights for implicitly flattering us, letting us persist in our complacent illusions—imagine the chorus, in unison now: oh, I'm not like that, not at all!—so that we can stride out of the theater with renewed confidence in our good intentions? Do stage villains and their occasional real-life versions, like dear Christain Agor, stutteringly eager for my aid in carting his millions out of Nigeria, then encourage the rest of us in our less conscious knavery? Do the clumsy knaves who can't even carry off their plots do the same? "Why, what a dunce you are!" sneers the intimidating district attorney as Clyde Griffiths sweats in miserable anxiety, "—what a poor plotter, without even the brains not to use your own initials in getting up those

[27] *The Mill on the Floss*, bk. 1, chap. 3. Compare Aung San Suu Kyi, *Letters from Burma* (London: Penguin, 1997), p. 131.

fake names you had hoped to masquerade under—Mr. Carl Graham—
Mr. Clifford Golden!"[28] No, you're not the sort who would head out to
murder your pregnant girlfriend and blunder so spectacularly. Should you
leap to the inference that your own blunders and complacencies don't conceal less lethal nastiness?

So our grasp of motives and intentions—our own as much as others'—
is uncertain, even feeble. That's one reason it's hard to figure out who's
cunning. Another is that we dispute the worth of different ends. Augustine borrows a story from Cicero about an exchange between Alexander
the Great and a pirate. What, demands Alexander, do you mean by plaguing the seas? Why, responds the pirate, just what you do in beleaguering
the earth. With my one boat, the pirate continues, I'm a robber; with your
navy, you're an emperor. Augustine's inference is that unless political rule is
just, the pirate is dead right and kingdoms are nothing but robbery on a
grand scale.[29] But that will make our assessment of Alexander's cunning
depend in part on the justice of his rule, a subject on which we should expect sustained debate. Augustine's inference aside, the pirate's view that
nothing succeeds like success is disturbing.

The pirate's challenge resounds through the centuries and allows the
knaves to turn the tables, indicting their accusers for employing the same
cunning tactics the knaves do. In 1592, Cuthbert Cunny-catcher vigorously
defended petty thieves.[30] (A cunny or conny or cony or coney is a rabbit or
dupe, his catcher then the knave who skins him alive.) "We Conny-
catchers," he protested, "are like little flies in the grass, which live [on] little leaves and do no more harm: whereas there be in England other profes-
sions that be great Conny-catchers and caterpillars, that make barren the
field wherein they bait." Usurers charge exorbitant interest, millers surrep-
titiously steal fine flour, retail merchants use false weights, butchers tamper
with meat to make it look better than it is, drapers keep their shops dark to
disguise the flaws in their wares, vintners dilute wine, tailors stash away extra material while working on garments, and more: one "vile and injurious
caterpillar" after another, all masquerading as upright members of society,
all audacious or smug enough to look down on conny-catchers—and nary

---

[28] Theodore Dreiser, *An American Tragedy*, bk. 3, chap. 9.

[29] *De re publica*, III.xiv.24; *City of God*, bk. 4, chap. 4.

[30] Cuthbert Cunny-catcher, *The Defence of Conny Catching* (London, 1592).

a one able to succeed without indulging in some conny-catching of his own. He who does not cheat does not advance. He doesn't even survive. So, too, "Your Tradesmen have their Mysteries," conceded Thomas Allen in 1616. The word then doubled as trade secrets, but Adams promptly alluded to stirring biblical imagery. "Mysteries indeed, for the mystery of Iniquity is in them: they have a stock of good Words, to put off a stock of bad Wares: in their particular qualities they are able to school *Machiavell*."[31] The bourgeoisie haven't always been ridiculed as sedate, domestic, effeminate.

In his own pirate tales, Defoe offered a complex biter-bit dilemma. One Avery proposed to the pirates of some smaller sloops that for safety's sake he should take their treasure on board his stronger, faster ship. They agreed. Then he urged the pirates on his ship to abandon the others and hustle away with all the treasure. They set sail at night; "nor do I find that any of them felt any Qualms of Honour rising in his Stomach, to hinder them from consenting to this Piece of Treachery." Back in England with fabulous if ill-gotten riches, Avery decided to cash in his chips and retire. But how could he sell his gold and diamonds without provoking awkward inquiries? A friend served as intermediary with some Bristol merchants, who gave him a small advance payment and relieved him of his plunder. Curiously, the rest of his promised money dribbled out to him slowly in minuscule amounts. So Avery went to Bristol to confront the merchants, "where instead of Money he met a most shocking Repulse, for when he desired them to come to an Account with him they silenced him by threatening to discover him," that is, to reveal his identity, "so that our Merchants, were as good Pirates at Land as he was at Sea."[32] As good or as bad? Were they obliged to try to restore the wealth to its rightful owners? Or at least to turn it over to government authorities? What if those authorities might well have cheerfully pocketed it? It wouldn't have surprised Defoe, who also invited the reader to condemn the glib rationalizations of yet another pirate band, who "sat down to spend the Fruits of their dishonest Industry, dividing the Spoil and Plunder of their Fellow-Creatures

[31] Thomas Adams, *The Sacrifice of Thankefulnesse* (London, 1616), p. 58; see 2 Thessalonians 2:7.

[32] Captain Charles Johnson [Daniel Defoe], *A General History of the Robberies and Murders of the Most Notorious Pyrates, and Also Their Policies, Discipline, and Government* (London, 1724), pp. 32–36.

among themselves, without the least Compunction or Remorse for what they had done; satisfying their Consciences with this Salvo, that other People would have done the same Things, if they had had equal Courage, and the like Opportunities." Then Defoe wheeled and jabbed at some prestigious profiteers we've already encountered. "I can't say, but that if they had known what was doing in *England*, at the same Time, by the *South-Sea* Directors, and other Persons, they would certainly have had this Reflection for their Consolation, *viz. That Whatever Murders and Robberies they had committed, they were not the greatest Villains that were then living in the World.*"[33] Criminals, merchants, statesmen: rogues one and all.

Defoe wasn't alone in bewailing the state of England in the early 1700s. Pope charted the triumph of vice:

In Soldier, Churchman, Patriot, Man in Pow'r,
'Tis Av'rice all, Ambition is no more!
See, all our Nobles begging to be Slaves!
See, all our Fools aspiring to be Knaves!
The Wit of Cheats, the Courage of a Whore,
Are what ten thousand envy and adore:
All, all look up, with reverential Awe,
At Crimes that 'scape, or triumph o'er the Law:
While Truth, Worth, Wisdom, daily they decry—
"Nothing is Sacred now but Villainy."
    Yet may this Verse (if such a Verse remain)
Show, there was one who held it in disdain.[34]

No wonder he addressed his jeremiad to posterity. In a world avidly pursuing cunning, what else could he do?

Maybe Defoe, Pope, and the period's other naysayers were just cranky. Maybe prime minister Walpole's Robinocracy was great and glorious, England thriving, and Mandeville wrong to uncover the links between com-

---

[33] *General History*, p. 142. Compare A Jobber [Defoe?], *The Anatomy of Exchange-Alley: or, A System of Stock-Jobbing* (London, 1719), pp. 16–25, for the argument that self-interested "jobbers" or stockbrokers, playing havoc with public finances, are essentially traitors.

[34] Alexander Pope, "Epilogue to the Satires," Dialogue 1, ll. 161–72. See Peter Dixon, *The World of Pope's Satires: An Introduction to the Epistles and Imitations of Horace* (London: Methuen, 1968), esp. pp. 100–105.

mercial greatness and vice. But surely some societies are dreadfully corrupt. Today an outfit named Transparency International publishes a Global Corruption Barometer and other materials of dispiriting interest to businessmen and investors, human rights activists, and melancholy observers of the human condition.[35] Suppose tossing literary bottles, mournful messages enclosed, into the oceans of time isn't your thing. If you live in such a society—and many millions today do, and sometimes we may be among them; our policemen too have been known to sell drugs, run protection rackets, pummel their critics; I say nothing of our adorable elected officials—do you want to risk being the cully of your integrity? Or do you want to learn how to dirty your hands, how not to be good?

Fantasies of Detachment

The question sometimes gets framed as if rationality and self-interest were concrete but obligations were ethereal phantoms no one should fear. Young Hegelian Max Stirner, hero of individualist anarchists, defiantly swept aside all kinds of obligations: "What is not supposed to be my concern! First and foremost the Good Cause, then God's cause, the cause of mankind, of truth, of freedom, of humanity, of justice; further, the cause of my people, my prince, my fatherland; finally, even the cause of Mind, and a thousand other causes. Only *my* cause is never to be my concern." Stirner would have none of these pernicious abstractions. "Away, then, with every concern that is not altogether my concern!"[36] But the idea that self-interest is real, obligations evanescent, begs one question after another.

We can start thinking about your rights and obligations as partly given by the social roles you occupy. A role, that is, a position within some institution (say, CEO's secretary), or, to extend the scope of the concept, a social position that by conventional understanding is reasonably clearly structured (say, street-corner preacher), is defined by a set of rights and obligations. To be a teacher is to be entitled to lecture a semi-captive audience and to

---

[35] See www.transparency.org.

[36] Max Stirner, *The Ego and His Own*, trans. Steven T. Byington (New York: Benj. R. Tucker, 1907), pp. 3, 6.

interrupt yourself to ask the students questions. To be a teacher is also to be obliged to prepare for class and to meet with students having problems with the material. When societies are corrupt, plenty of others aren't adhering to the rights and obligations of their roles. They're pocketing bribes and taking kickbacks, selling documents supposed to remain confidential, using the Internal Revenue Service to hassle their political opponents. The indignation we summon up at such scoundrels, the very vocabulary in which we assail them—a bribe is simply a payment they're not entitled to—registers their departure from the conventional understanding of their roles. The question "Should you join them?" is then a question of whether you too should flout the rights and obligations supposed to attach to your roles.

I say start thinking about your rights and obligations, not finish, because there is more to it than that. We can always criticize the conventional understanding of some role. The claim that it's wrong for overseers to whip slaves isn't rebutted by the reminder that administering those whippings is a right, even an obligation, of the role. Then too, there are moral issues that don't arise in any straightforward way from the roles you occupy. For instance, how much of your income and wealth should you give to the poor? These points are vital, but they don't mean we should drift away from the sociological landscape and pretend to entertain freefloating speculations about the right and the good.

Instead, contrast two ways of occupying a role. You can take its obligations for granted, even internalize them. If you're a father, say, you take care of your children, play with them, review their homework, and so on, because that is what fathers are supposed to do, even if sometimes they don't like it, even if they have other things they'd rather do. Or you can take the role's obligations as alienated social facts and then wonder whether you should comply with them. That latter stance, another version of instrumental rationality, can be nauseating. We recoil at the father who thinks, "I guess I should take an interest in my children, I mean after all I am their father, probably it is a good thing on balance for parents to care for children, it has socially useful payoffs; I wonder what payoffs would accrue to me if I did things these other dads do, like show up to soccer games; I wonder what costs I'll incur if I keep ignoring them." We recoil even at the father who thinks, "I should go watch my children play soccer because that is the right thing for a father to do." We don't want deliberation, or at least that kind of deliberation.[37] Deliberation about how to navigate conflicts among obligations is another matter. Ordinarily, though, we want the obligations to be so thoroughly internalized that they no longer feel like obligations; we want the agent to cultivate dispositions that make the relevant actions enjoyable. In a similar vein, notice what's defective in the hyperrational agent, a caricature of Kantian autonomy, who wants to deliberate about everything. "Should I molest this innocent child in the park? No, that would be wrong." He has a defective character if such possibilities routinely occur to him in the first place, even if he promptly rejects them.

The cunning man excels in detachment from his social roles, from the demands of morality, from any requirement that stands in his way. Odysseus thumbs his nose at justice and honor, principles that help define what it means to be a hero. If he needs Philoctetes's bow, he'll trick him. If he wants to kill Trojan soldiers, he'll slink out at night and slit their throats as they snore. Those aghast at this hero's decidedly unheroic ways think they have a weighty complaint. He'll probably see them as chumps all the more ready to be deceived by their unthinking belief that he will play the heroic game by its official rules. (Or he might launch a flank attack of Machiavellian rhetoric. Heroes, he could remind them acerbically, are also supposed to prevail come what may. So the lexicon of heroism is internally incoherent and they ought to junk their commitments to justice and honor.) Think of the cunning man as the fellow who sees "Do Not Trespass" signs as decoys for the unsuspecting, even as invitations promising attractive surprises. Or think of him as the man who picks and chooses, who's opportunistic, even unscrupulous, in some roles, faithful and reliable in others. Recall Dr. Johnson's unruffled suggestion that the lawyer sheds his apparent facile dishonesty as he leaves the courtroom. Or ponder Whopper, imprisoned in nineteenth-century America and introduced here in another criminal's colorful autobiography:

---

[37] Compare Bernard Williams's influential and provocative views—see especially the treatment of integrity in J.J.C. Smart and Bernard Williams, *Utilitarianism: For and Against* (Cambridge: Cambridge University Press, 1973), pp. 108–18, and the worry about "one thought too many" in "Persons, Character, and Morality," in Williams, *Moral Luck: Philosophical Papers 1973–1980* (Cambridge: Cambridge University Press, 1981), p. 18, with Peter Railton, "Alienation, Consequentialism, and the Demands of Morality," *Philosophy & Public Affairs* 13:2 (Spring 1984):134–71.

I am now about to make a statement that may appear a strange one to some readers. It is that this pickpocket—this jail and prison-bird—*was a man of honor*. He had adopted crime as a profession, and was as proud of it as any honest tradesman is of his own occupation. Outside of that he was perfectly reliable, his advice being sought by those in his own line, who placed unbounded confidence in his honesty. He was very particular to conceal his mode of life from his family, to whom he was a kind husband and father, having taught his children to be scrupulously honest; and they are to-day respectable and thriving tradesmen in London. They never discovered, until after I became acquaintanced with him, that their father had been engaged in any dishonorable business, or had been in jail and prison.[38]

Whopper's pride in his criminal enterprises might be that of any other expert practitioner. But he wasn't all that expert; after all, he landed in jail. More likely, I think, is that he knew his crimes enabled him to support his family, not just to procure filthy lucre but to pose as the man of the house, no, actually to be the man of the house, to radiate kindness, to dispense proper moral education, to establish his children in gainful employment and respectable society, feats he might never have been able to pull off had he been a virtuous but unemployed worker. Crime and a stint in jail? A price any loving father would pay gladly, his cunning both in picking pockets and in maintaining appearances at home the farthest thing from base self-interest. I bet that like many another father, Whopper welcomed his arduous sacrifices as guaranteeing his children a boost into easier lives.

Did Whopper's children know him? There he was, in the flesh, but he was invisible, leading another life they never caught a glimpse of. If you were literally invisible, what could you do? What would you do? H. G. Wells's prototype is a scientist captivated by "a magnificent vision of all that invisibility might mean to a man,—the mystery, the power, the freedom." But he discovers that he's committed to "judicious slaying" and a "Reign of Terror" in order to survive.[39] Ralph Ellison's model, enraged and doomed in his romance with a thinly veiled U.S. Communist Party, is terrified the first time he will take the lectern by the realization that he'd gain

---

[38] *Forging His Chains: The Autobiography of George Bidwell* (Chicago, 1888), p. 514.

[39] H. G. Wells, *The Invisible Man*, chaps. 19, 24.

a new identity, a real one, not just the false name assigned him by his radical overseers. "Not just a nobody with a manufactured name which might
have belonged to anyone, or to no one. But another personality." But he
learns that the notoriety he gains as passionate advocate dissolves the moment he puts on a hat and sunglasses. Then he looks like Rinehart, a flashy
criminal. "They see the hat, not me. There is a magic in it. It hides me
right in front of their eyes." Later, he discovers that Rinehart poses as a
reverend, a "spiritual technologist" promising in handbills to let his audience "Behold the Invisible." Entering the storefront church, he is over-
whelmed. "The world in which we lived was without boundaries. A vast
seething, hot world of fluidity, and Rine the rascal was at home. Perhaps
only Rine the rascal was at home in it. It was unbelievable, but perhaps
only the unbelievable could be believed. Perhaps the truth was always a
lie." Closing his gutwrenching tale, he confesses that he's been "hurt to the
point of abysmal pain, hurt to the point of invisibility."[40]

Tales of invisibility haven't always provoked such vertigo. In one medieval Japanese tale, some men figure out how dried mistletoe can make
them invisible: "Now these three men did just as they pleased: they stuck
charms for invisibility into their hair and went into the King's palace and
violated the royal ladies." The king managed to find them. Realizing that
even invisible men leave footprints, he sprinkled rice powder through the
palace corridors.[41] In one folktale from the Chuan Miao of western China,
a man gets hold of an invisible cloak. He quickly escalates from piling up
wealth to getting the emperor's daughter pregnant.[42]

There are all too many closely connected stories; I'll restrict myself to
three. In a Punjab tale, Prince Bahrmâgor yearns for his fairy princess wife,
locked in the innermost of seven nested prisons. Wearing a *yech*-cap sup-
plied by an obliging demon, the prince is invisible. He manages to slip his
way in to reclaim her—and dislodges the cap only far enough to appear to
her as a ghost before his embrace throws her into raptures.[43] In another In-

---

[40] Ralph Ellison, *Invisible Man* (New York: Random House, 1982), pp. 254, 366, 376, 437.

[41] *Konjaku monogatari shū*, in Marian Ury, *Tales of Times Now Past: Sixty-Two Stories from a Medieval Japanese Collection* (Berkeley, CA: University of California Press, 1979), p. 50.

[42] David Crockett Graham, *Songs and Stories of the Ch'uan Miao*, in *Smithsonian Miscellaneous Collections* 123:1 (8 April 1954):219.

[43] "The Faithful Prince," in Flora Annie Steel, *Tales of the Punjab: Told by the People* (London, 1894).

dian tale, a fakir gives a prince a magic ring of invisibility to help him solve the mystery of his wife's seven veils and nightly absences. He follows her and discovers she's a gorgeous fairy. But he forgets the fakir's caution and tells her about the ring. She unveils herself one last time and flies off for good.[44] In a shocking 1796 English novel of sex and intrigue in the church, Matilda poses as a young man and spirits herself into a monastery. She seduces the monk Ambrosio, despite his reputation for great holiness. Ditching her, he lusts after Antonia. Still Ambrosio's friend, Matilda bends Lucifer to her will. With the myrtle she gives the depraved monk, locked doors will be no barricades. He can use it to make his way into Antonia's chamber, "then breathe upon it thrice, pronounce her name, and place it upon her pillow." She will descend into a deep sleep and he can ravish her without her budging in protest. But it doesn't work out quite that way. Antonia's mother interrupts him, he murders her, and Matilda turns out to be the devil.[45] In a recent novel, Arno Strine can stop time— for everyone else. What does he like to do when he stops time? Well, no, he has his reservations about rape. But he undresses women, fondles them, masturbates. "I know that I could probably make much better use of my gift than I do," he admits; "government secrets, technological espionage, etc." No doubt Bach used his gift to write more cantatas. But he does what he does.[46]

Why do these tales of invisibility take this shape? The psychoanalytically inclined will remind us of the prince's manhandling Fortuna, of Callimaco's rollicking his way to sexual conquest and bliss, and suggest that seduction or rape—or, better, that blurry border between the two—is the primal scene of cunning. Whatever we make of that suggestion, the invisible man is detached from every social role. Why shouldn't he grab some sex with a desirable woman? Well, what's so great about having sex with a woman who doesn't want to be having sex with him, who can't even see him, who might even be sleeping? Okay, so change his magic spell. It will make him not invisible but the spitting image of whomever she'd most like

---

[44] "The Perfumer's Daughter," pt. 1, in Mark Thornhill, *Indian Fairy Tales* (London, 1888).

[45] Matthew Lewis, *The Monk*, chaps. 7–8.

[46] Nicholson Baker, *The Fermata* (New York: Random House, 1994), p. 22. For a provocative romp on an adjacent body of material, see Wendy Doniger, *The Bedtrick: Tales of Sex and Masquerade* (Chicago: University of Chicago Press, 2000).

to have passionate sex with. And it will make her readily aroused while he's at it. Then she'll be responsive, not inert. Anything wrong with that? Well, again, what matters is not just the ends he attains, but how he attains them. If he tricks a woman into sleeping with him, it's not as good as if he doesn't trick her. And there's a sense in which she isn't sleeping with him: a precious mutuality is missing.[47] But now suppose the trickster fires back, "yes, but my choice isn't between sex on my sneaky terms and sex on your high-minded terms of mutual clear-sighted consent. My choice is between groping this beautiful body and no sex at all." Is he better off not groping?

The invisible man is a fantasy, an appearance, no, not even that, a lack of an appearance. However fictive and shadowless his existence, though, he captures something real, because there are actual occasions on which people can go on holiday, depart from the demands of their everyday roles, and be confident they won't be caught. Recall Lady Mary's fornicating Schemers. The invisible man is also close kin to the shapeshifter who adopts Odysseus's slogan—as the occasion demands, such a one am I—as his own. That needn't be mythological. The cunning man, doing what it takes to realize his ends, holding his obligations at arm's length, in the social world but not quite of it, is protean, for sure, but he's as familiar as your next-door neighbor, indeed as yourself in the mirror, at least in some moods, at some moments, for some purposes. Recall the fellow selling groceries wholesale and his mocking the thought that he was stuck in a rut. Or take this 1889 account of another professional shapeshifter of everyday life:

> The detective must be able to adapt himself to all circumstances of time, place and society. He should be able to talk intelligently upon, and show some degree of familiarity with all trades and professions. There is no field of knowledge that may not at some time become practically useful to him. He must be all things to all men; a gentleman among gentlemen; a tough among bummers. He must be as familiar with the slang of thieves and low people as he is with the elegant phrases of polite society.

[47] See Simon Blackburn, *Lust: The Seven Deadly Sins* (Oxford: Oxford University Press, 2004), esp. chap. 10.

He fakes it nonchalantly, unlike the real gentleman or real tough wracked with doubt about his ability to perform competently.[48] Not shouldering the burdens of actually belonging in the role, he may well find it easier to render his performance persuasive. There's another wrinkle on the appearance/reality distinction: the fake gentleman carries himself elegantly enough to look real; the real gentleman stumbles and looks fake. And then another paradox for Plutarch: the real gentleman is the one whose manners seem inelegant, overdone, ungentlemanly. Then, too, the detective must be a master of masks:

> One of the first requisites of a good detective is perfect self-control. This should be both mental and physical, as far as possible. Control of the mind should extend to the suppression of the passions, anger, joy, fear; to the habit of composed and rapid thought under exciting and trying circumstances; to mental versatility in diverting attention from a danger point, or leading the conversation skillfully and without apparent design to a desired subject and eliciting information thereon. Physical control should extend principally to facial expression, although cases frequently arise in which many physical infirmities must be simulated. The face must sometimes express joy and delight when the real feeling of the mind is one of disgust and aversion. Intense hate must sometimes frown from the face when the real feeling behind it is that of admiration and love. Words, conduct and facial expression must be consistent, otherwise a charge of insincerity will be preferred by people whose observation would not ordinarily be considered acute.[49]

In this account, the role of detective is not a blank check, but it licenses a lot. One supposes the detective is loyal to his clients, intrepid in tracking down criminals. But within those toothless constraints, he not only can but must be a great pretender. An accomplished social actor, he revels in as-if games, ironic quotation marks invisibly bracketing his every sentence, every gesture. Surrounded by bullets and betrayal, he can't afford attachment.

---

[48] See William Ian Miller, *Faking It* (Cambridge: Cambridge University Press, 2003).

[49] *Grannan's Warning against Fraud and Valuable Information* (Cincinnati, OH, 1889), pp. 206, 207.

There are other ways to be a detective—Mycroft Holmes and Nero Wolfe were too corpulent to stir themselves, let alone be masters of masquerade. But the 1889 account isn't idiosyncratic in fastening on detachment. As detective Black ferrets out information, he relies on "his usual facility for playing fictitious roles."[50] The detective's moral ambiguity, much remarked on, his serving as carnival mirror twin to the cunning criminal, is wrapped up in this sociological detachment. The authors of the classic American detective stories dramatized this eerie detachment, too. Dashiell Hammett's Continental Op doesn't even merit a name, though we know he's short and fat. Take the self-description Raymond Chandler puts in Marlowe's mouth:

> I'm a lone wolf, unmarried, getting middle-aged, and not rich.
> I've been in jail more than once and I don't do divorce business.
> I like liquor and women and chess and a few other things. The cops
> don't like me too well, but I know a couple I get along with. I'm a
> native son, born in Santa Rosa, both parents dead, no brothers
> or sisters, and when I get knocked off in a dark alley sometime, if it
> happens, as it could to anyone in my business, and to plenty of
> people in any business or no business at all these days, nobody will
> feel that the bottom has dropped out of his or her life.[51]

Or again, in one dour moment (but you wouldn't be too happy either if someone sank an ice pick into your back and the cops rewarded you with a drubbing):

> I was a blank man. I had no face, no meaning, no personality,
> hardly a name.[52]

Yet again, returning to his office after the bitter end of another case:

> The room was stuffy and dull and impersonal as always. I opened
> a couple of windows and mixed a drink in the kitchen. I sat down
> on the couch and stared at the wall. Wherever I went, whatever I

[50] "No Motive," in Daphne du Maurier, *The Rendezvous and Other Stories* (London: Victor Gollancz, 1980), p. 34.

[51] *The Long Goodbye*, chap. 13, in Raymond Chandler, *Later Novels and Other Writing* (New York: Library of America, 1995), p. 493.

[52] *The Little Sister*, chap. 25, in Chandler, *Later Novels*, p. 354.

did, this was what I would come back to. A blank wall in a
meaningless room in a meaningless house.[53]

The magical reappearance by telephone of Linda Loring, with whom
Marlowe once had a brief adoring encounter, promises to relieve that te-
dium. She's on her way and the novel quits. Happy prospects beckon,
right? Chandler did begin drafting a novel where the two were married,
but his heavy drinking killed him before he could finish it.[54] I find it hard
to imagine any happily-ever-after loving relationship. Marlowe seems in
his element with one-off sexual encounters, no more, and Chandler knew
it. He once scribbled in a notebook, "A really good detective never gets
married. He would lose his detachment, and this detachment is part of his
charm."[55] (Want to be charming?) He expressed more specific reservations
about marrying off Marlowe. "I feel that your idea that he should be married, even to a very nice girl, is quite out of character. I see him always in a
lonely street, in lonely rooms, puzzled but never quite defeated."[56]

These examples suggest a blunt moral: role identification is good, role
distance bad. But that can't be right. If some role requires loathsome actions, stepping back and scrutinizing its demands should be embraced as
autonomy, not indicted as alienation. Unless we cling to some odd story
about the guaranteed larger rationality of society and history,[57] we can't be
confident that the demands of our roles are acceptable. But the problem
isn't just that you might do something loathsome if you don't appraise the
demands of your role. Suppose you somehow knew that your role would
never require you to do anything wrong or even slightly disreputable.
(Suppose someone you trusted assured you that that was true and you had
no reason to doubt her.) Or suppose you doubted your own ability to distinguish the occasions on which your role was requiring you to do wrong
and thought that on balance you'd do best if you never questioned it. Still,
there is something weirdly mechanical in doing what you're supposed to

---

[53] *Playback*, chap. 28, in Chandler, *Later Novels*, pp. 869–70.

[54] For the fragment of *The Poodle Springs Story*, see *Raymond Chandler Speaking*, ed. Dorothy
Gardiner and Kathrine Sorley Walker (Plainview, NY: Books for Libraries Press, 1962),
pp. 253–64.

[55] "Twelve Notes on the Mystery Story," in Chandler, *Later Novels*, p. 1008.

[56] Chandler to Maurice Guinness, 21 February 1959, in *Speaking*, p. 249.

[57] So for instance Bradley's reception of Hegel: "My Station and Its Duties," in F. H. Bradley,
Ethical Studies, 2nd ed. (Oxford: Clarendon Press, 1927), pp. 160–206.

do just because you're supposed to do it—even if the examined life isn't so hot, either. Then too we have holy images of radical role distance. Jesus relentlessly spurns family ties. Not only does he brush off Joseph and his mother, responding to their sorrow at missing him by briskly demanding, "How is it that ye sought me? wist ye not that I must be about my Father's business?" He also insists more generally—and ominously—that "If any man come to me, and hate not his father, and mother, and wife, and children, and brethren, and sisters, yea, and his own life also, he cannot be my disciple."[58] This ultimatum underlines what's at stake in a Christian renunciation of this world, which remains part of the tradition. John Bunyan's Christian abandons his family to pursue his salvation, racing off with fingers stuck in his ears and nary a backwards glimpse, to avoid their importunate cries. Instead Christian and his compatriots adopt voluntary or fictive kinship relations, saluting their fellow believers as brother and sister.[59]

It's hopeless to say anything sweeping or wholesale about the merits of role identification and role distance. We also need to distinguish different styles of identifying with, immersing ourselves in, roles. I don't know whether to laugh or cry—smirking is too easy—at the language of a 1956 company guide to organizing Tupperware parties. "The whole party plan," explains perky Betty, "is built on the basic needs of human beings. People need to express themselves. And one of the best ways of doing it is by putting on a Tupperware party." When should the faithful Tupperware vendor think about scheduling a party? *"Think about it all the time!"* Betty's acolyte soon gets the message: "from now on you can call me Party Planning Ann!" Ann's prattling makes her sound like a stooge or a spoof on Weber's Protestant ethic or Foucaultian discipline. "I guess the main idea is just not to WASTE time, is that right?" "That's it," beams Betty. Plan ahead, she urges. Do more work. Ann hesitates. "It seems that if I get that wrapped up in the work, my family will also become involved." "They will," agrees inexorable Betty. "And it's wonderful! The best dealers we have are those whose families are Tupperized." Now Ann's not hesitating, she's trailing off wordlessly. "Are what . . . ?" Betty, I think, is prim in her

[58] Luke 2:49, 14:26.

[59] John Bunyan, *The Pilgrim's Progress*, ed. Roger Sharrock (Harmondsworth, Middlesex: Penguin, 1973), pp. 41, 135, 242.

persistence. "Tupperized. We have children who sometimes bag orders for their mothers!"

It would be nasty to speculate on exactly why that image revives Ann's spirits, but it sure does. "That's wonderful!" she exclaims. Better yet is Betty's next revelation. "That's the way husbands get into the business, too. When your husband finds how happy you are and how wrapped up in your work, he begins to get enthusiastic about it, too, and can be of great help to you." "I hope I can Tupperize my family!" gushes Ann.[60] Now there's a woman who could use a bit more role distance. Identified with her role as Tupperware party hostess, Ann doesn't seem happily at home in the social world. Or if or insofar as she is happy, the happiness is that of a zombie or happy slave, a happiness you would avoid claiming for your own even if you understood that the day after it was yours nothing in it would seem objectionable to you. You wouldn't—shouldn't—get a lobotomy even if you were persuaded you'd be more cheerful after you had it, either. Ann seems like a mindless pawn in a corporate game or, to ratchet up the rhetoric, like a proletarian who's relieved the capitalist of the burden of having to exploit her by learning how to exploit and even colonize herself.

Her heart fluttering as she awaits the epiphanies of Tupperization, Ann is after all fictional. Not so everyone like her. Amway's corporate tactics cry out for a latter-day Cuthbert Cunny-catcher. Amway dealers make money not just by selling Amway products, though no matter how high in the organization they climb, they still have to close ten sales every month. They make their serious money by recruiting others as dealers. Then they get a cut on anything those new dealers sell, in perpetuity; and a further cut on whatever dealers recruited by those new dealers sell, in perpetuity; and so on, each aspiring to the lucrative day on which he has spawned prodigious schools of dealers. To become a dealer, you have to buy a pricey startup kit from the corporation. Sounds like another Ponzi scheme, but in a landmark decision the Federal Trade Commission decided that it wasn't.[61]

---

[60] *Know How! The Guide to Making Money with Tupperware* (n.p.: Tupperware Home Parties, 1956), pp. 34, 38, 109, 166–67.

[61] *In re Amway Corp.*, 93 FTC 618 (1979). Compare *In re Koscot Interplanetary, Inc.*, 86 FTC 1106 (1975), *aff'd sub. nom. Turner v. FTC*, 580 F.2d 701 (DC Cir. 1978). For an adoring encomium to Amway, see James W. Robinson, *Empire of Freedom: The Amway Story and What It Means to You* (Rocklin, CA: Prima Publishing, 1997); for confessional agitprop of a lapsed dealer, see Stephen Butterfield, *Amway: The Cult of Free Enterprise* (Boston: South End Press, 1985).

Somehow selling detergent, therapeutic magnets ("the *first* and *only* thera-peutic magnets that contain the exclusive, patented quadrapolar technol-ogy"),[62] and just about anything else imaginable on this basis lands the company starry-eyed zealots for dealers. Amway's in-house magazine is studded with testimonials—or fervent declarations of undying faith. "Our whole family enjoys using AMWAY BODY SERIES™ Bath Care products. AMWAY BODY SERIES Sensitive Skin Body Wash is extremely mild and gentle, so we use it to cleanse our 1-year-old daughter's skin. Miranda Beth is totally an Amway baby and enjoys bathtime with SUDZY SATINIQUE® Bubble Bath and Shower Gel. AMWAY BODY SERIES Sensitive Skin Body Powder helps keep her tender skin dry and comfortable between baths." Then there's the man on vacation who runs out of Amway's shaving cream. Because he flatly refuses "to buy a store-brand product," he impro-vises with Amway's "ARTISTRY® Clarifying Cleansing Gel. What an excit-ing find! The cleansing gel worked better than any shaving creme I've ever used."[63] Amway isn't the domestic equivalent of the Nigerian letter scam, but these rhapsodies do seem more troubling than the usual product en-dorsements. Is that because of the ignoble politics of culture? The name Amway is unsavory in fastidiously granola circles for summoning up im-ages of preened and paunchy men, garish women with bleached blonde hair piled high, the archconservative politics of the reigning DeVos fam-ily. Or is it because we discount for Madison Avenue hype but know that real people spontaneously produced this language? (Do we know that? How do we know the magazine editors don't make up the letters?) If they're ventriloquizing commercials, are they using the real speech of real people? or a facsimile thereof, suitable for framing, the speakers and their audience in turn suitable for being framed? But maybe images of false consciousness and foolish gullibility are obscenely out of order. Like Tupperized Ann, these correspondents are full of good cheer. Why second-guess them?

Because it's hard to justify having Tupperware or Amway assume such prominence in life. Nifty plastic containers and low-phosphate detergents are fine, but not finally important. Recall the example of health: what peo-ple prefer or want or choose isn't necessarily what's good for them. Play fill-in-the-blank: "My life is worth living because. . . ." Some candidates are nonstarters on their face: ". . . I Tupperized my family"; ". . . I shunned

---

[62] *Amagram* (May 1999), pp. 6–8, 16–24; see www.magnabloc.com.
[63] *Amagram* (November 1998), p. 45; *Amagram* (January 1999), p. 44.

stores and bought as much merchandise as I could from Amway." As always, it's possible to imagine heroically creative stories that shed surprising new light, so someone could in principle explain why those candidates are satisfactory, even ideal. Has Ann or the man quivering over cleansing gel's excellence as shaving cream got such a story? If, instead, the impatient response is, "but I don't *want* to live a worthwhile life, I don't care about that at all," the rejoinder is, "You should." Not caring is a theatrical gesture of despair.

In modern society, you occupy many different roles: employee, parent, child, faithful member of the congregation, softball coach, and so on. Plenty of those roles are voracious, happy to consume more and more of your time, your energy, your identity. The more you put into them, the better you perform within them, the more rewards you garner—and the more you neglect your other roles. So you have two problems. One: for any given role, should you identify with it or be distant from it? The cunning man counsels you to keep your distance. If you raise your eyebrows, he obligingly pops on a new mask. Now he is the defender of autonomy and he demands to know if you intend to become a robot. Two: how should you allocate your time among your roles? The cunning man now celebrates the possibility of your playing Don Juan or Casanova, occupying some role when things are going well for you, skipping out or retreating to other roles when you need time to plot your next conquest or lick your wounds. Here today, gone tomorrow; you can't catch me; now you see me, now you don't: these are his slogans. They are, he says, the slogans of anyone who wants to succeed. Knowing that the devil quotes Scripture but that the devout do, too—and which is he? and how can you tell? and how can *he* tell?—the cunning man pleads the example of Jesus scorning his family, and urges you on to heroic feats of agility.

While you're contemplating his counsel, perch on your other shoulder a 1710 writer on Christian prudence and listen to his more than faintly disapproving comment: "This is the very notion we have of a Politic or Cunning Man, we mean one that knows how to compass his End: that is, to use fit means for the obtaining of it." What might be pejorative about using fit means for realizing your ends? Any adequate account of prudence, he continues, would have to take up the worthiness of the ends and the lawfulness of the means. The cunning man's rationality, then, is radically deficient.[64] But for the cunning man, moral obligations and the requirements of our roles are barriers in the path of realizing our ends, no different in principle from Scylla and Charybdis.

In the introduction, I voiced a suspicion that the allure and disgust of instrumental rationality, role distance and role identification, and the justification of morality, all cluster tightly together, that they might even be different facets of the same problem. Once again, let's bring the theory down to the ground with an example. Would you steal twenty dollars from a close friend? Should you? Your friend's wallet is on her dresser and she's downstairs getting some drinks. You can pad over noiselessly on her plush carpeting, lift a twenty, cram it in your pocket, all the while murmuring, "As the occasion permits, such a one am I," and she'll never have a clue. Even if she notices that the twenty is gone, she wouldn't dream that you were the culprit. Don't quibble with the example; don't say that you might get caught. No one else is in the house and her creaky stairs will warn you if she suddenly returns. Again, nothing in the machinery of instrumental rationality requires that your ends be selfish. But aren't you better off with the twenty? If you don't want to buy yourself a treat, donate it to Oxfam. They need it more than your friend does. So there's a straightforward sense in which instrumental rationality seems to counsel grabbing the twenty, though—Silly Putty time again—I grant wearily that you can always stipulate that your ends include not ripping off your friend. Regardless, lifting the twenty is such a violent departure from our understanding of friendship that it wouldn't occur to anyone in the role. "How can a man not blush to think such things?" you might wonder. Suppose the answer is that when one does something for gain, one need not blush. And the betrayal of friendship would count as grotesquely immoral. Here again it won't do to plead the brute fact that you will feel guilty or anxious if you take the twenty. That emotion is parasitic on the judgment that you would have done something wrong. And it's evasive to plead that you've been so brainwashed that you can't wrest free of the emotion. Should you teach your children to plunder their friends when they can get away with it? Will

[64] John Norris, *A Treatise on Christian Prudence: or The Principles of Practical Wisdom, Fitted to the Use of Human Life, and Designed for the Better Regulation of It* (London, 1710), pp. 95–97. Similarly, Benjamin Bayly, *Fourteen Sermons on Various Subjects*, 2 vols. (London, 1721), 2:206.

you benefit them if you liberate them from the alleged superstitions of morality and social life? No, sorry, it's also evasive to plead that you've been brainwashed into giving your children a more conventional upbringing.

Philosophers have described a strategy of justification they call foundationalist: begin with self-evident or otherwise undeniable premises and then use only logical deduction to derive your desired conclusion. Such justifications, if they existed, might seem marvelously all-purpose. Whatever doubt or worry or criticism you were facing, you could produce the same justification. But then we should replace "might seem marvelously all-purpose" with "would be conversationally unresponsive." It's as if you wanted a single club to bludgeon your opponents into submission regardless of what their grounds of opposition were. Anyway, foundational justifications are philosophers' pet unicorns: their colorful folklore tells us what they look like, but we have yet to see one. Real justifications—this is a vital step in learning to shrug off toxic wholesale skepticisms—are responses to particular doubts, particular objections.[65] They may be persuasive against those, irrelevant against others. So: Larry's friend Bill angrily confronts him in the café. "I can't believe you're drinking coffee!" he snarls. "I guess it is addictive," concedes Larry. "But missing it causes only a headache, and I never miss it. There don't now seem to be any other health issues. I know," he rattles on, "they thought it caused cancer of the pancreas. It turns out that was a bad study—" but suddenly Larry notices that Bill is more hostile, his snarl now rabid, and it turns out he thinks Larry is complicit in the exploitation of third-world peasants. Were he solicitous of Larry's health, Larry's observations would comprise a perfectly good justification. But they're wholly unhelpful, given Bill's actual concerns. Worse, Larry's concern for his health betrays his narcissistic blindness to others' suffering. So what might have been a justification has actually dug him in deeper. Now he needs to find something else to say.

So what's the justification of coffee-drinking? Absent any context, any particular doubt, there is and could be no such thing. I think the point quite generally true of justification. So there is and could be no such thing as the justification of morality full stop or absent any particular doubt or criticism. So who's the critic who wants a justification of morality? What

---

[65] See especially Ludwig Wittgenstein, *On Certainty*, ed. G.E.M. Anscombe and G. H. von Wright, trans. Denis Paul and G.E.M. Anscombe (New York: Harper & Row, 1969).

are his doubts or objections? The usual (melo)drama conjures up a skeptical egoist, intent on pursuing selfish ends, who unimaginatively imagines morality as a set of proscriptions, a secular decalogue of "thou shalt nots." One time-honored justificatory strategy fails instructively.

Thomas Hobbes's fool denies the claims of justice.[66] He understands that it's called unjust to break covenants, but sometimes, he urges, it serves his interests to do so. The fool urges—shades of Machiavelli, though he appeals to pagan mythology—that some political rulers grab power by flagrantly unjust means, but still they rule and their title is taken to be legitimate. So if Justice is opposed to Reason, which the fool takes to be a tool for realizing his ends, "Justice is not to be approved for good." The fool's perspective echoes much of Hobbes's own position, yet Hobbes insists that the fool is mistaken. He concedes that it may sometimes turn out that injustice serves one's interests. But *ex ante*, he suggests, it is an imprudent bet. Once others realize that the fool will flout justice when he believes it serves his interests, they will cast him out of society. Yes, they may not figure out what a blackguard he is. They may stupidly go on trafficking with him. Now he is what economists call a free rider. He profits doubly, first, from the benefits of social cooperation, and second, from exempting himself. But again, Hobbes suggests, *ex ante* injustice is an imprudent bet. Once he realizes that others are likely to detect his shenanigans and sanction him accordingly, he should realize that justice is in his interests.

Hume wrestles with the same puzzle. "That *honesty is the best policy*, may be a good general rule, but is liable to many exceptions; and he, it may perhaps be thought, conducts himself with most wisdom, who observes the general rule, and takes advantage of all the exceptions." Hume acknowledges that those attracted by this line of reasoning are hard to answer, but musters several observations. One echoes Hobbes. The honest man has "the frequent satisfaction of seeing knaves, with all their pretended cunning and abilities, betrayed by their own maxims; and while they purpose to cheat with moderation and secrecy, a tempting incident occurs, nature is frail, and they give into the snare; whence they can never extricate themselves, without a total loss of reputation, and the forfeiture of all future trust and confidence with mankind."[67] And—it is not Hume's only suggestion about moral

---

[66] *Leviathan*, chap. 15.
[67] *An Enquiry Concerning the Principles of Morals*, sec. 9, pt. 2.

motivation, but he does like it—the honest man can bask in his vanity or "feel an accession of alacrity" when he reflects on how others admire him.[68]

I'd long thought that "honesty is the best policy" came from Ben Franklin's *Poor Richard's Almanac*. People I had no reason to doubt assured me it was. It turns out it's not there. (Franklin does endorse the maxim, apparently as a familiar bromide, in a letter he wrote decades after *Poor Richard*.[69]) It was, though, an eighteenth-century commonplace—and its age means that the slogan doesn't mean what it used to. Now *policy* means *course of action*. That renders the maxim a bit of bland moralism. But in the eighteenth century, *policy* meant prudence or statecraft. It was surrounded with intimations of base self-interest, even sly corruption, and so tipped over right into cunning. *Honesty* has shifted, too. It once referred not to truthfulness or integrity but to lofty social status or more generally, a reputation for being honorable. If you adopt the earlier senses of both words, once the maxim meant that it will strategically serve your interests if people think you're honorable. It's amusing to transform today's bland moralism into yesteryear's Machiavellian sentiment. But the right reading, I think, has to take *policy* in the older sense but *honesty* in its now familiar one, available since the late sixteenth century.

That surely is the reading Franklin would have endorsed. He reports in his *Autobiography* that early on he "grew convinc'd that *truth*, *sincerity* and *integrity* in dealings between man and man were of the utmost importance to the felicity of life," and he vowed to "practice them ever while I lived." Truthfulness and integrity, I imagine Franklin holding with his usual impish seriousness, are the best strategies for realizing even mischievous ends. Or, put differently, if you think you can advance your ends by lying and cheating, think again. Better to earn a reputation for being thrifty and industrious. There's room in Franklin's world for a bit of policy in cultivating the reputation. Staying up late to repair a broken typesetting form, returning to work early in the morning, he attracted approving attention. I don't suppose he pulled his curtains to conceal the shop lights. But the incipient Machiavellianism here doesn't erupt into the worry that maybe the appearance of honesty has nothing to do with honesty itself. Instead, the best

[68] *Treatise*, bk. 3, pt. 3, sec. 6.

[69] Franklin to Edward Bridgen, 2 October 1779, in *The Papers of Benjamin Franklin*, ed. Leonard W. Labaree and others, 36 vols. to date (New Haven: Yale University Press, 1959–), 30:430. Thanks to Alan Houston for the reference.

way to earn a reputation for honesty is to be honest. We can grant that the connection between reputation and actuality is contingent and still endorse Franklin's suggestion as an *ex ante* strategy.

Poor Richard adds some pithy observations. "One Man may be more cunning than another, but not more cunning than every body else." Fill in the unstated thought: that Man will be hard-pressed to figure out ahead of time who's even more cunning than he. Fancying himself a knave among fools, he may ruefully discover himself the biter bit. But then we have to assume too that if he weren't playing the knave, the more cunning wouldn't bother with him. So too with these cautions: "You may be too cunning for One, but not for All"; "Don't think so much of your own Cunning, as to forget other Men's: A cunning Man is overmatch'd by a cunning Man and a Half." But the cunning man might think he needn't be master demon of the social universe to play his rascally games and count himself a winner. Less concisely, Poor Richard launches into a sermonette on cooperation. "Man is but of a very limited Power in his own Person," he reminds the reader. It takes "Society and Conjunction with others" to get things done. But, he continues, they won't cooperate with you unless they trust you, so insincerity can doom you. "A discovered Dissembler can achieve nothing great or considerable."[70] Franklin concedes that on occasion deception will seem to serve your interests. But he insists that you fasten on the mistakes you might make in identifying those occasions and the crushing punishments you will suffer if detected.

The core insight here is straightforward. Yes, occasions when self-interest and morality diverge will tempt the fool to be immoral and keep it dark. But he should remember the risk that he'll be caught and punished. We can trick out the argument with bells and whistles: the fool might not be good at identifying the relevant occasions; he might succumb to unthinking temptation while flattering himself that he's clear-sighted in his calculations; maybe as a matter of psychological fact he can't turn his dispositions on and off, so he will feel guilty and anxious when he plays the cunning rogue. Overall, then, for us creatures of limited judgment and capacity, honesty is the best policy.[71]

---

[70] *Poor Richard's Almanack*, August 1745, September 1750, August 1754, April 1757.

[71] For a recent elaborate version of the argument, see R. M. Hare, *Moral Thinking: Its Levels, Method, and Point* (Oxford: Clarendon Press, 1981), chap. 11.

The problem with the argument is obvious. The fool can always propose to take his chances. He might be caught. But he might not be. He might feel guilty. But he might feel exhilarated in playing knave, in running circles around more innocent fools, and he might recollect his feats with smug delight. This game could be worth the candle. The fool's rejoinder depends on what economists call his level of risk aversion. He might be willing to stake his assets, his reputation, his liberty, his life, on the chance of being cunning and succeeding. The rewards on offer are princely. Is it reasonable to gamble? Ironically, the economist's theory of instrumental rationality leaves us with nothing to say about that. It takes levels of risk aversion as brute facts not themselves open to rational appraisal or criticism.

The allegorical literature is chock full of characters supposed to horrify us. John Skelton's *Magnificence* of 1515 treats us to Counterfeit Countenance, Cloaked Collusion, Double Dealing, Courtly Abusion, and Crafty Conveyance. Do you want to emulate them? As the occasion requires? Hobbes, Hume, and Franklin instruct you that you shouldn't—because doing so is actually an imprudent strategy for securing your ends. At best, that looks like giving the right answer for the wrong reason. At worst, it looks like the wrong answer. Either way, their discussion ignores historical and sociological problems all three men knew all too well.

Satan, God, and Cunning Bands

To be fair, Hobbes does hint at one of those problems. Like the fool of the Psalms, Hobbes's fool denies there is a God. So we can't try to persuade him that morality is in his long-term interest by reminding him of the horrors of hellfire. Even if he did believe in the afterlife, we'd run smack into another limit in the theory of instrumental rationality. Economists define time preference or your discount rate as how much more you value what occurs sooner than later, not because you're more confident it will occur—that goes to risk and uncertainty—but just because it comes sooner. (So the theory pictures us as greedy little kids who can't wait for the chocolate cake, not people who might savor anticipating far-off pleasures, though—grab that trowel and spread another chunk of Silly Putty here—I suppose an economist could always assign someone negative time preference.) And they take time preference as another brute fact not open to rational appraisal. So if your time preference is high enough, it's rational, according to the theory, to cash in on worldly pleasures now at the price of brimstone later. The possibility might seem fanciful, but one currency counterfeiter in colonial Pennsylvania seized on it. Scurrying off, the authorities in hot pursuit, he scoffed at the idea that he should fear arrest. "No, damn me!" he replied. "A man whose pockets are lined with money, and his heart with courage, has nothing to fear but God; and before I am heard of again in Pennsylvania, I shall be out of the reach of pursuit."[72] Now there's a man who's resolved his priorities. Does anything in the off-the-shelf story about instrumental rationality expose him to criticism? Suggesting that hell is infinitely painful and fiddling with the mathematics of the problem won't do. "I have already since my twenty-first year been wed with Satan, and in full knowledge of the peril and with duly considered valour, pride, and presumption, I did, out of a wish to find fame in this world, make a bond and league with Him, in such wise that what I would complish within the term of four and twenty years and what men would rightly regard with distrust, would come to pass solely by His help and is Devil's work, poured out by the Angel of Poison."[73] So spoke Faustian composer Adrian Leverkühn. Instead of chalking that up as the delusion of a man about to collapse from advanced venereal disease, think again about why we might properly shrink away in terror. Is it really because Leverkühn has calculated imprudently?

Regardless, it's worth pausing over how cunning shifts with the presence—or absence—of God. Recall Machiavelli flicking aside the divine in his account of princely politics. It's tempting to surmise that in a thoroughly religious world, or maybe just a thoroughly Christian one, problems of cunning wouldn't arise. After all, if everyone were devout, everyone would be trustworthy. Reverence for God, not just fear of hellfire, ought to help motivate moral behavior. Certainly that's the story line of gallows speeches from colonial America. Edmund Fortis, in jail after confessing to the rape and murder of a young teenager, recounted his wrestling

---

[72] Kenneth Scott, *Counterfeiting in Colonial Pennsylvania* (New York: American Numismatic Society, 1955), p. 128.

[73] Thomas Mann, *Doctor Faustus*, trans. John E. Woods (New York: Alfred A. Knopf, 1997), chap. 47, p. 521.

with conscience, God, and Satan. Rousing himself before his trial, he discovered that "the Devil was with me and said 'if you had killed your wife
I should have had you.'" There was nothing stony and blank about his
prison cell, with divine light flooding it, angels' singing resounding
through it, and a red fire he thought was Satan gleaming in it. "I prayed,
and said, O Lord, for thy dear Son Jesus' sake, who died for sinners, have
mercy on me! And immediately the same angels began to sing again; and I
believed in the Lord, and loved every body. I felt cool and calm; all the
dread and fear which I had suffered were gone."[74] I can't help wondering if
deathbed repentance, the triumphant return of the prodigal son, offers the
right incentives to would-be criminals. More appropriate, perhaps, Isaac
Frasier, only 28 years old and already facing execution, implored his readers to learn from his ignominious career. "Young people, may this my violent death be a solemn warning to you, to shun the paths of wickedness I
have trod, nor to put your trust in uncertain riches, but to remember your
Creator in the days of your youth, and to put your trust in the living
God."[75] His profaning the Sabbath, he warned, had yielded Satan the advantage. Aren't Fortis and Frasier shockingly literate for criminals? Isn't it
funny how they could turn out such convincing imitations of the bloated
syntax of the sermons they'd skipped? Not that funny: these gallows confessions were routinely written by ministers, not criminals.[76] Just another
pious fraud, another innocent deception brought off to serve God. In a
book that opened with a murdering minister and kneeled to the Constantine Donation, isn't it too late to take seriously the thought that religion
would preclude cunning?

And don't religious traditions celebrate the cunning exploits of their
good guys? Genesis is unflinching. Esau was "a cunning hunter," that is,
skillful at his trade, but he didn't have the cunning that counts. His twin,
Jacob, abundantly blessed in the dark arts of social life, had no problem

---

[74] *The Last Words and Dying Speech of Edmund Fortis, A Negro Man* (Exeter, [NH,] 1795),
pp. 8–11.

[75] *A Brief Account of the Life, and Abominable Thefts, of the Notorious Isaac Frasier* (New London,
[CT,] 1768), p. 16.

[76] For a study of the changing genre, see Daniel A. Cohen, *Pillars of Salt, Monuments of Grace:
New England Crime Literature and the Origins of American Popular Culture, 1674–1860* (New York:
Oxford University Press, 1993). For a sampling of primary texts from 1699 to 1796, see *Pillars of
Salt: An Anthology of Early American Criminal Narratives*, ed. Daniel E. Williams (Madison, WI:
Madison House, 1993).

swindling him. He made Esau, faint with hunger, sell him his birthright for some pottage. Their poor blind father Isaac preferred Esau, but Jacob tricked Isaac into blessing him. No mean blessing, either: "Let people serve thee, and nations bow down to thee: be lord over thy brethren, and let thy mother's sons bow down to thee: cursed be every one that curseth thee, and blessed be he that blesseth thee." No incidental pranks of a young scamp, those steps were required to make Jacob one of the three great patriarchs of Judaism. The church fathers faltered over this episode and similar ones.[77] Make of it what you will, we know God's verdict, because He reports it: "I loved Jacob, and I hated Esau."[78] If you stipulate that the genuinely religious couldn't be cunning, you have no great insight, but an arbitrary tautology, which ignores the historical record.

It's tempting to imagine, too, that for centuries the West was suitably religious and moral. Distinguished scholars cater, pander, to that temptation. One English historian insists, "All our ancestors were literal believers, all of the time."[79] One French historian argues that the sixteenth century was so drenched in religiosity that atheism was inconceivable.[80] Finally, it's tempting to think modernity means secularization. However familiar that script, the flaccid abstractions ought to alert us that something screwy is going on.[81] (Unless perhaps *modernity* just means Scandinavia.) Prophets of secularization ought to ponder the commentary of early Christians on their pagan ancestors. So, for instance, extended fragments of an acerbic ancient text, Oenomaus's *Detection of Impostors*, survive because church father Eusebius quotes them. When Oenomaus sardonically denounces Greek oracles as the tools of cunning phonies, Eusebius sternly corrects him: no, he urges, they were demonic.[82] So here we have secularization in reverse, and on its face it's the replacement of cunning with devilry. But a world of devilry isn't a world without cunning. On the contrary, it's a

---

[77] Saint John Chrysostom, *Homilies on Genesis*, no. 26; Origen, *Homilies on Jeremiah*, no. 20.

[78] Genesis 25:27–34, 27:1–29; Malachi 2–3.

[79] Peter Laslett, *The World We Have Lost*, 3rd ed. (New York: Charles Scribner's Sons, 1984), p. 71.

[80] Lucien Febvre, *The Problem of Unbelief in the Sixteenth Century: The Religion of Rabelais*, trans. Beatrice Gottlieb (Cambridge, MA: Harvard University Press, 1982).

[81] Bernard Yack, *The Fetishism of Modernities: Epochal Self-Consciousness in Contemporary Social and Political Thought* (Notre Dame, IN: University of Notre Dame Press, 1997), is full of arresting insights.

[82] Eusebius, *Preparation for the Gospel*, bk. V, chaps. 20–21.

world opening up new possibilities for the cunning. Anyway it's a bit rich, surely, to suggest that the United States is a secular society or even to forecast the death of religion. We may not be in the midst of another Great Awakening, but religion is flourishing. Nor is the United States unique. Respectable, well-educated, middle-class Britons still pursue witchcraft and magic.[83] So we need to think not just about the presence or absence of God, but that of Satan, too.

A centralized state presiding over a reasonably orderly administration of criminal justice is a historical rarity. Socrates blanches at Euthyphro's prosecuting his father for murder.[84] Yet Athens had no district attorney, so private parties brought criminal charges; and Euthyphro would have been worried about *miasma*, pollution of his blood, as a result of his father's crime.[85] London didn't gain a regular police force until Robert Peel steered the Metropolitan Police Bill through Parliament in 1829[86] (so "bobbies" and "peelers"), and—"the Anglo-American regime of ordered liberty"[87] ain't what it used to be—critics pounced on it as an affront to English civil liberties.[88]

In the absence of 911 and the cops, God was awfully useful. Justification by works or reminders of the hellfire awaiting sinners didn't hurt either. And God was wont to command supernatural agents to help Him. Consider the lurid title of a 1659 London pamphlet, *Strange and Wonderful News from Lancaster: Or A Dreadful Account of a Most Inhumane and Bloody Murther, Committed upon the Body of One Mr. Carter, by the Contrivance of His Elder Brother, Who Had Hired Three More Villains to Commit the Horrid Fact, and How It Was Soon After Found Out by the Appearance of a Most Dreadful and Terrible Ghost, Sent by Almighty Providence for the Discovery: as also The Manner of Its Appearance in Several Shapes and Forms, with Fresh Bleeding Wounds, Still Pursuing the Murtherer from Place, to Place; with the Relation of How He Endeavoured to Conjure It Down, and of Its Appearance and Declaration of the Murtherers, and of the Confession of the*

---

[83] T. M. Luhrmann, *Persuasions of the Witch's Craft: Ritual Magic in Contemporary England* (Cambridge, MA: Harvard University Press, 1989).

[84] *Euthyphro* 4a.

[85] Antony Andrewes, *The Greeks* (New York: W. W. Norton, 1978), pp. 179–81.

[86] 10 Geo. IV c. 44.

[87] *Duncan v. Louisiana*, 391 US 145 (1968), 149 n. 14.

[88] *Blackwood's Edinburgh Magazine* 29:175 (January 1831): 82–104.

Murderer when Apprehended, with Many Other Remarkable Circumstances.[89] But not everyone found the threat of divine punishment compelling. Several years before this ghostly policing, one moralist tweaked the Gospel sentiment and lamented, "What care men, so they get money, and great places? though they lose their souls."[90] The moralist had good cause to lament. Take some raucous pirates, captured, dragged back to London, convicted at trial, facing the welcoming gallows. The authorities solemnly urged them "to turn their Minds to another World, and sincerely to Repent": "'Yes,' answered one of them, 'I do heartily Repent; I Repent I had not done more Mischief, and that we did not cut the Throats of them that took us, and I am extremely sorry that you an't all hang'd, as well as we.'"[91]

Jackdaws grabbing whatever lies to hand, the cunning turn even religious sanctity to their own uses. After an 1185 tour, Gerald of Wales shuddered over the remorseless Irish: "above all other peoples they always practice treachery." They carry axes as staffs—handy, that—and cheerfully trample on sacred ceremonies and spaces:

> Under the guise of religion and peace they assemble at some holy place with him whom they wish to kill. First they make a treaty on the basis of their common fathers. Then in turn they go around the church swearing three times. They enter the church and, swearing a great variety of oaths before relics of saints placed on the altar, at last with the celebration of Mass and the prayers of the priests they make an indissoluble treaty as if it were a kind of betrothal. For the greater confirmation of their friendship and completion of their settlement, each in conclusion drinks the blood of the other which has willingly been drawn especially for the purpose.
>
> O! how often in the very hour of this alliance has blood been so treacherously and shamefully shed by treacherous blood relations that one or other has been left entirely drained of blood. O! how

[89] See too Malcolm Gaskill, *Crime and Mentalities in Early Modern England* (Cambridge: Cambridge University Press, 2000), pp. 213–19, 222–23; and, more generally, Peter Lake with Michael Questier, *The Antichrist's Lewd Hat: Protestants, Papists and Players in Post-Reformation England* (New Haven: Yale University Press, 2002), sec. I.

[90] Junius Florilegus [Richard Younge], *Philarguromastix: or, The Arraignment of Covetousnesse, and Ambition, in Our Great and Greedy Cormorants* (London, 1653), pt. 1, p. 9. Compare Matthew 16:26, Mark 8:36, Luke 9:25.

[91] Johnson [Defoe], *General History*, p. 53, italics removed and quotation marks introduced.

often a bloody divorce immediately follows within the same hour, or precedes, or even—and this is unheard of elsewhere—interrupts the very ceremony of the "betrothal"![92]

These Irish don't need to believe themselves empowered by Satanic darkness to behave so shamelessly. They need believe only that their enemies are stupidly devout, that religion makes them patsies. So religion enables cunning, as the devout have always known: "If a Man would effectually Cheat his Neighbor, or put the Dice upon him, he pretends to Piety to hide the Juggle, and under a cloak of Religion, acts and covers the foulest Frauds."[93]

Not one to play second fiddle to God, Satan pitched in, too. We can bookend that 1659 pamphlet on God's ghostly policeman with a massive 1658 compendium, painstakingly assembled by a bishop of the Church of England, of stories designed to heighten the reader's awareness—and terror—of Satan's malevolent doings.[94] Lesser angels and demons were busy little beavers, too. Martin Luther explained that the devil produces destructive thunderstorms, the angels good winds, indeed that winds are themselves good and evil spirits. The devil and his minions are always there, trying to harm people, and angels are always there, trying to protect them, but sometimes the angels fail. And the devil is so resourceful! why, he even alters medicines inside their boxes to render them powerless. He afflicted Luther with grave doubts about his attack on the monasteries and his sundering the unity of Christendom; he tortured him in his sleep with wretched dreams that left him soaked in sweat. Happily, Luther could drive him away, sometimes by quoting Scripture, sometimes by farting (though the latter tactic, cautioned the great theologian, was dangerous).[95]

Luther is not alone in imagining an everyday world chock-full of otherworldly actors. Others, at various historical moments, would have

---

[92] Gerald of Wales, *The History and Topography of Ireland*, trans. John J. O'Meara (London: Penguin, 1982), pp. 106–8.

[93] A. B., *The Mystery of Phanaticism: or, The Artifices of Dissenters to Support Their Schism* (London, 1698), p. 28.

[94] Thomas Bramhall, *An History of Apparitions, Oracles, Prophecies, and Predictions, with Dreams, Visions, and Revelations; and the Cunning Delusions of the Devil, to Strengthen the Idolatry of the Gentiles* (London, 1658).

[95] Martin Luther, *Table Talk*, ed. and trans. Theodore G. Tappert, in *Luther's Works*, ed. Jaroslav Pelikan and Helmut T. Lehmann, 55 vols. (Philadelphia: Concordia Publishing and Fortress Press, 1955–67), 54:16, 82, 89–90, 96, 172, 237, 280.

added brownies, dragons, dryads, dwarfs, elves, fairies, fays, gargoyles, ghosts, ghouls, giants, gnomes, goblins, harpies, imps, incubi, kobolds, leprechauns, mermaids, nymphs, phantoms, pixies, poltergeists, satyrs, selkies, sprites, succubi, sylphs, trolls, uldras. Then we get another enticing population, that of human—or vaguely human, or formerly human, or undead human, or superhuman; the boundaries here are disgustingly, eerily, amorphous—figures marked and changed by their commerce with these otherworldly actors: alchemists, astrologers, augurs, conjurers, exorcists, golems, magicians, mediums, necromancers, prophets, psychics, saints, seers, shamans, sorcerers, theurgists, vampires, warlocks, werewolves, witches, wizards, zombies. Have we really committed implacable genocide against this exotic cast of characters? Consider the range of associations summoned up by the opening of Francis Bacon's essay: "We take *Cunning* for a Sinister or Crooked Wisdom."[96] "Sinister or crooked" today most easily stands for, oh, evil or duplicitous. But *sinister* was once strongly tied to *left-handed*, understood not just as wicked but as Satanic. This belief shows up in the usual pale, vestigial way in the educational practice (my grandmother was one victim) of slapping left-handed students on their knuckles to get them to write with their right hands. It shows up too in our disapproval of those who work the system, cut corners, exploit ambiguities in the rules to their own advantage. They're creepy, we say, and the sentiment isn't only one of disgust; it also summons up the uncanny.[97] In this way, our vocabulary of moral appraisal remains otherworldly.

Henry Tufts was eager to break out of Exeter jail in the late 1700s. A resourceful handyman, he managed to drill and conceal a hole in the wall. His fellow prisoner thought Tufts a wizard in cahoots with Satan, who would engineer his escape. Inspired, Tufts instructed the poor guy to fling his clothes over the prison wall and then, ten minutes after he had left, to recite this unassuming incantation: "Come in old man, with that black ram, / And carry me out, as fast as you can." Somehow the incantation failed, but by then Tufts was long gone, happy to command a change of clothes. Another time, he needed to get away on a stolen horse. To defeat

---

[96] "Of Cunning," in *The Essayes or Counsels, Civill and Moral*. "I would rather say that it is a part, but the lowest part of Wisdom," offered Bolingbroke: *The Idea of a Patriot King* (London, 1740), p. 72.

[97] On disgust as a moral sentiment, see William Ian Miller, *The Anatomy of Disgust* (Cambridge, MA: Harvard University Press, 1997), chap. 8.

some sentries, he rigged up his very own cloven foot by doubling his leg back at the knee and lashing on an ox's leg he got from a butcher. Staggered by the real presence of Satan, the sentries let him pass.[98] Here a secular skeptic cunningly runs circles around the devout. It's a common motif. The mistake is imagining that it represents some world-historical transition from a medieval religious world where people behave well to a modern secular one where they're cunning. Gerald of Wales's story about the terrible Irish boasts the same motif; religious actors are often cunning, too; and anyway, the world remains religious. The secularization narrative is another illusory appearance, an opiate of the intellectuals. Time for its dreamy proponents to wake up and smell the coffee.

Hobbes never made their mistake. Perched in Paris, Hobbes watched parliamentary maneuvering against Charles I lead to civil war and the king's execution at the hands of Puritan fanatics. He knew how the Puritans used religion to whip their followers into bloody frenzies. Members of Parliament were subjected to, subjected themselves to, hundreds of inflammatory sermons.[99] One such sermon wielded a chilling biblical episode ("Curse ye Meroz, said the angel of the Lord, curse ye bitterly the inhabitants thereof; because they came not to the help of the Lord") to urge the merits of self-immolation in the service of God. "Give up your selves and all you have, so wholly to the Lord, and to his Church, that all your other outward occasions may not so much as dare to expect any thing from you, so long as the Church hath need of it": give up "pleasures," "profits and sometimes necessities," even life itself.[100] Here it's religion against self-interest. That means the challenge posed by Hobbes's atheistic fool is easier than that posed by contemporary religious believers. It means too that Hobbes's attempt to show that morality was a prudent strategy for securing self-interest had nothing to offer the very people who were setting England on fire. Again, justifications that help with one critic may be fruitless with another; but now I can add that the point is politically crucial. Nor would

---

[98] *A Narrative of the Life, Adventures, Travels and Sufferings of Henry Tufts* (Dover, NH, 1807), pp. 58–60, 228–29. For another rogue perceived as the devil incarnate, see *Memoirs of the Notorious Stephen Burroughs of New Hampshire* (New York: Dial Press, 1924), p. 70.

[99] They're collected in *The English Revolution: Fast Sermons to Parliament,* ed. Robin Jeffs, 34 vols. (London: Cornmarket Press, 1970–71).

[100] Judges 5:23; Stephen Marshall, *Meroz Cursed. Or, A Sermon, Preached to the Honourable House of Commons, at Their Late Solemn Fast, February 23 1641* (London, 1645), p. 50.

Hobbes's attempt offer anything to many of those assaulting our world. Solemnly memorize Hobbes's rejoinder to the fool. Now imagine reciting it to a fundamentalist lurking around abortion clinics, hoping to execute another doctor murdering babies; to a Palestinian suicide bomber; to Osama bin Laden. Every one of them is cunning—it's no easy matter to escape the shackles of everyday morality and law, to evade Israeli guards and roadblocks, to orchestrate the simultaneous hijacking of four airplanes—but not one is selfish. Self-interest isn't the most potent threat to morality. Yet Hobbes had no fantasies about turning England into a society of men as skeptical, secular, and timid as he was.[101] The seeds of religion "can never be so abolished out of human nature, but that new Religions may again be made to spring out of them," he declared.[102]

And again, those old-time religions continue apace, along with magic and folklore supposed to have vanished from the scene centuries ago. Demons are comfortably at home in modernity, thank you very much. They send email. Once they've possessed someone, they take over while their victim is sitting at her computer terminal. Here they hurl reckless defiance and shards of broken syntax at those attempting to deliver one such unlucky lady:

> No one forgives you of your sins!! You are all a bunch of faithless fools!! So, if she dies we do lose our house and go onward elsewhere. At least, no one else gets her. We are speaking of your dead Jesus, the God who lost to the Dark One. He has lost her, and she is ineffective for him or anything He has for her to do. We either keep her, and remain where we have been for 46 years, or she dies. It is this simple, yet, *your prayers make it much more complex.* I hereby curse you. The curses fall upon you and your families and loved ones; your ministry is rendered inoperative and destined to failure. Leave us and this girl alone. She will be harmed for every prayer uttered; every one of you who comes to befriend her, either on this computer or in person, and for any further attempts at making

---

[101] Contrast David Johnston, *The Rhetoric of Leviathan: Thomas Hobbes and the Politics of Cultural Transformation* (Princeton, NJ: Princeton University Press, 1986). For my own account of Hobbes, see *Happy Slaves: A Critique of Consent Theory* (Chicago: University of Chicago Press, 1989), chap. 3.

[102] *Leviathan*, chap. 12.

us leave. We have stolen her will. She does cry, even now, for
mercy. Yet, there is none. Hahahahahahahahahahaaha!! You have
lost!!

How would others try to befriend the poor possessed woman "on this
computer"? Well, this message is reported at www.demonbuster.com. (It's
bowdlerized: they decorously removed the demons' foul language, though
not the extravagant blasphemy.) The good-hearted folk at that website responded to a string of such messages by firing back Spiritual Warfare
Prayers: bits, bytes, and pixels doing the Lord's good work. It's unclear if
they succeeded in delivering the woman from her demons. Still, they offer
helpful free advice. A benevolent guy, I pass some on. Get those candles
out of your house: they host demons. Throw out any incense, especially
if you're experiencing intestinal distress. That Native American dream
catcher has to go, too. "You definitely do not want this thing in your
home." In fact, don't just throw it out. Burn it. What's cute about practic-
ing witchcraft? Unfazed, my daughters retorted that they'd take their
chances.

Another brave fellow, offering his services at www.exorcism.net, will exorcise your demons for a paltry $75. Demons are "a small percent" of the
host of "negative entities" afflicting us, he instructs the goggle-eyed reader,
but they are real. Hogwash? Here's one success story:

> Mrs. V. has a daughter 15 years old, we will call Mary. Mrs. V. and
> Mary have always gotten along very well. Mary told her mother that
> she started hearing voices in her head, these voices told her to do
> mean things to people and were extremely vulgar. Mrs. V. contacted
> me, told me the story and said the only new thing in their lives was
> a new neighbor girl that Mary had started hanging around. Mrs. V.
> also said that the new girl seemed to be rather crude.
>
> I checked Mary and found that she had 12 negative entities
> inside her body and 17 in and on her aura. I removed them and
> placed Mary in a protective sphere and a White Christ light. The
> last time Mrs. V. contacted me Mary had not heard the voices since
> the exorcism.

Do you summarily dismiss this tale? Are you sure that it's invented from
whole cloth or that Mary was suffering schizophrenia? How do you know?

If you want to sample the services on offer, you can fill out an online form. Those not as computer-savvy as today's demons can snail-mail their woes to a post office box. Either way, he does the exorcism online—if, that is, the Higher Self gives permission. No muss, no fuss, no incense, no crystals, no stranger poking around your home muttering Latin prayers or mystic incantations. (No, I do not get a commission for referring you.) Cut-rate capitalism and the internet meet chthonic and Satanic powers. Spotting the efficiency gains in television ministries, God too does His bit with modern media. "The reports seemed to be coming in almost as fast as I could read them," Jim Bakker recalled of his (or His?) exploits on Christian Broadcasting Network: "arthritis healed, kidney problem healed, bad back healed, problem with eyesight healed, loss of hearing healed, sinus healed. Tumors and cancers were dropping off people's bodies."[103] No bets from this quarter on which side will emerge victorious in this titanic struggle. But remember it the next time someone purrs—or yowls—about how secular modernity is.

So one wonders why Hobbes, Hume, and Franklin devoted so much energy to trying to show the skeptical, secular egoist that morality was in his interest. Each of them knew that such egoists were not in fact the central threat to social and political order. That aside, another objection is more devastating. Remember that all three caution the skeptic that if he gets caught in the cunning act, others will refuse to cooperate with him. Hobbes's forecast is the grimmest: he'll be "cast out of Society" and die. Really? People may not be so generously forgiving, but they have short memories. Anyway, he can always move and start over. (When social detachment fails, try spatial detachment.) Prison terms don't usually last forever. Even when the rickety criminal justice system secures a conviction, or more likely a plea bargain, even when the cunning knave obligingly does his time, he's likely to return to his scheming ways upon release. Prisons produce recidivism, not rehabilitation. Next time he may well be successful. No doubt he'll relish snickering at those merciful types intent on giving prisoners a second chance.

Worse yet, in this talk of "society" confronting "the individual" and banishing him, there is no glimpse of the actual problem, the one we gesture toward in referring to honor among thieves. Consider some more colonial

---

[103] Jim Bakker, *Move That Mountain!*, pp. 136–37.

counterfeiters. "Silver Sam" Casey had the members of his gang swear an oath to keep each other's secrets. Each added, "if I am not true to you and do not keep all your Counsel & your Secrets I pray God to shut me out of Heaven and to make all my Prayers to become Sin."[104] Here God underwrites solidarity, uniting the insiders so they can better prey on outsiders. Don't waste any time wondering at the naivete of those who'd imagine that God would stand behind their criminal activity. He's been enlisted for far worse causes.

And don't leap to the conclusion that these rogues will never be able to rely on each other. Yes, they might betray each other. Literature often consoles us with portraits of the rogues finally turning on one another, like the Vicomte de Valmont and the Marquise de Merteuil, the two sexual predators of *Les Liaisons dangereuses*. But—take the Mafia's code of silence—rogues can also rely not just on coercion but on loyalty, even love, to cement their cooperation. That "we" owe each other respect and painstakingly fair treatment but may or even must dish out contempt and savage injustice to "them," that it doesn't even qualify as injustice when dispensed to them because their filthy sort deserves it, indeed that our so treating them is a crucial part of what unites us and supplies our identity, is no occasional lapse from cosmopolitan decency and goodness. On the contrary, I daresay it's easily the most common social formation of human history. Whether the cleavage between us and them is articulated as clan, tribe, nation, sect, race, class, party, or whatever other weighty little-endian/big-endian distinction beckons, our license or duty to exploit them with as much cunning as we like is business as usual.

It furnishes cause for rejoicing, too, for warm embraces and convivial toasts, stories celebrating the clever ripoffs of the enemy, stories rather like those Odysseus treats us to, but these stories all too true. Frontinus tells a striking tale. His tone is dry, clipped, but surely admiring: he is exploring choiceworthy military tactics. Athenian general Melanthus and Boeotian king Xanthus have agreed to settle their conflict by one-on-one combat, a sensible convention for avoiding carnage. They near one another and Melanthus musters the tones of righteous indignation: how dare Xanthus bring a companion to help him fight? As far as Xanthus knows, he's by

---

[104] Kenneth Scott, *Counterfeiting in America* (New York: Oxford University Press, 1957), p. 231.

himself, complying with their agreement. Baffled, he looks around, and Melanthus promptly kills him.[105] Is there anything wrong with Melanthus's duplicity? Do you pause at enshrining Melanthus as the epitome of rationality? at taking Xanthus to be a chump who gets just what any chump deserves? Do you admire Melanthus? Do you want to strive to be more like him? Should you teach your children to emulate him? Are you blameworthy if you *fail* to teach your children to emulate him?

Is the worry reputational effects? But would anyone know? And—these are enemies, after all—Xanthus's followers presumably hate Melanthus already; why shouldn't Melanthus's followers applaud his deft action? As usual, the appeal to reputational effects seems invidiously parasitic on the first-order judgment it's trying to secure: absent some recondite handwaving, his action will harm his reputation only if the locals think he's behaved badly. But again, why should they? Should they worry that he's signaled that he's generally unreliable in schemes of social cooperation? But can't they distinguish different social settings? Don't they sensibly assume that how Melanthus behaves in one role doesn't reveal much about how he'll behave in another? Doesn't his betrayal of the outsiders cement his solidarity with the insiders? When Melanthus hosts dinner to celebrate his unscrupulous victory, do his followers have to inspect him warily when he cuts the cake? Is the reputational worry that if future potential combatants get wind of Melanthus's betrayal here, they'll prudently refuse one-on-one combat with him? But isn't it prudent of him and his followers to discount that future event by its (slim) likelihood and (remote) time in the future? So, all things considered, shouldn't Melanthus's troops burst into uproarious applause? Maybe you don't want to be like Melanthus or to have your children be like Melanthus. But maybe you'd rather your political leaders were (more) like him, resolute and daring as Machiavelli's prince, able and willing to be sleazy to safeguard your interests. Your side needs its scoundrels, too. When you notice that you rely on them, can you keep congratulating yourself on having clean hands?

The stability of honor among thieves is exhibited in a mask that curiously announces itself as a mask but still deceives: I mean criminal argot or lingo. Some picturesque words and phrases encapsulate scams gone by. Here are two from a century ago. A tin-mitten takes money from con men

---

[105] *Stratagems*, II.v.41.

and buys the unblinking ignorance of local authorities.[106] The donegan worker maneuvers in public restrooms. He enters the stall next to that of his intended victim and rolls, say, a collar stud on the floor. Then he asks the victim to retrieve it for him. While the victim leans down, he quickly reaches over the wall dividing them and removes the wallet from the victim's inside jacket pocket. He's out of the restroom before his victim knows what's hit him. Even the victim eager to chase the donegan worker will have to fumble around and pull up his pants—and figure out how to identify a suspect he's never seen.[107]

But the real point of this language is to allow trusting and trustworthy knaves to communicate in ways baffling the honest fools. The occasional dictionary sedulously catalogues and defines the day's reigning lingo and even offers examples with translations.

> Tim Sullivan buzzed a bloke and a shakester of a reader. His jomer stalled. Johnny Miller, who was to have his regulars, called out, "cop-bung," for as you see a fly-cop was marking. Jack speeled to the crib, when he found Johnny Doyle had been pulling down sawney for grub. He cracked a casa last night, and fenced the swag. He told Jack as how Bill had flimped a yack, and pinched a swell of a spark-fawney, and had sent the yack to church, and got half a century and a finnif for the fawney.[108]

---

[106] David W. Maurer, *The Big Con: The Story of the Confidence Man* (Indianapolis: Bobbs-Merrill, 1940; reprint ed. New York: Doubleday Anchor, 1999), chap. 7.

[107] *American Tramp and Underworld Slang*, ed. Godfrey Irwin (New York: Sears Publishing, 1931), p. 64; compare "Pickpocket Lingo (Maybe New York Only)," *Saturday Evening Post* (21 October 1950), in *The Notebooks of Raymond Chandler and English Summer*, ed. Frank MacShane (New York: Ecco Press, 1976), p. 63.

[108] George W. Matsell, *Vocabulum; or, A Rogue's Lexicon* (New York, 1859), p. 105:

> Tim Sullivan picked the pockets of a gentleman and lady of a pocket-book and purse. Tim's fancy-girl stood near him and screened him from observation. Johnny Miller, who was to have a share of the plunder, called out to him: "Hand over the stolen property—a detective is observing your maneuvers." Sullivan ran immediately to his house, when he found Johnny Doyle had provided something to eat, by stealing some bacon from a store-door. Doyle committed a burglary last night, and disposed of the property plundered. He told Sullivan that Bill had hustled a person, and obtained a watch, and also robbed a well-dressed gentleman of a diamond ring. The watch he sent to have the works taken out and put into another case, or the maker's name erased and another inserted; the ring realized him fifty-five dollars.

Sure, the people sharing this vocabulary can betray each other. But its shared use testifies to their ongoing reliable cooperation.

Honor among thieves punctures efforts to show that the cunning operator must be incurably lonely, unable to enjoy the great goods of friendship and love. "*Knaves* I know there are *in Notion* and *Principle*, as well as *in Practice*: who think all Honesty as well as Religion a mere Cheat; and, by a very consistent reasoning, have resolv'd deliberately to do whatever by *Power* or *Art* they are able, for their private advantage." So admitted that philosophical optimist—we might instead christen him a complacent moralist—Shaftesbury in 1711. "But such as these never open themselves in Friendship to others." Or again,

> There can never be less *Self-Enjoyment* than in these suppos'd *wise Characters*, these *selfish* Computers of Happiness and private Good; whose Pursuits of *Interest*, whether for this World or another, are attended with the same steady Vein of cunning and low Thought, sordid Deliberations, perverse and crooked Fancies, ill Dispositions, and false Relishes of *Life* and *Manners*. The most negligent undesigning thoughtless *Rake* has not only more of Sociableness, Ease, Tranquillity, and Freedom from worldly Cares, but in reality more of Worth, Virtue, and Merit, than such grave Plodders, and *thoughtful* Gentlemen as these.[109]

These remarks would plausibly rebut anyone who set himself the daffy goal of always being ready to rip off anyone and everyone else. But when Odysseus and Diomedes slip off for their moonlit murders, Diomedes doesn't have to fret that Odysseus might stab him in the back. The snoring soldiers are Trojan enemies; he's an Achaian friend. So the two heroes work together. Their calculating distance from the dictates of honor and their cunning joint enterprise redouble their trust and friendship. Plato hated the suggestion that justice is doing good to friends and harm to enemies, but he didn't invent it. It lived in social practice, so the two heroes can see themselves as not just devious, but just.[110]

---

[109] Shaftesbury, "Sensus Communis," II.ii, in *Characteristicks*; "Miscellaneous Reflections," V.iii, in *Characteristicks*, small capitals removed.

[110] *Republic* 332d–335e; see generally Arthur W. H. Adkins, *Merit and Responsibility: A Study in Greek Values* (Oxford: Clarendon Press, 1960).

My favorite literary treatment of cunning is Melville's *Confidence-Man*, a book so rich that I have despaired of offering it more than a cameo appearance in these pages. It piles up confusing appearances and ironic inversions, delights in psychological ambiguities and moral paradoxes, presses on what's at stake in trusting others. It's April Fool's Day and the boat *Fidèle*—Faithful—is steaming down the Mississippi. On board is a confidence man, or maybe more than one confidence man, maybe working in concert, maybe not. In the novel's brief opening chapters, Melville sketches one unflinching ripoff after another. In one, a confidence man assists a bedridden miser crying out for water. In saccharine tones that put us on warning, he coos, "And did they let you lie here, my poor sir, racked with this parching thirst?" The miser ignores the query but "in a voice disastrous with a cough" asks, "How can I repay you?" The answer is startling, vague, menacing: "By giving me your confidence." "Little left at my age," shoots back the miser, "but take the stale remains, and welcome."

"Such as it is, though, you give it. Very good. Now give me a hundred dollars." You might be amused at the effrontery—I am—but the miser is terrified and erupts into another explosive coughing fit. "What a shocking cough," commiserates the confidence man. "I wish, my friend, the herb-doctor was here now; a box of his Omni-Balsamic Reinvigorator would do you good." (The herb-doctor may be another confidence man or he may be this same one in a different costume.) Too bad, he continues, that the miser hasn't got a hundred dollars; if he did, he could invest and triple it. The miser is intrigued—at least his interlocutor isn't a shameless beggar—but also mystified. Why does he run around the world offering to invest others' money? "How is the gain made?" "To tell that would ruin me. That known, every one would be going into the business, and it would be overdone. A secret, a mystery—all I have to do with you is to receive your confidence, and all you have to do with me is, in due time, to receive it back, thrice paid in trebling profits." Tempted but wary, the miser wants evidence, the sight of an honest face—the cabin is dim, his vision bad, the confidence man almost invisible—or at least a promise of when he can look forward to the return on his investment. The confidence man is obdurate. "No ifs. Downright confidence, or none. So help me heaven, I will have no half-confidences." Still the miser is afraid to hazard his gold, so the confidence man heads off: "You won't confide. Good-bye!"

"'Stay, stay,' falling back now like an infant, 'I confide, I confide, help,

friend, my distrust!'" The passage echoes the Gospels. A father has asked
Jesus if He can help his son, possessed by a spirit. "Jesus said unto him,
If thou canst believe, all things are possible to him that believeth. And
straightway the father of the child cried out, and said with tears, Lord, I believe; help thou mine unbelief."[111] Melville's allusion casts the confidence
man as Jesus. It's just one of the book's recurrent fiendish puzzles, put in
play as the boat sets sail, when a man with "flaxen head" and "lamb-like figure" inscribes scriptural sentiments on charity on his slate and earns jeers
and shoves from the crowd. The puzzle deepens with another biblical allusion.[112] The miser finally disgorges his gold. "'I know not whether I should
accept this slack confidence,'" said the other coldly, receiving the gold, 'but
an eleventh-hour confidence, a sick-bed confidence, a distempered, deathbed confidence, after all.'" No hosannas over the eleventh-hour conversion
of this sinner. Instead the confidence man really is leaving this time—no
point lingering now that he's clutching the hundred dollars—and with a
"final flicker of reason," a reason apparently set obstinately against such
trust or confidence, the miser, his coughs now a death rattle, summons him
back in vain. "Nay, back, back—receipt, my receipt! Ugh, ugh, ugh!
Who are you? What have I done? Where go you? My gold, my gold!
Ugh, ugh, ugh!"[113]

If the miser doesn't trust, he dies a lonely miser. If he does trust, he risks
betrayal and dies a death even lonelier. The confidence man needn't be the
least bit lonely. Even if he is doing all the work on that boat—that would
make him one remarkable quick-change artist and strenuously busy guy—
he can carve the world in two, the valuable us he has warm and trusting relationships with and the contemptible them he mercilessly exploits. Then
again, the barrier between us and them is often porous, transgression of official strictures about those contemptible others always possible, even enticing in its way, not only for cosmopolitan moralists but also, you guessed
it, for cunning opportunists wondering if here too they might profit by
flouting the rules.

Compare a moment toward the dreary closing of *Beowulf*. Our hero has
been abandoned by most of his followers. Wiglaf, the one sticking by

[111] Mark 9:23–24.
[112] Matthew 20:1–16.
[113] Herman Melville, *The Confidence-Man: His Masquerade*, chap. 15.

Beowulf in his fight against the dragon, upbraids those who've fled: when
word of their disgraceful cowardice gets out, he warns, foreign princes will
invade and conquer.[114] They can rule out this bad publicity easily enough.
All they have to do is kill Wiglaf. Are they restrained by fear that the
nearby retainers will witness their dastardly deed? They're not *that* nearby:
Wiglaf has to send word to them to explain what's been going on. So do
the yellow-bellied followers lack the courage of their cowardly convictions?
If they're not willing to stick with Beowulf, should they be willing to follow
through on their betrayal? Or is it easier to excuse them their cowardice because they don't relinquish all the commitments of honor and glory?

Or consider the Arthurian romances, magically populated with dragons
and the like, but realistic in thinking about honor. The locals frequently
report—and endorse—the norm that it is dreadfully dishonorable for two
or more knights to attack one.[115] Sure, the norm is sometimes trans-
gressed: what norm isn't?[116] And some don't fall within its jurisdiction:
when puissant knight Erec fights two giants at once, I doubt the reader is
supposed to wax indignant.[117] But Erec also meets a wicked knight and his
two followers. The three live by robbing others, and they wouldn't mind
gaining Erec's purse or his lovely wife. The narrator reminds the reader of
the norm, central to grasping his tale: "In those days it was the custom and
practice that in an attack two knights should not join against one; thus if
they too had assailed him, it would seem that they had acted treacher-
ously." The robbers dutifully attack Erec one at a time and decorously lose
one at a time: one killed, one wounded, one unhorsed.[118] Is it irrational of
them not to gang up on Erec? Are they rule-worshippers? The virtuous
Knights of the Round Table aren't going to salute them for fighting gal-
lantly in such a bad cause. Their fellow thieves might well snicker at their
stupidity. After all, as robbers they've already opted out of the central aspirations of the official script. So why should they stick to any of it? And
why do they? Notice that the robbers might want not only to win purse
and wife alike, but to win them in the right way. Even if they don't care

---

[114] *Beowulf*, ll. 2860–91.

[115] For instance, Sir Thomas Malory, *Le Morte D'Arthur*, bk. 8, chaps. 27, 40; bk. 10, chap. 1;
bk. 18, chap. 24.

[116] Malory, *Arthur*, bk. 7, chap. 5; bk. 8, chap. 13.

[117] Chrétien de Troyes, "Erec et Enide," vv. 4381–579.

[118] "Erec et Enide," vv. 2765–94, quoted from Chrétien de Troyes, *Arthurian Romances*, trans.
W. W. Comfort (London: Dent, 1975), p. 37.

about winning the approval of more conventional knights, their subscribing to the same standards bars some betrayals and so keeps them partly loyal to, partly members of, the community they've allegedly renounced. Once again, we can ask not just, what should they do? but also, who should they be? and even, what is actually in their interests? We can't intelligently answer those questions by deferring to their current preferences or desires. Every one of those questions presupposes that they may need to revise or discard their preferences. Or again, we can also ask, what communities should command their loyalties? on what occasions, in what settings, for what purposes?

That loyalty is a loser, that rationality dictates that you maintain only the semblance of loyalty and only as long as it serves your interests, that you should be ready to betray not just your country or your clan but your friends and loved ones: this bizarre fantasy is at home in literature or perhaps psychopathology, also in the blackboard scribblings of crude economists, but nowhere else in daily life, and emphatically not because we are lamentably weak. What about the opposite view, that no matter what, we should be unflaggingly loyal to the dictates of principle and our social obligations? Dress it up in Kantian garb as the slogan that moral considerations are overriding, or spoof it in *The Pirates of Penzance*'s breathy cadences about the slave of duty: either way it's every bit as bizarre.

Once again, morality and self-interest seem diametrically opposed. If we relinquish the strategy Hobbes, Hume, and Franklin adopted, that of harnessing instrumental rationality and showing that morality is the means to self-interested ends, can we say anything else? Let's return to the fantasy of the invisible man grabbing sex with a high-status woman. Theorists will recall yet another version from the opening gambit of Plato's *Republic*.[119] Suppose you had a ring that would turn you invisible, so you could get away with doing whatever you liked. (The ancient Greeks actually employed such magic.)[120] Armed with such a ring, Gyges' ancestor

---

[119] *Republic* 359d–361d. Contrast the version in Herodotus, *Histories*, I.8–12.

[120] Christopher A. Faraone, *Ancient Greek Love Magic* (Cambridge, MA: Harvard University Press, 1999), pp. 103–4, has some magical rings recorded several centuries after Plato; for other invisibility spells, see *The Greek Magical Papyri in Translation: Including the Demotic Spells*, ed. Hans Dieter Betz, 2nd ed. (Chicago: University of Chicago Press, 1992), pp. 9–10; see too *Curse Tablets and Binding Spells from the Ancient World*, ed. John G. Gager (New York: Oxford University Press, 1992). For evidence of the use of magic in the heyday of classical Athens, see *Republic* 364c, *Laws* 933a.

slept with the king's wife, enlisted her assistance in murdering the king, and took over the kingdom. Would any just man go on being just if he had such a ring? That's a question about moral motivation. Is it finally reputation, fear of punishment, an accession of alacrity in basking in others' admiration, that in fact make people moral? Is that all there is? Glaucon raises the stakes. Suppose, he says, that the unjust man always gets away with his misdeeds and enjoys a stellar reputation; and suppose that the just man's reputation is dreadful, that people believe him thoroughly unjust. Is it still better to be just? Why? That's a question about justification, set up—some will say unfairly tilted—to rule out any probabilistic calculations on why honesty might be the best policy.

Plato's strategy, more promising than that of Hobbes and company, is to challenge the background understandings of rationality, self-interest, and morality.[121] Blithely skipping over exegetical complications, and adding some insights from Aristotle and Kant, I might summarize the argument this way. If your conception of rationality is that which we also found in Hobbes and Hume, something like finding the way to the things desired, you're a slave to your desires. Instead you should be asking yourself what makes a life worth living. And if your conception of morality is a laundry list of "thou shalt nots," you have an impoverished account of something like a dictator's snarls. Instead you should be thinking about stances that express care and respect for others. The aspiration is to make self-interest and morality converge, to show that on reflection the best way for you to live is in part to be moral.

From this point of view, the mistake is imagining that we start with fixed and independent conceptions of self-interest and morality and then have to reconcile them. That project left one singularly able ethicist sounding lachrymose, melodramatic, about the dualism of practical reason, "an ultimate and fundamental contradiction in our apparent intuitions of what is Reasonable in conduct."[122] Better, surely, to back up and ask a more general question: what should we care about? And again, if a choiceworthy life includes genuine care and regard for others—for friends, family, fellow citizens, strangers around the globe, if in varying degrees and settings; for

---

[121] Terence Irwin, *Plato's Moral Theory: The Early and Middle Dialogues* (Oxford: Oxford University Press, 1977).

[122] Henry Sidgwick, *The Methods of Ethics*, 7th ed. (London: Macmillan and Co., 1907), p. 508.

that matter, refusing to carve the world into an *us* worthy of trust and respect and a *them* worthy only of being victimized—then the apocalyptic conflict between self-interest and morality is a nonstarter. Instead we can say forthrightly that the cunning rogue who rips off others in the name of his self-interest is making a mistake about what's valuable, what's worth pursuing, where those categories are prior to talk of interest or moral duty.[123] Jonathan Swift probably intended his dry comment—"I have known Men of the greatest Cunning, perpetually cheated"[124]—as a reminder of the biter-bit problem, of how easy it is for the clever to get tripped up in their own machinations. But it's tempting to take that "perpetually" as meaning that such men constantly cheat themselves. Nor is this response to the cunning rogue exulting in his interests a bit of banal mystification or saccharine moralism: it's hard-edged and sober.

So if cunning prompted the anxiety that you have to be a chump to care about morality, to refuse to exploit others when you can get away with it, that anxiety is misplaced. That's why I declare that mine, finally, is no counsel of despair. All well and good, but it's not going to settle all the vexing difficulties posed by cunning. No matter what your ends, you will confront occasions on which it is tempting to evade some obstacles, moral ones included, in order to attain something valuable. I much doubt that we can say anything interestingly general about how to resolve the exquisite difficulties that arise. Ours remains ineluctably the terrain of casuistry even after we wryly acknowledge that corrupt churchmen and cunning operators turned *casuistry* into a dirty word.[125] But we should resist stupid slogans and siren songs. If we construe theories of practical reason— instrumental rationality, expressive accounts, utilitarianism, Kantianism, and so on—as idealizations of particular facets of our deliberations, I've no objections to them. But if we construe them as rival candidates, so that it's incumbent on us to choose one and live by its mandates, well, count me a refusenik.

---

[123] See especially Barbara Herman, "Training to Autonomy: Kant and the Question of Moral Education," in *Philosophers on Education: Historical Perspectives*, ed. Amélie Oksenberg Rorty (London: Routledge, 1998).

[124] *Thoughts on Various Subjects*, small capitals removed. Or consider Bierce, *Dictionary*: "*Rascal, n.* A fool considered under another aspect."

[125] For a more temperate overview, see Albert R. Jonsen and Stephen Toulmin, *The Abuse of Casuistry: A History of Moral Reasoning* (Berkeley: University of California Press, 1988).

CODA

I return briefly to the world of Odysseus and the attractions and repulsions of cunning that launched this circuitous fox hunt. In a familiar Greek way, *métis* wasn't only the abstract quality of cunning. Hesiod tells us that she was one of the daughters of Ocean—and that "Zeus, as King of the gods, / took as his first wife Mêtis, / and she knew more than all the gods / or mortal people." He fathered Athena, goddess of wisdom, by her—and swallowed her in a vain attempt to avoid a dire prophecy and so that she might plan for him.[126] Apollodorus adds that Mêtis provided a drug that got Kronos to vomit up Zeus's siblings, who helped him conquer Kronos and the Titans, and that she used her shapeshifting skills in vain to avoid Zeus's sexual embrace.[127] These myths portray the mightiest of gods, off to rule on Mount Olympus, orally incorporating cunning so that he can forever draw on her advice. No surprise there. But the myths also cast cunning not as the skill enabling rape or sexual conquest, but as what gets raped. And they don't cast cunning as wisdom's bitch daughter. They cast wisdom as cunning's bitch daughter. What then?

---

[126] *Theogony*, ll. 358, 886–900, 929a. I've quoted from *Hesiod*, trans. Richmond Lattimore (Ann Arbor: University of Michigan Press, 1959), p. 176. For cunning as the offspring of wisdom and envy, see "Origin of Cunning: An Allegory," *The Wit's Magazine; or, Library of Momus* (July 1784):263–65.

[127] *The Library*, 1.i.1, I.iii.6.

AFTERWORD

꩜ Another century, another country, another murderous churchman.[1]

The victim: Master James, "a man well-reckoned in the general report of all" and a minister in Norfolk. James held two benefices or livings: that is, he had the income from two parishes but also the responsibility for running them. (In these years, the practice of treating benefices as property to be bought, sold, assigned by local aristocrats, and the like was an everyday scandal.) Getting older and tired, he hired a curate to handle the responsibilities of one parish.

The villain: Master Lowe, the very curate in question, whose salary was supplemented with room and board in James's house. Satan spotted a promising opportunity, or so the recorder of this sorry tale informs us. The "sweet milk of preferment"—the pleasures of knowing that he'd gotten a job—curdled in Lowe's mouth. Satan afflicted him with gnawing envy. Wasn't he "born to higher fortunes" than being a poor curate with an ignominious master? Satan suggested a solution, too. James's wife—"a woman of good Parentage, virtuous education, and (to the outward eye) of civil and unblemished reputation"—was close at hand. If he could win her love, murmured the tempter, he could "raise his estate, to the very height and top of his desires."

Was this wife victim, villain, or something altogether different? It's hard to tell at the story's launch, but she soon succumbed to Lowe's advances. Our recorder hurries past their unseemly assignations to report that Satan wasn't satisfied. No, he "loves to have his bondslaves sooted all over with the Coal of damnation," so he continued whispering his sour somethings in Lowe's haunted ear. Yes, he was sleeping with his master's wife. What of it? Their sex was furtive, fearful, infrequent. Master James was still master of the household. An amiable enough master, willing roundly to reject whispered word that "Master Lowe dieted at Master James his board, and

---

[1] *A Trve Relation of the Most Inhumane and Bloody Murther, of Master Iames Minister and Preacher of the Word of God at Rockland in Norfolke. Committed by one Lowe His Curate, and Consented vnto by His Wife, Who Both Were Executed for This Fact This Last Assizes: He Being Drawne and Hanged, and Shee Burned, Who at His Death Confessed the Murther of His Owne Child, Vnlawfully Begotten, and Buried It Him Selfe* (London, 1609).

lodged in his wife's bed" without even accosting curate or wife, but still master. By such seductive pleas, Lowe's "learned counsel the Devil" prevailed on his reluctant client—yes, reluctant, now recalling James's hiring him, trusting him, even loving him—to murder his master. He already was damned to hell as an adulterer. Murder could make him no worse off in the afterlife. But it could improve his worldly life.

A series of attempts failed, but perseverance is a virtue. (Isn't it?) Lowe finally managed the trick. Christmas celebrations included nightly festivities with the neighbors. Afterward, James headed off to share his bed with his eight-year-old daughter, their way lit by a servant who lived in town. No, there's no hint of incestuous child abuse here. The sleeping arrangements of Norfolk in 1609 weren't ours. And if Lowe was gnashing his teeth at his poverty, there's no reason to think that a vicar with two livings was wealthy. The recorder adds that he doesn't know why James's wife "bedded not with him." Perhaps she was still nursing or perhaps she'd made a "secret promise to Lowe." James and daughter lay in one bed; a trusty servant in the adjacent room; James's wife in a room under his; Lowe, "molding his villainy," at the other end of the house. Lowe's stay in bed was short and sleepless. He slipped into James's chamber. Nature exploded in protest, with fierce winds, lightning, thunder: none of it halted Lowe, now Satan's remorseless instrument. "Like a bestial savage . . . he laid violent and bloody hands upon the body of his sleeping Master: And offering to smother him after some violent strugglings, Master James was overheard by the fellow in the next room to utter these words, what do you mean, come you to murder me." James's daughter, "like a silly lark trembling," implored Lowe not to kill her father. He told her to shut up, adjusted the bedcovers, and left. Cloaked by darkness, he retreated to bed: maybe his own, maybe his lover's. Now dead, James was still warm and quiet. Thinking he was peacefully sleeping, his daughter hugged him and fell back asleep.

The next day, the alarmed servant from the adjacent room discovered "the close and horrid actions of the night." Frightened, he headed into town, where he met the servant who'd led James and daughter to bed, told him what he'd heard, and declared that he hoped their master was okay. The other returned, found "the pretty child sweetly sleeping, having twined her tender arms about his murdered body," and dashed downstairs to alert the mistress of the house, who remained silent. Not Lowe, who leaped from his bed, demanded where were the murderers, and returned to the scene of the crime. Finally the daughter roused herself and burst into tears at the sight of her dead father. Soothing her, a maid offered to put her in Lowe's bed. No, said the girl, she wouldn't go there because he had killed her father. The maid kept quiet and brought the girl to her mother, who listened as her daughter repeated the charge. "Peace, fool," replied the widow, "hold thy tongue, he loved us all too well to hurt thy father." She left the room only to hear James's servant telling the maid the lethal words he'd overheard in the night. "Peace, wretch," she sputtered again. Worse, she and Lowe were soon overheard muttering about a secret plan.

Still, she had the church bells rung, assured everyone that James had died a natural death, and arranged for his burial, his winding cloths right over his bloody nightclothes. (An extra fee procured that suppression of evidence.) Meanwhile Lowe seized on inspiration to dispose of the distressingly garrulous servant. He assigned him an urgent errand: the servant's uncle, Lowe explained, was on his deathbed, eager to make the servant his heir, but wanted to see him. The servant balked: he hadn't the money or gear to make a long trip. Lowe generously lent the servant what he needed. So the fellow set off. "The intent of Lowe's sending him thus away was this, to accuse him for the murder, which done, his present and secret flight should confirm him guilty of it, and clear himself." Not bad, as rapid improvisations go.

Happily, the hapless servant was intercepted by a neighbor who'd heard rumors of the truth. The servant yet again chattered his ingenuous way through the story of James's last words. The neighbor ushered him to a nearby justice of the peace and had him swear to it. The servant he'd confided in swore to the exchange, too. The justice wanted to know why they'd been silent so long. They explained that James's wife had commanded them to: "peace, wretch, know you what you do, will you cast away a man without cause?" Hearing that the second servant had been summoned to testify, Lowe boldly showed up himself, hoping to make his case that one servant or the other was the real killer. Canny in the ways of law enforcement, the justice didn't reveal that he already knew that Lowe had suggested and funded the apparent getaway. Instead he indicated that he distrusted the servant but decided to hold runaway servant and Lowe alike until the next court of sessions convened. Graciously, he added that he'd be happy to make himself responsible for Lowe's appearance, provided that Lowe would stay with him, an offer the curate couldn't refuse.

The neighbor popped up again, this time to commiserate with Lowe and warn him that alas, the justice was collecting not just suspicions but evidence against him. He urged Lowe to confess, and added that he had friends who knew the king: for a fee, they could get him pardoned. Lowe thought, and "after certain broken and distracted pausings, replied, if I should trust my life in your hands, would you prove faithful? I would, replied his seeming friend, and deal for you as effectually as were you mine own son." Betrayed by appearances, Lowe was delighted. He confessed, but added that if the neighbor couldn't procure his pardon, he'd deny that he'd ever acknowledged his crime. Not to be outdone, the neighbor slyly suggested that he needed a written confession for a petition of pardon to be granted. Desperate, Lowe obliged. Was the killer faithful to his mistress? He kept insisting that she'd had nothing to do with the killing, but he conceded that they'd had intimate relations. So where, demanded the neighbor, did the poor curate hope to get the money for the pardon? It wouldn't be a trivial sum. Lowe declared that the woman would provide it, but adamantly refused to implicate her.

Clutching his valuable text, the neighbor made a beeline—not to those shadowy friends of the king, but to the solid and substantial justice of the peace. One down, one to go: how could they make the widow confess? Donning yet another mask, the neighbor went to the James residence and found the widow nursing her child. He "told her as in great secrecy" that Lowe wanted to meet with her. "Out upon him," she responded, "hath he not brought me to shame enough, but he would draw my life likewise in question?" Then she hesitated. Hoping "to draw her further on," the neighbor echoed, "your life?" Warier than her fool of a lover, the woman shot back daringly, "I know your policies better than you imagine, but you both are and shall be deceived in me, and as for master Lowe, pray return this, I have nothing to do with him, neither will I stir over the threshold to meet or speak with him (be he guilty of my husband's death) would it save his life." She wouldn't budge.

The justice now consigned Lowe to jail and kept the widow in his house. One day, the justice was questioning Lowe, who insisted yet again that he had nothing to do with James's death. The neighbor now showed up and "plucked a paper out of his pocket." Fooled yet again, Lowe inferred that it was the long-awaited pardon and "grew very pleasant and content." His sunny mood darkened into consternation when the neighbor gazed at the paper and started reciting the words of his confession. The betrayal now manifest, Lowe sounded the anguished tones of crucified righteousness, and I bet his was no faltering pose. "Villain," he demanded, "hast thou betrayed me?"

To the bitter end, though, Lowe refused to incriminate his mistress. He almost escaped from jail. The attempt earned him leg irons and the dungeon. There he rotted until court finally convened. He and the widow were convicted of the killing. Lowe was sentenced to be hanged, she to be burned. (As a woman who'd murdered her husband, she was guilty of petit treason under a 1351 statute. The gruesome penalty—comparing it to the disemboweling and drawing and quartering suffered by treasonous men, Blackstone explained that "the natural modesty of the sex forbids the exposing and publicly mangling their bodies"—wasn't repealed till 1790. In 1828 the crime lapsed back to murder.)[2] She went first: he got to witness her constancy, or anyway her stubbornness, as she acknowledged that she'd tried to conceal the murder but still insisted she'd had nothing to do with planning or executing it. Ascending the gallows, he confessed to the murder—and to another crime. Before this tawdry tale commenced, he had fathered a child by a wealthy man's daughter. He'd sought her hand in marriage, but the father refused him. He tried saving everyone from some arson he'd engineered, but the heroics didn't come off and he was dismissed. After arriving at Master James's, he'd summoned his child, claiming he'd found a new nurse. He took the child, suffocated it—murderers do have their pet tactics—and buried it in a field. Unburdening himself of this horror, admitting too that he'd killed Master James, "requesting all such as were there to pray for him, with hearty penitence, and outward patience, he seemed to embrace his death." But did he? And did God embrace him?

What a puzzling cast of characters! Master James, respected, innocent, a victim, was also something of a fool. Master Lowe, despised, guilty, displayed his own fierce loyalty to his mistress in resolutely denying that

[2] 25 Edw. III st. 5, c. 2; 30 Geo. III c. 48; 9 Geo. IV c. 31, sec. 2. William Blackstone, *Commentaries on the Laws of England*, 4 vols. (Oxford, 1765–69; reprint ed. Chicago: University of Chicago Press, 1979), 4:93. For more on these matters, see Shelley A. M. Gavigan, "Petit Treason in Eighteenth Century England: Women's Inequality before the Law," *Canadian Journal of Women and the Law* 3:2 (1989–90):335–74.

she'd participated in planning or executing the murder. Maybe he displayed integrity, too: the court was satisfied with her guilt, but there's not a bit of evidence in the pamphlet that she was indeed guilty. What, then, was the mistress of the tale? She strayed from the path of marital fidelity. Did she murder her husband? Was she Lowe's victim? or the victim of English criminal law? And that crafty duo, the justice of the peace and the neighbor, running their good-cop/bad-cop routine and deceiving Lowe into a confession: do you want to qualify your applause for them? Should you?

INDEX